2014年外研社大学外语教学科研项目
以内容为依托的"影视作品中的跨文化交际"课程的教学模式和学生跨文化交际能力的培养（项目编号：20140041）

Intercultural Communication in Movies

影视作品中的跨文化交际

主编◎马晶文
编者◎畅青霞　Brent Pinkall
审校◎Brent Pinkall

西南交通大学出版社
·成都·

图书在版编目（CIP）数据

影视作品中的跨文化交际 = Intercultural Communication in Movies：汉英对照 / 马晶文主编.
—成都：西南交通大学出版社，2015.6（2020.1 重印）
ISBN 978-7-5643-3919-7

Ⅰ. ①影… Ⅱ. ①马… Ⅲ. ①英语 – 高等学校 – 教材 ②电影影片 – 文化交流 – 鉴赏 – 世界 Ⅳ. ①H319.4：J

中国版本图书馆 CIP 数据核字（2015）第 111500 号

Intercultural Communication in Movies
影视作品中的跨文化交际

主编　马晶文

责任编辑　祁素玲
特邀编辑　尹多智
封面设计　何东琳设计工作室

西南交通大学出版社出版发行　（028-87600564　028-87600533）
地址　四川省成都市二环路北一段111号西南交通大学创新大厦21楼
邮政编码　610031
网址　http://www.xnjdcbs.com
印刷　四川煤田地质制图印刷厂

成品尺寸　185 mm×260 mm　　印张　12　　字数　392 千字
2015 年 6 月第 1 版　　2020年 1 月第 6 次印刷
ISBN 978-7-5643-3919-7　　定价　29.00元

课件咨询电话：028-81435775
图书如有印装质量问题　本社负责退换
版权所有　盗版必究　举报电话：028-87600562

前　言

　　2007年，教育部颁布的《大学英语课程教学要求》指出：大学英语教学应以英语语言知识与应用技能、学习策略和跨文化交际为主要内容。同时，大学英语课程不仅是一门语言基础知识课程，也是拓宽知识面、了解世界文化的素质教育课程。因此，大学英语课程应充分考虑对学生文化素质的培养和国际文化知识的传授，要尽可能地利用语言载体，让学生了解科学技术、西方社会、文化等知识，以提高学生的跨文化交际意识，培养其跨文化交际能力。

　　在经济全球化迅速发展的今天，不同文化背景的个体和群体之间的交流日益增多。文化是个广义的概念，文化差异包罗万象，文化的显性和隐性特性在人们的交际中起着很大的作用。因此，掌握语言并不能实现有效的交际，文化的差异会产生误解和冲突。

　　本教材对跨文化交际的主要理论进行了简要介绍，并将跨文化交际理论作为分析工具，通过对大量中外影片的文化分析，使学生对跨文化交际理论的学习达到一定的深度。同时培养了学生对目的语文化的兴趣和理解力，并将这种意识有效地运用在实践当中，使学生能够较为客观、全面地认识英语国家的文化，开拓学生的文化视野，提高跨文化交际意识，增强跨文化交际能力。本教材主要针对非英语专业的学生，可作为他们大学英语后续课程或通识类选修课程的教材。

　　本教材的特点在于将单纯的跨文化交际理论知识的学习与语言的实践自然、有效地结合起来。每一个单元都会介绍几个跨文化交际的术语，为使学生得到身临其境的学习体验，选择数个针对这一文化现象的影视片段作为该理论的具体案例，帮助学生在近乎真实的文化语境中对这些跨文化知识进行更好的理解。此外，每个单元所提供的两篇阅读材料也紧扣该跨文化交际的术语展开，介绍东西方具体的文化现象、风俗习惯和做法，使学生将理论学习与实践结合起来，对目的语文化有更深层次的理解和认识。再次，为巩固学生对理论知识的学习效果，又给出相关影视作品和生活中的具体案例进行分析，拓宽学生的外语习得环境。最后，以任务为驱动，提供相关开放式、拓展性练习，使学生融入角色，完成这些练习。这些精心设计的课堂活动使学生仿佛身临其境，去感受异国文化，体验真实的跨文化交际语境，在提高语言能力的同时，以轻松愉快的方式了解文化差异，从而达到最终的教学目的。

　　在本教材的附录中，提供了课文中所用影视片段的脚本，在帮助学生更好地欣赏电影的同时，可作为听力材料让学生自学。另外，提供了数十部跨文化交际的中外电影名称，供教师和学生在课堂或课后观赏和学习。此外，考虑到非英语专业学生的具体情况，在附录中还给出了课文中所涉及的跨文化交际理论的中文定义，以帮助学生更好地理解所学的内容。

本书阅读材料源于英美国家的杂志和网站，选用时进行了不同程度的修改，以更好地适应本书的特点和学生的学习需求；同时，为保证选篇语言的纯正性，由美籍教师 Brent Pinkall 对本书做了整体的审阅和修订。对有作者姓名的文章进行标注，作者姓名不详的标明出处，在此谨向所有作者表示感谢。

参与本书编写的中国和美国教师均具有一定的跨文化交际经历，所有案例均为一手资料。跨文化交际是一门新兴学科，所涉及知识十分广博，本书中有很多不尽之处，敬请各位批评指正。

如果需要相关的影视资料，请发电子邮件至 574220551@qq.com 邮箱联系。

编　者

2015 年 1 月于兰州

Contents

Introduction ··· 1

Unit 1　Intercultural Communication ·· 2

　I. Definition of Intercultural Communication ·· 2
　　　1. Introduction to Intercultural Communication
　　　2. What Is Communication?
　II. Content-based Activities ·· 5
　　Section A　Movie Clips
　　Section B　Intercultural Communication Reading
　　　Passage 1　Cross-cultural Communication
　　　Passage 2　Teaching Our Kids about Cultural Diversity
　　Section C　Case Studies
　III. Task-based Activities ·· 13
　　Exercises
　　Group Work
　　Assignment

Unit 2　Culture and Communication ·· 15

　I. Definition of Culture and Communication ·· 15
　　　1. What Is Culture?
　　　2. The Iceberg Model of Culture
　　　3. The Lewis Model of Culture
　II. Content-based Activities ·· 18
　　Section A　Movie Clips
　　Section B　Intercultural Communication Reading
　　　Passage 1　Intercultural Communication and Cultural Differences
　　　　　　　　 – How People Are the Same and How They Are Different
　　　Passage 2　Differences between American & Chinese Culture
　　Section C　Case Studies
　III. Task-based Activities ·· 25
　　Exercises
　　Group Work
　　Assignment

Unit 3 Cultural Value Orientation ·················· 28

I. Definition of Cultural Value Orientation ·················· 28
1. Kluckhohn and Strodtbeck's Value Orientation
2. Traditional Chinese Value Orientation: Confucianism

II. Content-based Activities ·················· 31
Section A   Movie Clips
Section B   Intercultural Communication Reading
   Passage 1   Eastern Culture vs. Western Culture
   Passage 2   The Values Americans Live by (I)
Section C   Case Studies

III. Task-based Activities ·················· 41
Exercises
Group Work
Assignment

Unit 4 Cultural Diversity ·················· 44

I. Definition of Cultural Diversity ·················· 44
Hofstede's Dimensions of Cultural Diversity:
1. Power Distance
2. Uncertainty Avoidance
3. Individualism vs. Collectivism
4. Masculinity vs. Femininity
5. Long Term Orientation

II. Content-based Activities ·················· 48
Section A   Movie Clips
Section B   Intercultural Communication Reading
   Passage 1   Hofstede's Asian Cultural Factors
   Passage 2   The Values Americans Live by (II)
Section C   Case Studies

III. Task-based Activities ·················· 56
Exercises
Group Work
Assignment

Unit 5 Context and Social Norms ·················· 59

I. Definition of Context and Social Norms ·················· 59
1. Edward T. Hall's High-context and Low-context Culture
2. Social Norms

Contents

 II. Content-based Activities ·········· 62
  Section A Movie Clips
  Section B Intercultural Communication Reading
   Passage 1 American Culture & Social Life
   Passage 2 The Values Americans Live by (III)
  Section C Case Studies
 III. Task-based Activities ·········· 72
  Exercises
  Group Work
  Assignment

Unit 6 Time and Space across Culture ·········· 75

 I. Definition of Time and Space across Culture ·········· 75
  1. Time: Monochronic Time vs. Polychronic Time
  2. Proxemics
 II. Content-based Activities ·········· 78
  Section A Movie Clips
  Section B Intercultural Communication Reading
   Passage 1 Time Sense: Polychronicity and Monochronicity
   Passage 2 How to Use Proxemics in the Corporate Classroom
  Section C Case Studies
 III. Task-based Activities ·········· 87
  Exercises
  Group Work
  Assignment

Unit 7 Verbal and Nonverbal Communication ·········· 90

 I. Definition of Verbal and Nonverbal Communication ·········· 90
  1. Verbal Communication
  2. Nonverbal Communication
 II. Content-based Activities ·········· 95
  Section A Movie Clips
  Section B Intercultural Communication Reading
   Passage 1 Nonverbal Aspects of Language (Paralinguistics) I
   Passage 2 Nonverbal Aspects of Language (Paralinguistics) II
  Section C Case Studies
 III. Task-based Activities ·········· 105
  Exercises
  Group Work
  Assignment

Unit 8 Culture Shock and Adaptation ... 108

    I. Definition of Culture Shock and Adaptation ... 108

        1. What Is Culture Shock?

        2. Intercultural U-Curve and W-Curve Adjustment Model

        3. Intercultural Competence

    II. Content-based Activities ... 112

      Section A   Movie Clips

      Section B   Intercultural Communication Reading

        Passage 1   Cultural Adjustment

        Passage 2   Cultivating Intercultural Communication Competence

      Section C   Case Studies

    III. Task-based Activities ... 120

      Exercises

      Group Work

      Assignment

Appendixes ... 122

    Appendix I   Cultural Terms ... 122

    Appendix II   List of Recommended Movies ... 129

    Appendix III   Scripts of Movie Clips ... 131

    Appendix IV   Keys to Exercises ... 164

Bibliography ... 182

Introduction

As the world becomes smaller, people of different countries are interacting more and more increasingly, which means the study of intercultural communication is becoming ever more important. In order to live and function in this multicultural environment as effectively and meaningfully as possible, people have to be competent in intercultural communication. Since 1960s, the study of intercultural communication has progressed rapidly. It was introduced to China in 1980s. There are multiple ways to think about intercultural communication. Many textbooks emphasize the theories of intercultural communication. However, we begin this textbook by using a different method.

We believe that the best way to learn about intercultural experiences is to engage in real life. As we all know, learning about intercultural communication is not about learning a finite set of skills, terms and theories. It is about understanding cultural realities. But how do we do this?

We cannot always see what is happening when we communicate within intercultural contexts. We all suffer from various intercultural blind spots. Communication is a two-way street. If neither side knows how to communicate clearly and concisely, miscommunication is inevitable.

Movies are cultural products that contain representations of people and places, and therefore visions of how the world is or should be. We have found that films are very effective media to introduce culture, people's value orientation and communication styles. Because movies are entertaining, engaging, and in many cases they stimulate curiosity toward other cultures, they can provide many real-life scenarios to serve as case analyses for intercultural adjustment, which may avoid simplistic cultural input and provide a cross-cultural experience. Furthermore, they can enhance the learning of intercultural communication and help create an intercultural experience for people, especially those who study intercultural communication only by means of textbooks or theories. Through watching and learning movie clips and many cases, people can gain a lot of knowledge from intangible meaning to tangible cultural concepts and real life experience. Finally, these movie clips and cases will enrich and expand classroom discussions to broader and more relevant issues so as to broaden people's perspectives and inspire them to further reflection, learning and research.

In conclusion, specific movies or specific approaches to be used in teaching about culture can be very beneficial for people to study intercultural communication. By means of these movies we can well understand some cultural theories and improve our cultural competence in order to bridge the gap between our culture and other cultures. We hope you can begin your intercultural journey from an interesting and different perspective. Let's get started.

Unit 1　Intercultural Communication

I. Definition of Intercultural Communication

1. Introduction to Intercultural Communication
2. What Is Communication?

1. Introduction to Intercultural Communication

1) What is intercultural communication?

What is intercultural communication? Since 1963 many researchers have begun to study this field and have suggested various terms, such as transracial communication (Smith, 1973); interracial communication (Rich, 1974); interethnic communication (Scollon & Scollon, 1981) and cross-cultural communication (Ruben, 1986). Here we use David Pinto's viewpoint to define this term. Intercultural communication can be defined as the communication between individuals and/or groups from different cultures (p14). It is a form of communication that aims to share information across these various cultures and social groups. Intercultural communication describes a wide range of communication processes and problems that naturally appear within a group which is made up of individuals from different religious, social, ethnic, or educational backgrounds. In this sense it seeks to understand how people from different countries and cultures act, communicate and perceive the world around them. In a word, intercultural communication is communication between people of different cultures.

In the study of intercultural communication, there are two terms that we should know: intercultural communication and cross-cultural communication. In this distinction, Gudykunst believes that cross-cultural communication involves the study of similar communication situations or behaviors in different cultures. Intercultural communication, in contrast, involves the study of the process of communication between people from different cultures.

Here we use David Pinto's and Samovar & Porter's theories to explain intercultural communication and its process. According to Pinto, intercultural communication (ICC) is a discipline that studies the interaction between individuals or groups with different backgrounds. ICC aims to enhance intercultural awareness, encourage the use of a double-perspective approach and offer a systematic method for analyzing cultural differences in order to increase the effectiveness of communication between these individuals or groups (Pinto, p15, 2000). And Samovar & Porter define that intercultural communication is communication between people whose cultural perceptions and symbol systems are distinct enough to alter the communication events (2013, p48).

2) What are the elements and methods of intercultural communication?

Pinto points out that if ICC is to achieve its objectives, it must involve the following elements. Firstly, intercultural awareness is very significant, that is knowledge of various concepts in communication science and certain aspects of culture. Secondly, people should have double-perspective (2P) while looking at a situation, that is viewing it from the viewpoint of one's own culture as well as from the viewpoint of the other person's culture. Finally, the three-step method (3SM) is an effective way to solve problems that arise within intercultural communication.

The three-step method seeks to remove obstacles that hinder effective communication. Since we are often unaware of the norms, values and rules we adopt during socialization, every individual thus perceives and interprets everything around him from the limited perspective of his own norms and values. As a result, the individual tends to regard his own norms and values as universal. People tend to project their own norms, values and perceptions onto other people, and consequently they fail to fully express them to each other.

In intercultural communication, Pinto finds that many obstacles have their origins in the differences of norms and values between different cultures. He provides the following three steps to deal with those obstacles:

Step 1 is to get to know one's own norms, values and behavioral codes. Which rules and codes influence one's ways of thinking, acting and communicating?

Step 2 is to get to know the norms, values and behavioral codes of the other party. In doing so, opinions about the behavior of the other party should be separated from facts. What is the meaning behind the "unusual" behavior of the other party?

Step 3 is to determine how to deal with the observed differences in norms, values and behavioral codes in the given situation. Each party must decide the extent to which he is willing to adjust and accept the behavior of the other party.

2. What Is Communication?

The term "communication" refers to many forms of information transmission. It is a process involving a sender, a recipient and a message (Pinto, p19, 2000). A message is sent by the sender through a communication channel to a receiver, or to multiple receivers. It is a two-way process of reaching mutual understanding, in which participants not only decode information, news, ideas and feelings, but also encode the message into a form that is appropriate to the communication channel, and give feedback. Samovar & Porter define communication as "a dynamic, systematic process in which meanings are created and reflected in human reaction with symbols" (2013, p24).

The word "communication" comes from the Latin "communis", meaning "to share", and includes verbal, non-verbal and electronic means of human interaction. Communication Channels is the term given to the way in which we communicate (see Figure 1.1 below). There are a number of communication channels available to us today.

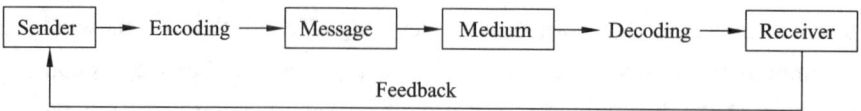

Figure 1.1　Classic Model of Communication

Humans convey information through a variety of channels, including face-to-face conversations, telephone calls, text messages, email, blogs, the Internet, radio and TV, written letters, brochures and reports, gestures, facial expressions, body languages and even social contexts, to name just a few. Communication can occur instantaneously in closed, intimate settings or over great periods of time in large public forums, like the Internet. In general, communication is a means of connecting people or places. In today's globalized, media-driven world, effective communication is essential.

Questions

1. What is intercultural communication?

_____

2. What is communication?

_____

3. What are the three elements of intercultural communication?

_____

4. Why do we need to study intercultural communication?

_____

Cultural Comprehension

Decide whether the following statements are true or false according to what you read.

(　　) 1. The terms "intercultural communication" and "cross-cultural communication" have the same meaning.

(　　) 2. International communication only takes place between groups like African Americans and Americans.

(　　) 3. All people who come from the same country will have the same culture.

(　　) 4. The double-perspective (2P) refers to looking at intercultural communication from the viewpoint of different cultures.

(　　) 5. Humans convey information through a variety of channels; therefore, intercultural communication happens in different contexts.

Unit 1　　Intercultural Communication

II. Content-based Activities

Section A   Movie Clips

 Introduction to the movie *The Terminal*

The main character Viktor Navorski is a man from an Eastern European country and he has just arrived in New York Airport. However, after he left his country war broke out. Suddenly, Navorski becomes a man without a country – or at least one that the U.S. cannot recognize – and therefore he is forbidden to enter the U.S. However, he also cannot be deported, so the security manager tells him that he has to remain in the airport until his status can be fixed. What's more, Navorski does not speak English, so he cannot communicate with others. But he somehow adapts and sets up residence in the airport, which makes Frank Dixon who places him there unhappy because he is on the verge of a promotion, and Navorski's presence might complicate that. Therefore Frank tries to get Navorski to leave, but Navorski refuses. This is because Navorski makes friends with some workers in the airport and is attracted to a stewardess.

Introduction to movie clip 1

In the selected scene, Viktor Navorski has just arrived at New York City's John F. Kennedy International Airport. Since he cannot understand English very well, it is very difficult for the officers to communicate with him. Although Viktor has his passport, he cannot enter the U.S. because a war has broken out in his country. His passport is therefore invalid until America can establish diplomatic relationships with the new government. In the clip, the officers try hard to explain what has happened in Viktor's country.

 Introduction to the movie *Gua Sha Treatment*

Gua Sha Treatment is a Chinese movie released in 2001. It is a story about cultural conflicts experienced by a Chinese family in the U.S.A.

Grandfather Xu comes from China to visit his son, Datong Xu's family in St. Louis. In order to treat a slight fever, he gives his grandson, Dennis Xu, a treatment of Gua Sha. But the authorities mistake the harmless traditional Chinese medical treatment for child abuse because of the obvious marks left on Dennis' back. According to the American law, the child is taken away by Child Welfare Bureau. Meanwhile, Grandfather Xu leaves America because he thinks that the living environment is not suitable for him. In his eyes, Gua Sha is so simple, common and harmless in China, while in America, it is regarded as child abuse. Furthermore, he cannot speak English. In the end, an American friend of the father, Benton Davis, tries Gua Sha and proves that the treatment leaves painful-looking marks that are not actually painful or harmful at all. Finally, the grandson is able to return home and the family is reunited.

Introduction to movie clip 2

In the selected movie clip, Datong Xu is charged by the American Child Welfare Bureau for

Intercultural Communication in Movies
影视作品中的跨文化交际

abusing his son. The plaintiff lawyer tries to prove Datong Xu is a brutal man who loves violence, as demonstrated by his computer designs of Sun Wukong. Because of their different cultural perspectives, they argue heatedly in court. Datong Xu regards Sun Wukong as a kind-hearted, righteous hero; however, the American lawyer thinks Sun Wukong is a naughty and violent monkey.

Exercises

Task 1: Fill in the blanks to the following lines spoken in the movie clips you just watched.

1. This is just a standard_____.
2. All the flights in and out of your country have been_____.
3. The new government has_____all borders, so your visa is no longer valid.
4. You have no right to enter the U.S. and I have no right to_____you.
5. Sun Wukong is a good-hearted compassionate righteous hero. He_____our traditional value and ethic.
6. And when the poor farmer_____him he totally destroyed their poor trees.

Task 2: Watch the movie clip for a second time and decide whether the following statements are true or false.

(   ) 1. Viktor Navorski is denied entrance to the U.S. because his passport was lost.
(   ) 2. The security manager of the airport told Viktor Navorski that he could return to his country.
(   ) 3. Viktor Navorski has a good command of English, and he can easily understand the American officers at the airport.
(   ) 4. Viktor Navorski is free to go anywhere he likes in the International Transit Lounge.
(   ) 5. Datong Xu is a man interested in violence.
(   ) 6. Both the American people and Chinese people have the same attitude towards Sun Wukong.

Task 3: Discussion: Divide students into several groups to discuss the clips and the problems of intercultural communication.

1. Why does Viktor Navorski fail to understand what happened in his country?

_____

2. Do you think Viktor Navorski encounters culture shock? Why?

_____

3. What kind of impression does Sun Wukong leave on Chinese people? Positive or negative?

_____

4. Why does the plaintiff lawyer in the clip have a different understanding of Sun Wukong from Datong Xu?

_____

Unit 1  Intercultural Communication

Section B Intercultural Communication Reading

Pre-reading Task

1. Why is cross-cultural communication important in the business world?
2. What kind of role does language play in intercultural communication?
3. Is it necessary for children to learn about intercultural communication in a globalized context?

Passage 1

Cross-cultural Communication

Business is not conducted in an identical fashion from culture to culture. Consequently, business relations are enhanced when **managerial**, sales, and technical personnel are trained to be aware of areas likely to create communication difficulties and conflicts across cultures. Similarly, international communication is even further strengthened when business people can anticipate areas of **commonality**. Finally, business in general is enhanced when people from different cultures find new approaches to old problems creating solutions by combining cultural perspectives and examining the problem at hand from each other's differing cultural perspectives.

The Factors

Culture directly affects the communication process in an international business setting through seven **variables**:

- language;
- environmental and technological considerations;
- social organization;
- contexting and face-saving;
- authority conception;
- nonverbal communication behavior;
- time conception.

These seven items form the **acronym** LESCANT. Most barriers when communicating across cultures derive from the communicator's **misgauge** of the LESCANT factors. By assessing in advance the roles these variables play in business communication, one can improve one's ability to convey those messages effectively to an audience from a different culture.

The seven LESCANT factors alone do not provide a thorough knowledge of another culture. Moreover, these seven dimensions of culture are not intended to represent the only causes of intercultural communication difficulties. Being aware of these factors does, however, provide an underlying foundation for understanding business people from other cultures. In short, these seven factors represent an approach for asking the right questions needed to see the most significant cultural differences and similarities. The answers to those questions vary according to the individual experiences of those involved.

Intercultural Communication in Movies

Language

Among the most often cited barriers to conflict-free cross-cultural business communication is the use of different languages. It is difficult to underestimate the important role that an understanding of **linguistic** differences plays in international business communication. Difficulties with language fall basically into three categories: **gross** translation problems, problems in conveying subtle distinctions from language to language, and culturally-based **variations** among speakers of the same language.

Gross translation errors, though frequent, may be less likely to cause conflict between parties than other language difficulties for two reasons. First, they are generally the easiest language difficulty to detect. Many gross translation errors are either **ludicrous** or make no sense at all. Only do those errors that continue to be logical in both the original meaning and in the mistranslated version pose a serious concern. Nonetheless, even when easily detected, gross translation errors waste time and wear on the patience of the parties involved. Additionally, for some, such errors imply a form of disrespect for the party into whose language the message is translated.

The subtle **shadings** that are often crucial to business **negotiations** are also weakened when the parties do not share a similar control of the same language. In English, for example, the mild distinctions between the words "misinterpret" and "misunderstand" can prove significant in a sensitive situation. To a touchy negotiator, to say that he or she "misunderstands" may imply that he or she is **dim-witted**. To say that same negotiator "misinterprets" a concept, by contrast, allows the negotiator a way to save face since all interpretations are arguable. He or she has reached an understandable though inaccurate interpretation of the matter. In such a situation, the term applies more objectively to the matter at hand than to the specific negotiator. To a non-native speaker with inadequate control of the language, however, such subtle distinctions might be lost. When other parties with full control over the language with whom the non-native speaker communicates assume that knowledge of this distinction exists, conflict deriving from misunderstanding is likely.

Nor do such mistranslations need to actually cross languages in cross-cultural business situations. Dialectical differences within the same language often create gross errors. One frequently cited example of how variations within a single language can affect business occurred when a U.S. **deodorant** manufacturer sent a Spanish translation of its slogan to their Mexican operations. The slogan read "If you use our deodorant, you won't be embarrassed." The translation, however, which the Mexican-based English-speaking employees saw no reason to avoid, used the term "embarazada" to mean "embarrassed". This provided much amusement to the Mexican market, as "embarazada" means "pregnant" in Mexican Spanish.

(707 words)

(Adapted from http://info.communispond.com/blog/bid/243299/barriers-to-cross-cultural-business-communication)

Unit 1　　Intercultural Communication

Passage 2

Teaching Our Kids about Cultural Diversity

Jennifer Shakeel

There is no denying the fact that our children today are faced with more diversity than we parents were at their age. America is the "melting pot" of the world and that is a good characteristic. It is here in America that you can experience the different cultures of the world without leaving the country – and for many, without leaving their state or city. All of this diversity raises a very good question, though. How as parents do we teach our children about cultural diversity and **tolerance**?

First, in order to teach our children about cultural diversity and tolerance, we as parents need to figure out what our beliefs are about these two topics. How open are we to people from another culture or race? Do we have any **biases** or **prejudices** against people that are different? Knowing if we do, admitting that we do and then figuring out why we do is the first step. Our goal is to teach our children about different cultures and introduce them to the different ways people live. We do not want to **cloud** their judgment and give them biases.

As adults, it can be hard to open ourselves up enough to recognize and deal with our prejudices, but it is something we need to do for our children's sake. You want your child to be open to new experiences and new people. In order for them to be that way, you need to be that way yourself. Read books with your children about other cultures. Many libraries have wonderful selections about different cultures and societies from around the world. Talk to your local librarian and check out a few books and read them with your child. Make sure that they are age appropriate, and if your child has more questions, the two of you can use the Internet together to get answers.

Where we live, the schools have done a really nice job of bringing out the different cultures that are present among the students in the school. They all do reports about different cultures, which requires them to do research, write a report and create something from that culture to share with the class. They also do a "Cultural Awareness" night at school. For this, families are asked to set up a **booth** in the gym with **posters**, maps and traditional clothing and present something about their culture to the people that come through the "fair". Thankfully, many families participate and there is food, music, dances, art and toys from all over the world right there in the gym.

That is something that the kids really look forward to and that we enjoy doing with them. We participate in the fair. Our family has a nice cultural mix. I am from America and my husband is from Pakistan. We were both raised very differently but have come together and created a wonderful harmony that has allowed our children to experience many things that most of their friends haven't. They have friends from different cultures and we all get together and have dinners and celebrate different events together.

We decided as parents that we would educate our children about the different religions and **spiritualities**, and when they were ready, they could decide for themselves what they wanted to believe in. We do not eat pork, we do celebrate the holidays, and we honor diversity and celebrate the fact that we are our own culture. We do this because kids are smarter than many adults give them **credit for**. When we talk to our children about where we have come from or about other people that we know and that they are friends with, we talk to them intelligently. If we don't have an answer for a certain question, we tell them that we do not know and then we find the answer together.

The best way to teach your child about cultural diversity is to let them see that you are accepting and tolerant. Our children **emulate** us. They act the way they do because of what they see their parents do. If you are open to other people and make an effort to learn more about different cultures, your child will eagerly want to do the same.

Make an effort to get to know your neighbor. Have dinner with a family that is different than your own. Encourage your child to make friends with other children. Ask them about the other kids in their class. We taught our children that they need to look at each person as a person.

We all look different on the outside – different colors of hair, eyes and skin. We all believe differently about a lot of different things. Pointing out those differences and using those differences as reasons to not talk to someone is never acceptable. We have also told them that it is never okay for another person to do something to them that makes them feel bad or hurts them or others.

Tolerance means understanding and openness. It does not mean acceptance of cruel behavior. That goes for everyone, regardless of their culture.

(858 words)

After-reading Task

1. According to passage 1, what does "LESCANT" mean?

_____

2. According to passage 1, why can language lead to great barriers in communication?

_____

3. According to passage 2, what does "melting pot" mean?

_____

4. According to passage 2, what is the best way to teach children about cultural diversity?

_____

 WORDS LIST

Passage 1
managerial /ˌmænəˈdʒiːriəl/ *a.* 经理的；管理上的
commonality /ˌkɒməˈnælɪti/ *n.* 共同特征；共同性；共性；公共
variable /ˈveəriəbl/ *a.* 变化的，可变的
              n. 可变因素，变量

acronym /'ækrənɪm/ *n.* 首字母缩略词
misgauge /mɪs'geɪdʒ/ *n.* 误判
linguistic /lɪŋ'gwɪstɪk/ *a.* 语言的；语言学的
gross /grəʊs/ *a.* 总的
variation /ˌveərɪ'eɪʃn/ *n.* 变化；变量
ludicrous /'luːdɪkrəs/ *a.* 可笑的；荒唐的
shading /'ʃeɪdɪŋ/ *n.* 细微变化；细微差别
negotiation /nɪˌgəʊʃɪ'eɪʃn/ *n.* 协商，谈判
dim-witted /dɪm'wɪtɪd/ *a.* 笨的，傻的
deodorant /dɪ'əʊdərənt/ *n.* 除臭剂，防臭剂

Passage 2
tolerance /'tɒlərəns/ *n.* 宽容，容忍
bias /'baɪəs/ *n.* 偏见
prejudice /'predʒʊdɪs/ *n.* 成见，歧视
cloud /klaʊd/ *v.* 使难以理解；使……朦胧不清；混淆
booth /buːð/ *n.* 售货棚，摊位
poster /'pəʊstə(r)/ *n.* 海报，招贴，公告
spirituality /ˌspɪrɪtʃʊ'æləti/ *n.* 精神性，灵性
credit for 赞扬；认可
emulate /'emjʊleɪt/ *v.* （因为钦慕而）仿效，模仿

Section C　Case Studies

Case 1

Matthew, an American graduate student studying in China, was invited to his Chinese friend's home for the weekend. Upon entering the home, his friend's mother, Mrs. Wang, wants to welcome him by pouring him some tea.

Mrs. Wang: "Would you like some tea?"

Matthew: "No, thank you!"

Mrs. Wang then proceeds to pour Matthew a cup of tea and sets it in front of Matthew. Over a course of thirty minutes, Matthew drinks half of the cup. Mrs. Wang then proceeds to pour Matthew more tea, but Matthew tries to refuse her.

Matthew: "I have enough! Thank you!"

Mrs. Wang insists and fills the cup again. Matthew smiles and says, "Thank you!" This time, Matthew drinks the whole cup. Mrs. Wang again proceeds to fill the cup up with more tea, and Matthew again tries to refuse her.

Matthew: "Really, I don't need any more. Thank you!"

Mrs. Wang still insists and pours more tea. Matthew smiles and begins drinking again, but he is actually quite upset.

Intercultural Communication in Movies
影视作品中的跨文化交际

Reflection

1. Why do you think Matthew is upset?

2. What is Matthew trying to communicate with his words and body language? How does Mrs. Wang interpret his words and body language?

3. What is Mrs. Wang communicating with her words and body language? How does Matthew interpret her words and body language?

Case 2

John, an American college student studying abroad in China, has invited his Chinese friend, Dai Tong, to have lunch together at the school cafeteria.

John: "What time do you want to meet there?"

Dai Tong: "I don't care. You decide!"

John: "OK, how about 12:00?"

Dai Tong: "Sounds good. See you then!"

Later, John arrives at the cafeteria at 11:55, but he does not see his friend, Dai Tong. He waits and keeps looking at his watch. He checks his phone, but Dai Tong has not contacted him about being late. Almost 15 minutes later, at 12:08, Dai Tong finally arrives with a big smile. Dai Tong greets John and appears happy, however John feels upset and disrespected.

Reflection

1. What intercultural communication conflict has occurred in the example above?

2. What cultural expectations does John have of Dai Tong when they decide to meet at 12:00? What kind of communication does he expect when Dai Tong does not show up by 12:00?

3. What should John and Dai Tong do next time to avoid this communication conflict?

Case 3 Watch the movie clip "*Anna and the King*" and try to analyze the cultural phenomenon in an intercultural context.

Reflection

1. What can we learn from the movie clip?

2. How can people respect cultural diversity?

III. Task-based Activities

Exercises

Choose the best choice according to the cultural context.

( ) 1. You call your American friend on the phone to see if he is free to play basketball with you. When he first answers the phone, you want to begin with some small talk. You should say:
   a. "Hey, what are you doing?"
   b. "Hey, how are you doing?"

( ) 2. You help your foreign teacher Mr. Martin find his classroom.
   Mr. Martin : "Thank you!"
   a. "You're welcome."
   b. "You don't have to say thank you."

( ) 3. In class, your English teacher greets you. You should reply:
   a. "Good morning, teacher."
   b. "Good morning, Mr. Martin."

( ) 4. You meet an American for the first time and want to become friends with him. You should say:
   a. "If you're free, I'd love to hang out sometime."
   b. "Can we be friends?"

( ) 5. Your American friend has cooked you dinner at her house. After you take your first bite, she asks you, "So, what do you think?" You reply:
   a. "Not bad!"
   b. "It's great!"

Group Work

Discussion 1

Imagine that you are designing a course for American students coming to China. What would be important for Americans to know about China? What would you teach them about the perceptions of Chinese people?

Discussion 2

In groups, discuss the question: Why is intercultural communication more difficult than communication between people from the same culture?

Intercultural Communication in Movies
影视作品中的跨文化交际

Assignment

Presentation 1
Divide students into several groups to analyze the relevant movie clips and discuss the intercultural conflicts.

Presentation 2
How can people cultivate their awareness of intercultural communication? Try to use David Pinto's three-step method to illustrate how to effectively communicate in an intercultural context.

> *The gentleman pursues harmony instead of homogeneity; the vulgar man seeks uniformity at the sacrifice of harmony.*
> — Confucian saying
>
> 君子和而不同，小人同而不和。
>
> *Isn't it a pleasure for one to have like-minded people coming from faraway places?*
> — The Analects of Confucius
>
> 有朋自远方来，不亦乐乎？

Unit 2   Culture and Communication

I. Definition of Culture and Communication

1. What Is Culture?
2. The Iceberg Model of Culture
3. The Lewis Model of Culture

1. What Is Culture?

Culture is a complex system of behaviors, values, beliefs, traditions, norms, foods, art, jewelry, clothing, etc., that is transmitted from generation to generation. Every nationality has a different culture, which gives it an identity and uniqueness. This leads to misunderstanding and misinterpretation between people from different countries. As a result, it is very important to understand others' cultures – especially while communicating nowadays. There are numerous definitions of culture, but we have only selected a few of them to study.

Geert Hofstede (1984, p51) defines a very common set of models for international cultures. He says, "Culture is the collective programming of the human mind that distinguishes the members of one category of people from another. Culture in this sense is a system of collectively held values."

Kroeber and Kluckhohn (1952) believe culture "consists of patterns, explicit and implicit, of behavior acquired and transmitted by symbols, constituting the distinctive achievements of human groups, including their embodiments in artifacts; the essential core of culture consists of traditional (i.e. historically derived and selected) ideas and especially their attached values; culture systems may, on the one hand, be considered as products of action, and on the other as conditioning elements of further action".

Samovar & Porter (2013, p36) define culture as "the deposit of knowledge, experience, beliefs, values, actions, attitudes, meanings, hierarchies, religions, notions of time, roles, spatial relations, concepts of the universe, and artifacts acquired by a group of people in the course of generations through individual and group striving".

John Paul Lederach (1995, p9) says, "Culture is the shared knowledge and schemes created by a set of people for perceiving, interpreting, expressing, and responding to the social realities around them."

In short, from the perspective of intercultural communication, culture is defined as the shared patterns of behaviors, interactions, cognitive constructs, and understandings that are learned through a process of socialization. These shared patterns identify the members of a culture group while also distinguishing them from other groups.

2. The Iceberg Model of Culture

The *Iceberg Model of Culture* is suggested by Guy Rocher in 1969 (see Figure 2.1 below). The iceberg model demonstrates how culture is made up of a visible structure (above the water) and an invisible structure (below the water). He reasoned that if the culture of a society is an iceberg, there are some aspects visible above the water, but there is a larger portion hidden beneath the surface. Only about 10% of the iceberg is visible above the waterline – namely, external or surface culture. But 90% of the iceberg is invisible and hidden beneath the surface – namely, internal or deep culture.

Figure 2.1 Iceberg Theory of Culture

What does this mean? The external part of culture is what we can see, such as behaviors and traditions. The internal part of culture, however, is below the surface of a society and includes things like beliefs, values and perceptions.

While comparing the external and internal elements of culture, we can see great differences.

Internal	*versus*	*External*
Implicitly Learned		*Explicitly Learned*
Unconscious		*Conscious*
Difficult to Change		*Easily Changed*
Subjective Knowledge		*Objective Knowledge*

Cultural competence requires us to be consciously aware of the ways in which the invisible cultural elements can influence our relationship with others. We cannot judge a new culture based only on what we see when we first enter it. We must take the time to get to know individuals from that culture and interact with them. In order to understand others' values, it is important to situate ourselves by identifying our own culture's visible and invisible elements. Only by doing so can we understand the values and beliefs that underlie the behavior of another nationality.

3. The Lewis Model of Culture

Richard Donald Lewis is a British linguist who suggests the Lewis Model of Cross-Cultural Communication. His model provides a practical framework for understanding and communicating with people of other cultures. The core of the model classifies cultural norms into Linear-Active, Multi-Active and Re-Active (see Table 2.1 below). The Lewis Model can help us get along better both personally and professionally with other cultures because it allows us to predict how they are likely to act.

Table 2.1 The Characteristics of Each Cultural Type

LINEAR-ACTIVE	MULTI-ACTIVE	RE-ACTIVE
Talks half the time	Talks most of the time	Listens most of the time
Gets data from stats, research	Solicits information first-hand from people	Uses both data and people sources
Plans ahead step by step	Plans grand outline only	Looks at general principles
Polite but direct	Emotional	Polite and indirect
Partly conceals feelings	Displays feelings	Conceals feelings
Confronts with logic	Confronts emotionally	Never confronts
Dislikes losing face	Has good excuses	Must not lose face
Compartmentalizes projects	Lets one project influence another	Sees the whole picture
Rarely interrupts	Often interrupts	Doesn't interrupt
Job-oriented	People-oriented	Very people-oriented
Sticks to the facts	Juggles the facts	Statements are promises
Truth before diplomacy	Flexible truth	Diplomacy over truth
Sometimes impatient	Impatient	Patient
Limited body language	Unlimited body language	Subtle body language
Respects officialdom	Pulls strings	Networks
Separates the social & professional	Interweaves the social & professional	Connects the social & professional
Does one thing at a time	Multi tasks	Reacts to partner's action
Punctuality very important	Punctuality not important	Punctuality important

(Adapted from *When Cultures Collide: Leading Across Cultures* by Richard D. Lewis)

Linear-actives are cultures that plan, schedule, organize, and do one thing at a time. Germany, Switzerland, and the U.S. are in this group. Multi-actives are cultures that do many things at once, planning their priorities not according to a time schedule but according to the relative interest or importance that each appointment brings with it. Italy, Latin America and Arab countries are members of this group. Re-actives are cultures that prioritize courtesy and respect, listening quietly and calmly to others and responding carefully to their proposals. Vietnam, Japan, China and Republic of Korea are in this group.

Questions

1. What is the Cultural Iceberg Model?

2. What is the core of the Lewis Model of Culture?

3. What is the culture, according to Samovar & Porter?

4. Discuss with your partner what type of culture China belongs to and give some examples to illustrate.

Cultural Comprehension

Decide whether the following statements are true or false according to what you read.

( ) 1. The Lewis Model of cross-cultural communication helps people who come from different cultures to better understand cultural differences.

( ) 2. In the Cultural Iceberg Model, behaviors and customs are visible and subconscious, which account for 10% of culture.

( ) 3. Culture is the deposit of knowledge, experience, beliefs, values, attitudes, religions and possessions acquired by a group of people over the course of generations.

( ) 4. German and American people belong to the Linear-actives because they plan and organize things and do one thing at a time.

( ) 5. Arab, Japan, China and Republic of Korea belong to the cultural group of Re-actives.

II. Content-based Activities

Section A   Movie Clips

 Introduction to the movie *The Joy Luck Club*

The movie *The Joy Luck Club* is based on a novel with the same name. The novel is written by Amy Tan, a famous Chinese American writer. It is a story about four Chinese immigrant women and their American-born daughters.

Growing up in different cultures, the four mothers have different views of the world from their American-born daughters, which leads to countless conflicts. However, the mothers never cease to try to build bridges over the cultural differences and conflicts between them and their daughters. At first the daughters don't understand their mothers and the Chinese culture that their mothers represent, but as time elapses, the daughters begin to understand and appreciate their mothers' past and accept their mothers in the end.

Introduction to movie clip 1

In the selected clip, Waverly brings her American boyfriend Richard home to meet her family members. Richard knows little about the Chinese culture, especially table manners. At dinner, Richard behaves improperly by taking all of the shrimp before others eat them and bragging about his good use of chopsticks. What's worse, when Waverly's mother presents her best dish, she denigrates herself by saying, "This dish has no flavor; it's too bad to eat." However, Richard takes her seriously and adds a lot of soy sauce, ruining the whole dish.

 Introduction to the movie *Anna and the King*

This is the story of a romance between the King of Siam and the widowed British schoolteacher Anna Leonowens during the 1860s. Anna was invited by the king to teach his fifty-eight royal children in the exotic land of Siam. Since Siam is a traditional eastern country, after she arrives, she experiences various kinds of culture shock. Since she is a young widow who brings her little son with her, she has to adapt to the traditions of the Siamese, which are unbearable to her at times. This film explores the challenges different genders and cultures face in society.

Introduction to movie clip 2

In the selected clip, cholera breaks out and many people get infected, including the King's little daughter. She is in a critical condition and calls for her teacher Anna. After Anna is invited to the palace, the prime minister tells Anna not to weep, because this will cause the dead person to come back to comfort the living.

Exercises

Task 1: Fill in the blanks to the following lines spoken in the movie clips you just watched.

1. You should have taken only a small_____of the best dishes until everyone had had a helping.
2. He shouldn't have_____he was a fast learner.
3. When Rich_____my mom's cooking and he didn't even know what he had done.
4. As is the Chinese cook's custom, my mother always_____her own cooking, but only with the dish she serves with special pride.
5. The little one has made_____mention of Sir's name.
6. It is why man must not be heard_____.

Task 2: Watch the movie clips for a second time and decide whether the following statements are true or false.

( ) 1. Rich can use Chinese chopsticks very well.

Intercultural Communication in Movies
影视作品中的跨文化交际

(　　) 2. Waverly's mother holds very traditional Chinese values.

(　　) 3. Rich should eat up all the shrimps since he enjoys them.

(　　) 4. There is misunderstanding between Rich and Waverly's family members owing to the culture difference.

(　　) 5. While seeing the little princess, Anna is too sad to weep.

(　　) 6. Weeping is a way to show people's respect for the dead in Siam.

Task 3: Discussion: Divide students into several groups to discuss the clips and the problems of intercultural communication.

1. Why does Rich fail to leave a good impression on Waverly's parents?

_____

2. Do you think Waverly's mother will approve of their marriage? Why?

_____

3. What is the traditional Chinese cooking custom?

_____

4. What do Chinese people do to show their respect for the dead? Will they weep?

_____

Section B　Intercultural Communication Reading

 Pre-reading Task

1. Have you ever considered the differences between people? Why are people so different?

2. Do you think one culture is better than another? What factors cause you to think this way?

3. What differences are there between American and Chinese culture? Give some examples to support your opinion.

Passage 1
Intercultural Communication and Cultural Differences
— How People Are the Same and How They Are Different

Eisla R. Sebastian

"People are alike, and people are different." What a profound statement. This statement is an important concept in learning how to deal with intercultural communication issues, and with today's population shift it is more important than ever to grasp it. Here we will examine how people are alike, and how people are different in relation to intercultural communication.

First, let's look at how people are alike, and how these similarities relate to intercultural communication. Without trying to state the obvious, physiologically we all have basically the same heart, lungs, blood, brains, etc. Also we all try to "seek pleasure and avoid pain". (Samovar and Porter, 2001, p29). Protection of the **ego** is also a commonality among the human race as well. At

20

some point in life we all realize that life is finite, that we are "isolated from all other human beings" (p29), we all must make decisions, and that the world is given meaning by personal experiences. Also every culture has a language, a set of social rules based on the group members' ages and genders, and systems to **regulate** the community (p29). If we remember that we have these similarities, then it is obvious that we are more alike than different. Using these similarities we can then relate to someone we thought we could not understand because they were "different". And by altering slightly our views on the similarities, we can then begin to understand the differences in cultures.

"Members of different cultures look differently at the world around them. Some believe that the physical world is real. Others believe that it is just an **illusion**. Some believe everything around them is permanent, while others say it is **transient**. Reality is not the same for all people." (Samovar and Porter, 2001, pp29-30) Realizing that people "see" things differently is key to intercultural communication. Knowing how to "see" as a member of another culture is difficult, because no two people are exactly alike, and therefore no two people communicate exactly the same way. If you can pick out the key elements to that cultures' codes of conduct, it will greatly increase the success rate of your communication attempts. Such differences in communication may include personal conduct such as how close or far away you stand, whether touching is permitted, and if so, what kind of personal contact is permitted and what is expected. For example, because of the population density in Europe, people tend to stand very close together and touch a lot while conversing, while Americans, coming from a country with a relatively low population density tend to leave a great deal of space between themselves and others while they are speaking.

Another way in which people are different is their view of the world. For example, the Egyptian worldview is based on Arabic culture. Businesses are closed on Friday because that is their holy day, as opposed to the Christian holy day on Sunday, when most American businesses are closed. The **Hindus**' worldview, on the other hand, is based on "a set of interrelated assumptions and beliefs about the nature of reality, the organization of the universe, the purpose of human life, God, and other philosophical issues concerned with the concept of being" (Samovar and Porter, 2001). As you can see knowing some of these differences will greatly increase your ability to understand and communicate more efficiently in an intercultural situation.

Knowing that "people are the same, and that people are different" is essential to effective intercultural communication. By learning to identify commonalties and adjusting them to the culture you are trying to communicate, and by learning the key communication codes of a culture you can avoid misunderstandings, and get your intentions across clearly.

(635 words)

Passage 2
Differences between American & Chinese Culture
Rachel Bennett

Different countries have different social structures, business norms and ways of forming relationships. Analyzing cultural norms is not a means to determine a "model" way of life, but it is a way of understanding how countries and individuals interact on a local, national and international scale. China and the United States are leading global super powers, and yet they have very different cultural practices.

Social Structure

China has a very formal and **hierarchical** social structure that extends to business, institutional and family life. For example, children are expected to respect their elders with the oldest family member commanding the greatest respect. In America, there is greater fluidity between groups with workers, managers, children and adults often making joint decisions and enjoying social occasions together.

Collectivism vs. **Individualism**

In China, people think about ideas in a collective sense, often considering how their actions will affect their friends, neighbors and colleagues before making a decision. Decisions are more commonly made for the greater good as opposed to personal gain. In America, **prioritizing** individual goals and motives over collective ones is considered the norm. This **ethos** is often actively encouraged to stimulate ambition and a drive to achieve business and personal success.

Morals and Values

Humility and respect are very important in Chinese culture. Individuals are expected to treat each other well and to show modesty when discussing successes, or to not discuss them at all. In America, people are comfortable with openly discussing, playing up and praising success with humility being seen by some as a weakness.

Additionally, in China, there is a strong sense of right and wrong. In America, there are more gray areas with questions of morality being a matter for discussion as opposed to being **set in stone**.

Freedom of Expression

The Chinese are strictly bound by **protocol** and so it is better to "save face" by respecting and honoring the opinion of others, even if you believe what they are saying is incorrect, than to demand that others agree with your way of thinking. American culture is much more direct with people being encouraged to debate **contentious** issues even if it leads to confrontation.

Business Relations

Business relations reflect the collective and individual nature of both societies. One thing that often strikes newcomers to the United States is Americans' **gregariousness**. It's not unusual for strangers to get friendly and **strike up** conversations about a common interest. Yet in reality, Americans are likely to draw clear distinctions between acquaintances and business associates, and their personal friends. Conversely, while Chinese are often perceived as more reserved and distant than Americans, they seek genuine personal relationships with their business partners that go beyond networking and they actively work to build these connections. Consequently, securing a business deal in China is often a lengthy process. Business in the US is a more **cut throat** process with emphasis being placed on speed and efficiency over building relationships.

(493 words)

 After-reading Task

1. According to passage 1, why should we understand people's similarities before considering their differences?

2. According to passage 1, what's the purpose of understanding cultural diversity?

3. Do you agree with the analysis of collectivism and individualism of passage 2? Why?

4. According to passage 2, how do Chinese people deal with business relationships? How do Americans?

 WORDS LIST

Passage 1
ego /'i:gəʊ / *n.* 自我；自我意识
regulate /'regjʊleɪt/ *vt.* 调节
illusion /ɪ'lu:ʒən/ *n.* 错觉；幻想
transient /'trænzɪənt/ *a.* 短暂的；转瞬即逝的
density /'densətɪ/ *n.* 密度
Hindus /'hɪndu:z/ *n.* 印度人

Passage 2
hierarchical /ˌhaɪə'rɑ:kɪkl/ *a.* 等级（制）的
fluidity /flʊ'ɪdətɪ / *n.* 流动性
collectivism /kə'lektɪvɪzəm/ *n.* 集体主义
individualism /ˌɪndɪ'vɪdʒʊəlɪzəm/ *n.* 个人主义
prioritize /praɪ'ɒrətaɪz/ *vt.* 按重要性排列，优先处理
ethos /'i:θɒs/ *n.* 民族精神；精神特质
humility /hju:'mɪlətɪ / *n.* 谦逊，谦恭
set in stone 一成不变

Intercultural Communication in Movies
影视作品中的跨文化交际

protocol /'prəʊtəkɒl/ *n.* 礼仪
contentious /kən'tenʃəs/ *a.* 引起争论的，有争论的
gregariousness /grɪ'gerɪəsnəs/ *n.* 集群性
strike up 使开始；建立起
cut throat 割喉式的；快速的

Section C Case Studies

Case 1

Wang Li, a Chinese businesswoman, was working in the United States on a short-term project. One day, while she was walking by what seemed to be a park, she saw a long row of fancy, black cars driving slowly down the street led by a police car. "Wow, a wedding!" she thought. "I've never seen an American wedding before."

Suddenly, the cars stopped and parked on the edge of the street. A man and a woman got out of the first car. They were dressed very nicely. "This must be the bride and groom," she thought. Wang Li went up to them.

"Congratulations!" she said enthusiastically. "I'm sure this is the best day of your life!"

The couple looked at her with startled eyes. Suddenly, the woman yelled at her.

"Are you serious? Get out of here! And don't let me ever see you again!" Then the woman burst into tears. The man comforted her while Wang Li left very confused.

"What's their problem? I thought I was being nice," she thought to herself.

Reflection

1. Why did the woman yell at Wang Li? What were the cars doing?

_____

2. In what way was Wang Li assuming her culture was the same as American culture?

_____

3. If you were in America and saw a long row of black cars, would you assume the same thing Wang Li assumed? What could you do to ensure you are interpreting this cultural practice correctly?

_____

Case 2

Chen Na and Xiao Yu, two Chinese students studying abroad in the United States, went to a restaurant to celebrate their American friend Lisa's birthday. At the restaurant, Chen Na and Xiao Yu both gave Lisa a small birthday gift. Lisa was very happy, and told Chen Na and Xiao Yu, "Thank you!" In fact, Lisa liked the gift so much that she thanked them four or five times during the evening.

Unit 2   Culture and Communication

Chen Na and Xiao Yu, however, began to feel upset. In the past, they thought Lisa was their best friend, but now they were starting to have doubts. "Why is she acting so polite around us?" they wondered.

After they finished eating, the waitress came with the bill. Chen Na and Xiao Yu sat silently and looked at Lisa, waiting for her to pay the bill. Lisa, however, looked at Chen Na and Xiao Yu, expecting them to pay for her birthday dinner. Finally, Lisa took out some money and paid for the whole dinner. However, as she left, she was quite upset. "I thought Chen Na and Xiao Yu were my best friends. How could they expect me to buy them dinner on *my* birthday?"

Reflection

1. In what way did Lisa assume Chen Na and Xiao Yu's culture was the same as her own? What problem did this lead to?

   _____

2. In what way did Chen Na and Xiao Yu assume that Lisa's culture was the same as their own? What problem did this lead to?

   _____

3. How could these girls avoid a similar conflict in the future?

   _____

Case 3   Watch the following clip from *"The Mother PK Daughter-In-Law"* and try to analyze the cultural phenomenon in an intercultural context.

Reflection

1. Why is Emma so surprised when her husband explains the Chinese family?

   _____

2. What are the differences between western family and eastern family?

   _____

III. Task-based Activities

Exercises

Choose the best choice according to the cultural context.

(   ) 1. Your American friend, John, compliments you on your English.

   John: "Wow, your English is so good!"

   You should respond by saying:

   a. "No, no, my English is very poor."

b. "Thank you. I am glad you think so."

(　　) 2. You are eating at a restaurant with your American friend, Sarah, and you are looking at the menu deciding what to order. You are not really hungry for pizza, but everything else on the menu sounds good. Sarah asks you what you want to order.

Sarah: "What would you like to eat?"

You should respond by saying:

a. "Anything except pizza."

b. "Anything is fine."

(　　) 3. Your American friend, Steve, pays for the bill after you have lunch together. You should say:

a. "Thank you for dinner!"

b. You should not say anything because you two are good friends.

(　　) 4. While you and your friend are walking on the street, you see a tall American. You rarely see foreigners – especially tall foreigners – in your city, and you want to take a photo with him to show your friends. You should say:

a. "Hi, can we take a photo with you?"

b. You should not take a picture with him because Americans think it's rude for strangers to ask for a photo.

(　　) 5. While you are talking with your American friend, she mentions that her grandmother died last year. You should say:

a. "Oh, what a pity!"

b. "I'm sorry to hear that."

Group Work

Discussion 1

Discuss with your classmates about common misunderstandings and conflicts that occur between Westerners and Chinese. What are some differences and similarities between the two cultures?

Discussion 2

Now that you understand differences that arise between cultures, discuss with your partner about how you can avoid making mistakes when communicating cross-culturally.

Assignment

Presentation 1

Please use the "The Lewis Model" to determine which country and what kind of characteristics belong to each culture type by using √ and filling in the blanks. Make a brief presentation about this topic.

Unit 2   Culture and Communication

Nation	Linear-active	Multi-active	Re-active
USA			
UK			
Canada			
Australia			
China			
Republic of Korea			
Italy			

Presentation 2

Just like an iceberg, some cultural aspects are visible, while many are invisible. Think of cultures you've visited or learned about. Fill in the following blanks with at least five words and present them to the class, explaining each word.

Visible cultural characteristics   *Invisible cultural characteristics*
      Artifacts   *Ethical codes*
_____   _____
_____   _____
_____   _____
_____   _____

> *One man's meat is another man's poison.*
> 萝卜白菜，各有所爱！
> *So many countries, so many customs.*
> 百里不同风。
>
> – English proverb

Unit 3　Cultural Value Orientation

I. Definition of Cultural Value Orientation

1. Kluckhohn and Strodtbeck's Value Orientation
2. Traditional Chinese Value Orientation: Confucianism

1. Kluckhohn and Strodtbeck's Value Orientation

Nowadays, we are living in a global village. Technology has brought everyone much closer together, and this means that people of different cultures find themselves working together and communicating more and more. However, this also poses the question: How well do those people who come from different cultures communicate with and understand each other?

As we know, values are an important, generally invisible part of our culture. What is value? It refers to one's principles or standards or one's judgment of what is valuable or important in life. Values form the basis of all our attitudes and actions, and this brings us into harmony or conflict with those who share or do not share our own cultural values. Cultural values are indeed subjective, relative, and evaluative when it comes to understanding social norms. As a result, different countries, religions, societies, and people adhere to very different beliefs, traditions, and laws.

Cultural values are defined as culture-level dimensions that reflect a set of deeply held beliefs that characterize a culture's worldview with respect to humanity and its relationship to nature and time (Kluckhohn and Strodtbeck, 1961; Hofstede, 1984). The concept of the value orientation theory was created by Kluckhohn and Strodtbeck in 1961, according to Jandt (2009). There are five basic questions that need answering at the root of any culture: 1) What is the innate human nature? 2) What is the relation between man and nature? 3) What is the mode of human relationship? 4) What is the mode of human activity? 5) What is the orientation toward time? Based on these questions, Kluckhohn and Strodtbeck believe that value orientation is the dominant value system of a society that makes it distinct from other societies. Value orientation is made up of five categories relating to human activities and their relation to them. These five categories are man vs. nature orientation (defined by which one dominates the other), time orientation (past, present, or future), human nature orientation (good, evil, or a mix), activity orientation (doing, being, or growing), and relationships between humans (based on the individual, the group, or ancestors).

Kluckhohn and Strodtbeck propose that all human societies must answer a limited number of universal problems and that the value-based solutions are limited in number and universally known, but that different cultures prefer different ones. These value orientations impose parameters designed to establish larger patterns of cultural-specific behavior based on worldviews that can then be compared across cultures, as a way of understanding culture-group behavior. Ting-Toomey (1999) sums up their theory as follows (Table 3.1).

Table 3.1 Kluckhohn and Strodtbeck's Value Orientations

Orientation	Range of Value Orientations		
People and Nature	Subordination to Nature	Harmony with Nature	Mastery over Nature
Time Sense	Past Oriented	Present Oriented	Future Oriented
Human Nature	Basically Evil (mutable / immutable)	Neutral or Good and Evil (mutable / immutable)	Basically Good (mutable / immutable)
Human Activity	Being – who you are	Being in Becoming	Doing – what you are doing
Social Relations	Hierarchy (authoritarian decisions)	Group (group decisions)	Individualism (autonomy)

Klukhohn and Strodtbeck (1961); based on Ting-Toomey's summary (1999).

Ting-Toomey explains the value orientation patterns. Firstly, in the man vs. nature value orientation, mastering the environment means having control over nature; being harmony with nature emphasizes spiritual transformation or enlightenment over material gain; subjugation to nature means that nature is beyond the control of individuals. Secondly, in time sense, future-oriented time sense emphasizes planning and clear objectives; present-oriented time sense values here-and-now, especially relationships; and past-oriented time sense honors historic and ancestral ties and elders. Thirdly, in human nature orientation, "basically evil" implies that most people cannot be trusted, people are fundamentally bad and they have to be controlled; "basically good" means most people are by nature fundamentally good; and mixed nature suggests that there are both good and bad people in the world. People can be changed with proper guidance. Fourthly, in human activity, "doing" refers to achievement-oriented activities; "being" means living with emotional vitality and relational connection; and "being-in-becoming" refers to spiritual renewal and connection. Finally, there are three types of social relations. The first one is hierarchy, which shows that there is a natural order to relations. Some people are born to lead and others are followers; the second one is individual relation, which suggests that all people should have equal rights, and each person should have complete control over his own destiny; the third one is cooperation, which emphasizes organization and team work. Each member participates in decision making because it is important that significant decisions not be made alone.

From the observations above, we can see that there are completely different cultural value systems in Western and Asian societies, which explains the cultural diversity between the two to a certain extent. It is these value orientations that account for differences around the world between various people's customs, behaviors, etc.

2. Traditional Chinese Value Orientation: Confucianism

China is a country with an approximately five-thousand-year history, in which Confucianism has exerted a major influence in shaping its unique culture and values. Traditional Chinese value orientation is greatly influenced by Confucianism and other schools of thought, such as Taoism and Buddhism. Chinese value orientations have often been characterized as very different from those in the West.

During the Spring and Autumn Period (春秋) and the subsequent Warring States Period (战国), Chinese traditional philosophy flourished into what has become known as the Hundred Schools of Thought (诸子百家). During this period, the major schools of thought included Confucianism (儒家), Daoism (道家), Mohism (墨家) and Legalism (法家). All had considerable influence in the traditional Chinese and Asian value system.

Confucianism has many beliefs, but here we will only address its core theory of "Five Constant Virtues" (五常). The "Five Constant Virtues" are known as "benevolence" (仁), "personal loyalty" (义), "courtesy, politeness or propriety" (礼), "wisdom" (智) and "faith" (信). Among them benevolence can be regarded as the primary virtue. Chinese people believe that humans are fundamentally virtuous or virtue-oriented. Moreover, they think people should be in a harmonious relationship with nature; nature and people should be unified into one. As was discussed above, Chinese culture is collectivism-oriented, which pays more attention to group identities, emphasizes interpersonal and mutually dependent relationships within the group, shows great concern for mutual faces, and stresses consensus, cooperation and harmony. Because Chinese culture is primarily past-oriented, Chinese people cherish the past and respect their ancestors. These value orientations have provided a rich cultural legacy for Chinese, as well as other East Asians and Southeast Asians.

However, Confucianism has also had its negative influences. For example, women, such as wives and daughters, have a lower position in society than men. According to Confucianism, there are Three Obediences and Four Virtues for Women (三从四德). The Three Obediences are obeying one's father as a daughter, obeying one's husband as a wife, and obeying one's sons in widowhood. The Four Virtues are morality, proper speech, modest manners, and diligent work. Unfortunately, the low view of women according to Confucianism led to tragic fates for many women in early China.

Questions

1. What is cultural value orientation?

_____

2. What are the relationships between man and nature?

_____

Unit 3 Cultural Value Orientation

3. How many types of cultural value orientations are there according to Klukhohn and Strodtbeck?

_____

4. What is Confucianism? Talk to your partner about Chinese cultural value orientations and try to give some examples to illustrate.

_____

Cultural Comprehension

Decide whether the following statements are true or false according to what you read.
(   ) 1. Confucianism primarily holds the belief of the "Five Constant Virtues".
(   ) 2. Subjugation to nature means that nature is beyond the control of individuals.
(   ) 3. As far as time is concerned, people have different value orientations.
(   ) 4. Some people believe that we should all live harmoniously with one another because we are all creatures of the same universe.
(   ) 5. Collectivism is a common cultural pattern found in most northern and western regions of Europe and North America.

II. Content-based Activities

Section A   Movie Clips

 Introduction to the movie *The Pursuit of Happyness*

Starring superstar Will Smith, this film is about the true life story of Chris Gardner, a dream pursuer, who goes from living on the streets to owning his own brokerage firm. At the beginning of the story, Gardner spends all of his savings on high-tech medical equipments and tries his best to sell them to hospitals. However, owing to the high prices, the equipment is turned down by most hospitals, which makes it difficult for Gardner to support his family. Then his wife leaves him and he has to maintain custody of his son. After countless setbacks he finally becomes successful.

Introduction to movie clip 1

In this clip, Chris Gardner accompanies his son to play basketball one Saturday, even though their living conditions are terrible since his wife has left the family. Because they can't afford to pay rent, they have to move into a motel. Despite the setbacks life has brought them, they remain optimistic about their future. Most importantly, Chris Gardner keeps encouraging his son to pursue his dreams, which are the only hope for a better tomorrow.

 Introduction to the movie *Little Miss Sunshine*

This story is about a pudgy, bespectacled seven-year-old girl Olive who dreams of getting

Intercultural Communication in Movies
影视作品中的跨文化交际

first place at the coming Little Miss Sunshine beauty contest. In order to support her in the competition, all of her family sets out on a trip. What may attract the audience's attention is that her family consists of her father Richard, a former motivational speaker who still clings to his philosophy of success; her Nietzsche-reading elder-brother, who has taken a vow of silence until he achieves his dream of becoming a fighter pilot; her grandfather, who is a man with a penchant for creative profanity; her uncle, who is a gay and suicidal genius who lost his male lover and former colleague; and her mother, who seems the only normal one and bonds the whole family together.

Introduction to movie clip 2

Just before Olive goes on stage, both her father and older brother don't want her to continue with the competition because they think the other girls have performed too profanely and that it is not suitable for Olive. However, her mother supports her very much, since Olive has devoted so much time and energy for the chance to participate in the competition.

Exercises

Task 1: Fill in the blanks to the following lines spoken in the movie clips you just watched.

1. Don't ever let somebody tell you that you can't do something, _____ me.
2. You got a dream, you got to_____ it.
3. Are you_____ to be backstage?
4. You're the mom and_____ protect her.
5. Everyone is gonna_____ her, Mom. Please don't let her do this.
6. She has worked so hard. She's_____ everything into this.

Task 2: Watch the movie clips for a second time and decide whether the following statements are true or false.

(   ) 1. Christopher and his father moved into an expensive hotel since his father has a good job.

(   ) 2. Christopher dreams of becoming a basketball player in the future but his father disapproves.

(   ) 3. Concerning education, Chris Gardner prefers to encourage his son rather than discourage him.

(   ) 4. In the talent competition, other contestants have very excellent performances.

(   ) 5. In the middle of the competition, both Olive's elder brother and her father encourage her to go on with the competition.

(   ) 6. Only Olive's mother supports her continuing with the competition because she thinks Olive is the best one.

Task 3: Discussion: Divide students into several groups to discuss the clips and the problems of intercultural communication.

Unit 3　　　Cultural Value Orientation

1. What role does encouragement play in children's education in Western countries?

2. "Stand on one's own feet" is an essential philosophy for the growth of a person. Do you agree?

3. Why does Olive's mother support her to continue the competition?

4. Should parents make important decisions for their children? What is your opinion?

Section B　Intercultural Communication Reading

 Pre-reading Task

1. What are some differences between Eastern and Westerner cultures?
2. How do you learn about the life of ordinary Americans? Through movies or the Internet or other channels? Do you think how Americans are portrayed in these channels is accurate?
3. How do cultural differences lead to conflicts while people are communicating with each other?

Passage 1

Eastern Culture vs. Western Culture
Sagarika Goswami

"Oh, East is East, and West is West, and never the **twain** shall meet, till Earth and Sky stand presently at God's great Judgment Seat; but there is neither East nor West, Border, nor Breed, nor Birth, when two strong men stand face to face, **tho'** they come from the ends of the earth!"
– Rudyard Kipling

Labeling someone as a **stooge** of the West is one of the most common charges that is leveled at any Eastern today who is very critical of its tradition and culture. **Differentiating** philosophies, cultures and religions as Eastern or Western is illogical and does not make any sense. I agree that there are huge differences between Eastern and Western cultures, but as there is a head and a tail for a coin there are both positive and negative impacts of Western culture and Eastern culture. I think both cultures are unique in their own way and equally good. We should not think of which culture is better but should take the good qualities of both cultures and put them into use in our lives.

Broadly speaking, the world has been classified into Western and Eastern cultures. The East-West **dichotomy** is a sociological concept used to describe perceived differences between Western cultures and the Eastern world. Before being judgmental on such issues, we must first

Intercultural Communication in Movies

know what culture exactly means. Culture has been defined in a number of ways by different philosophers, but most simply it is defined as the learned and shared behavior of a community of interacting human beings. It describes what people develop to enable them to adapt to their world, such as languages, gestures, customs and traditions that define values and organize social interactions, religious beliefs, rituals, dress, art, and music to make symbolic and **aesthetic** expressions. It is culture that determines the practices and beliefs that are associated with an **ethnic** group and provide it with distinctive individual identity.

For an insightful understanding of Eastern culture vs. Western culture, I would like to present a pictorial **representation** (see Figure 3.1 below). Of course, I am not generalizing everyone into these categories, but the drawings do capture the essence of cultural differences between Western and Eastern cultures. Here WC represents Western culture and EC represents Eastern culture.

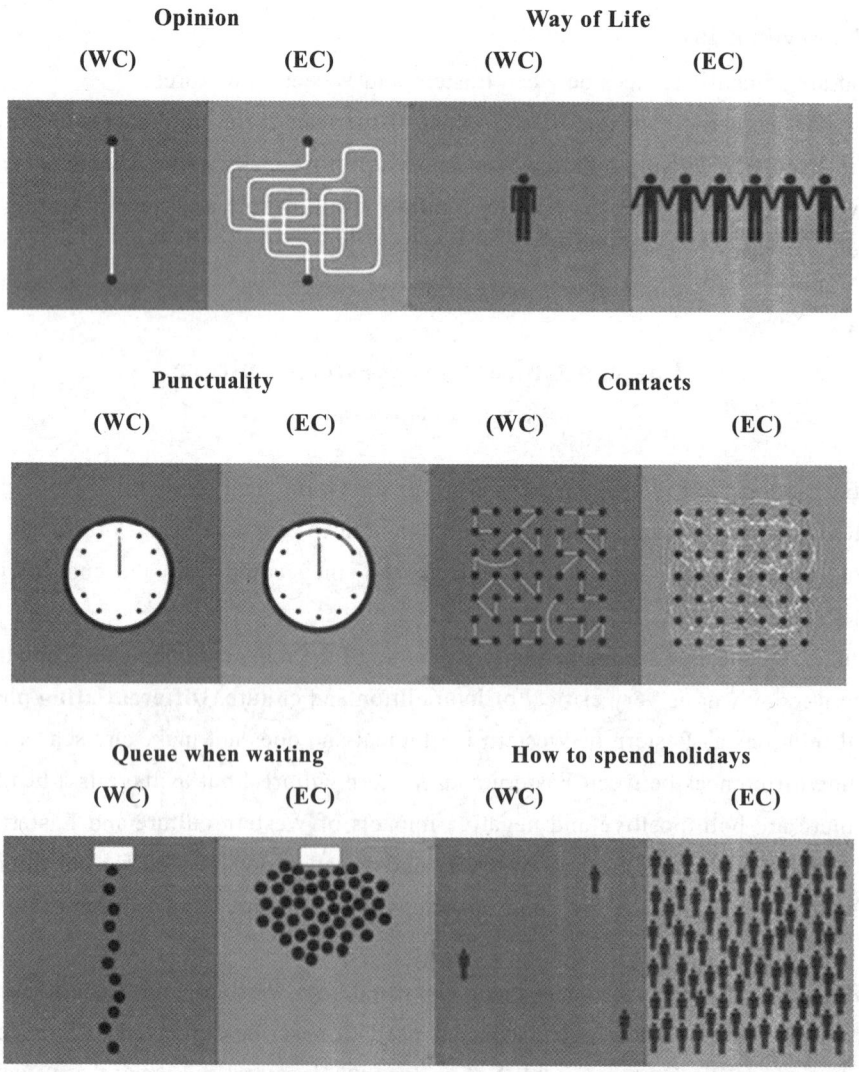

Unit 3 Cultural Value Orientation

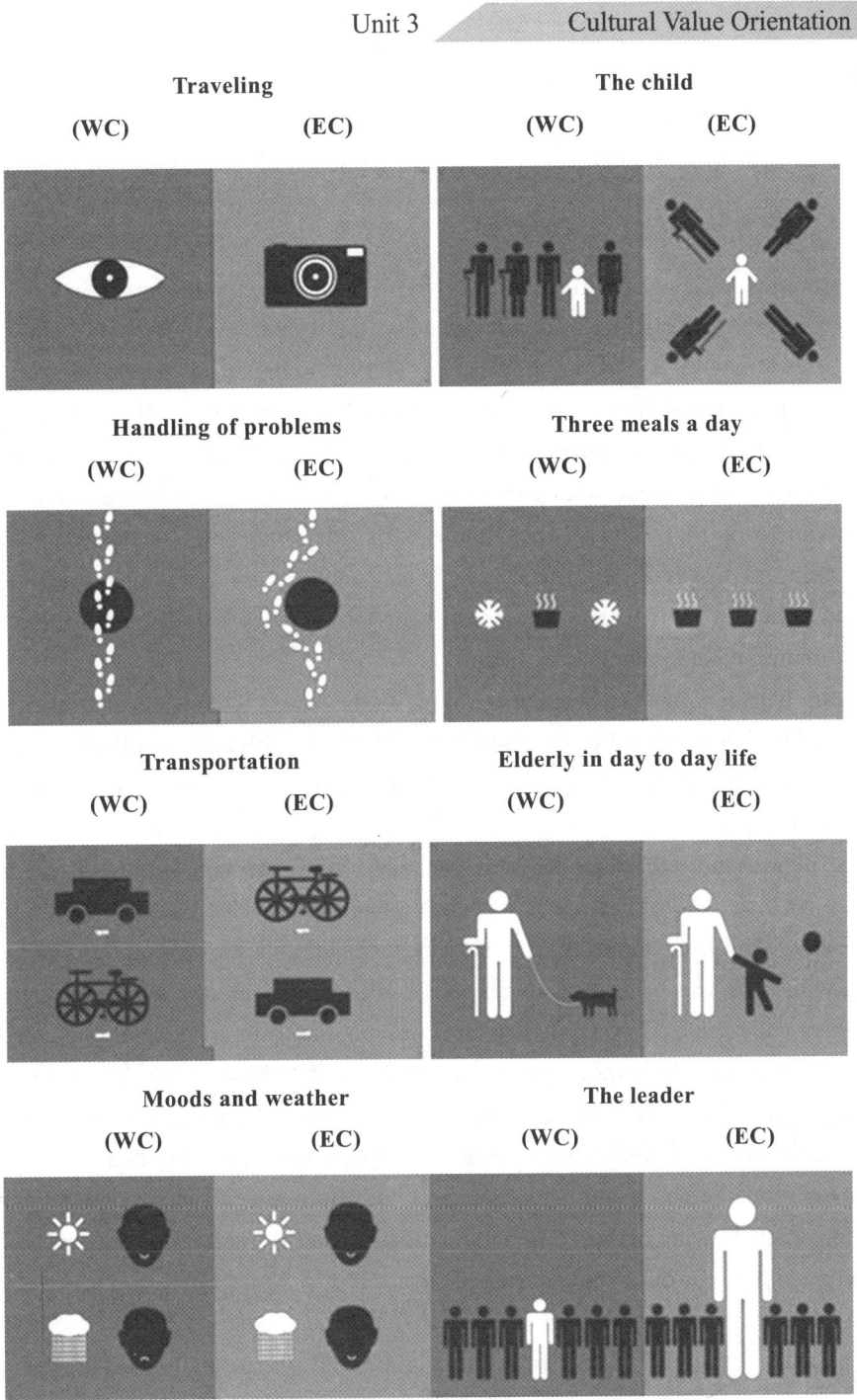

Figure 3.1 Pictorial representation of cultural differences between WC and EC

Below are few major differences that we can easily see between the two societies:

• Westerners place a high value on having fun. This doesn't mean that they don't care about serious issues. If they see someone upset, they will often assume that the person wants to be left alone, unless they are good friends. Easterners, on the other hand, prefer people to be concerned about them when they are upset or depressed. If your questions are not welcome, they will tell you

Intercultural Communication in Movies
影视作品中的跨文化交际

but will still generally appreciate the concern.

• Westerners can become intimate quite quickly in friendships, but that doesn't mean that they are committed. Commitment takes longer to happen. For Easterners, commitment is more closely tied to intimacy. There is an expectation that friendship, after a deep talk, will continue at the same level.

• Westerners can have **affectionate** guy-girl friendships without any romantic interest. Be cautious in assuming a Westerner is romantically interested, even if their behavior appears intimate. If you're not kissing or holding hands, you're probably not dating. Easterners tend to have a much lower **threshold** of what is considered a relationship. What Westerners might consider a normal guy-girl friendship can be read as definite interest in the other person. In particular, spending time alone with someone of the opposite sex is a strong sign of interest. Westerners tend to be more honest about their skills and value high self-esteem. They are not necessarily being **arrogant** if they openly admit that they are good at something. Easterners are less likely to volunteer their talents. They will wait for someone to ask them to use their skills, rather than jumping in and volunteering them.

• Equality between men and women is valued in the West. To imply that women are weaker, more emotional or that they need protection can be offensive. **Chivalry** is still alive and well in the East. Many women expect doors to be opened for them, to be served first at dinner, and for help in carrying heavy things.

• Westerners do not take their work as personally as Easterners tend to. It is not that they don't care about their work. They are more relaxed about their jobs. Easterners tend to take their work personally. **Tromping** across their freshly cleaned floor, or showing up late when you are to be working with them can be seen as disrespectful. Broadly speaking, Western society strives to find and prove "the truth", while Eastern society accepts the truth as given and is more interested in finding the balance. Westerners put more stock in individual rights; Easterners in social responsibility. While there are some good virtues as well as bad practices in Western culture, the same is true for Eastern culture. We must always remember every coin has two sides.

I hope next time before becoming judgmental we would give a second thought and present a **justified** view without being biased. It is we who decide what is good for us and what is not; but to blame a culture simply for our own convenience is not fair.

(971 words)

(This passage was slightly edited from the original to fit the format of this book.)

Passage 2

The Values Americans Live by (I)
L. Robert Kohls

Most Americans would have a difficult time telling you, specifically, what the values are that Americans **live by**. They have never given the matter much thought. Even if Americans consider this question, they would probably, in the end, decide not to answer in terms of a definitive list of values. The reason for this decision is itself an American value, in that every individual is so unique that the same list of values could never be applied to all, or even most, of their fellow citizens.

Although Americans may think of themselves as being more varied and unpredictable than they actually are, it is significant that they think they are. Americans tend to think they have been only slightly influenced by family, church or schools. In the end, each believes, "I personally chose which values I want to live my own life by."

Despite this self-evaluation, a foreign **anthropologist** could observe Americans and produce a list of common values that would fit most Americans. The list of typically American values would stand in sharp contrast to the values commonly held by the people of many other countries.

Here we can say that if the foreign visitor really understood how deeply **ingrained** these 13 values are in Americans, he or she would then be able to understand 95% of American actions – actions that might otherwise appear strange or unbelievable when evaluated from the perspective of the foreigner's own society and its values.

The different behaviors of a people or a culture make sense only when seen through the basic beliefs, assumptions and values of that particular group. When you encounter an action, or hear a statement in the United States that surprises you, try to see it as an expression of one or more of the values listed here. For example, when you ask Americans for directions to get to a particular address in their own city, they may explain, in great detail, how you can get there on your own, but may never even consider walking two city blocks with you to lead you to the place. Some foreign visitors have interpreted this sort of action as showing Americans' "unfriendliness". We would suggest, instead, that the self-help concept is so strong in Americans that they firmly believe that no adult would ever want, even temporarily, to be dependent on another. Also, their future orientation makes Americans think it is better to prepare you to find other addresses on your own in the future.

Before proceeding to the list itself, we should also point out that Americans see all of these values as very positive ones. They are not aware, for example, that the people in many Third World countries view change as negative or threatening. In fact, all 13 of these American values are judged by many of the world's citizens as negative and undesirable. Therefore, it is not enough simply to **familiarize** yourself with these values. You must also, so far as possible, consider them without the negative or **derogatory connotation** that they might have for you, based on your own experience and cultural identity.

It is important to state **emphatically** that our purpose in providing you with this list of the most important American values is not to convert you, the foreign visitor, to our values. We couldn't achieve that goal even if we wanted to, and we don't want to. We simply want to help you understand the Americans with whom you will be relating – from their own value system rather than from yours.

Intercultural Communication in Movies

1. Personal Control over the Environment

Americans no longer believe in the power of fate, and they have come to look at people who do as being backward, primitive, or hopelessly **naïve**. To be call "**fatalistic**" is one of the worst criticisms one can receive in the American context; to an American, it means one is **superstitious** and lazy, unwilling to take any initiative in bringing about improvement.

In the United States, people consider it normal and right that man should control nature, rather than the other way around. More specifically, people believe every single individual should have control over whatever in the environment might potentially affect him or her. The problems of one's life are not seen as having resulted from bad luck as much as having come from one's laziness in pursuing a better life. Furthermore, it is considered normal that anyone should look out for his or her own self-interests first and foremost.

Most Americans find it impossible to accept that there are some things that lie beyond the power of humans to achieve. And Americans have literally gone to the moon, because they refused to accept earthly limitations.

Americans seem to be challenged, even compelled, to do, by one means or another (and often at great cost) what seven-eighths of the world is certain cannot be done.

2. Change

In the American mind, change is seen as an **indisputably** good condition. Change is strongly linked to development, improvement, progress, and growth. Many older, more traditional cultures consider change as a **disruptive**, destructive force, to be avoided if at all possible. Instead of change, such societies value stability, **continuity**, tradition, and a rich and ancient **heritage** – none of which are valued very much in the United States.

These first two values – the belief that we can do anything and the belief that any change is good – together with an American belief in the virtue of hard work and the belief that each individual has a responsibility to do the best he or she can do have helped Americans achieve some great accomplishments. So whether these beliefs are true is really irrelevant; what is important is that Americans have considered them to be true and have acted as if they are, thus, in effect, causing them to happen.

(To be continued)

(976 words)

(The above passage is only the first portion of the entire work, the other portions are in Unit 4 and Unit 5)

 After-reading Task

1. According to passage 1, how do Westerners and Easterners solve their problems when confronted by them?

Unit 3   Cultural Value Orientation

2. According to passage 1, what is the attitude of Westerners and Easterners towards their job?

3. According to passage 2, what has a great effect on Americans' lives? Why?

4. According to passage 2, do Americans believe in fate? Why or not?

 WORDS LIST

Passage 1

twain /tweɪn/ *n.* <古>二；一对
tho /ðəʊ/ *abbr.* 虽然；可是（though）
stooge /stu:dʒ/ *n.* 喜剧里的配角或丑角
differentiate /ˌdɪfə'renʃɪeɪt/ *v.* 区分，区别，辨别
dichotomy /daɪ'kɒtəmɪ/ *n.* 一分成二
aesthetic /i:s'θetɪk/ *a.* 美学的；审美的
ethnic /'eθnɪk/ *a.* 种族的，民族的
representation /ˌreprɪzen'teɪʃn/ *n.* 表现；陈述
affectionate /ə'fekʃənət/ *a.* 深情的，挚爱的
threshold /'θreʃhəʊld/ *n.* 门槛，入口
arrogant /'ærəgənt/ *a.* 傲慢的，自大的
chivalry /'ʃɪvəlrɪ/ *n.*（中世纪的）骑士制度；骑士品质
tromp /trɒmp/ *v.* 践踏，跺脚
justified /'dʒʌstɪfaɪd/ *a.* 有正当理由的
Rudyard Kipling 鲁德亚德·吉卜林（1865—1936，英国著名小说家、诗人）

Passage 2

live by 以……为生
anthropologist /ˌænθrə'pɒlədʒɪst/ *n.* 人类学家
ingrained /ɪn'greɪnd/ *a.* 根深蒂固的；彻头彻尾的
familiarize /fə'mɪlɪəraɪz/ *v.* 使……熟悉，使通晓
derogatory /dɪ'rɒgətrɪ/ *a.* 贬低的；贬义的
connotation /ˌkɒnə'teɪʃn/ *n.* 内涵，含义
emphatically /ɪm'fætɪklɪ/ *ad.* 强调地，断然地
fatalistic /ˌfeɪtə'lɪstɪk/ *a.* 宿命论的
naïve /naɪ'i:v/ *a.* 天真的
superstitious /ˌsu:pə'stɪʃəs/ *a.* 迷信的

39

indisputably /ˌɪndɪˈspjuːtəblɪ/ ad. 无可置辩地，无法反驳地

disruptive /dɪsˈrʌptɪv/ a. 分裂性的；破坏的

continuity /ˌkɒntɪˈnjuːətɪ/ n. 连续性，连贯性

heritage /ˈherɪtɪdʒ/ n. 遗产

Section C Case Studies

Case 1

James, an American, was teaching English for his first time in China. On the first day of class the students all appeared to be paying attention to the lesson. James continually asked if any students had questions, but since no one raised their hands, James assumed everyone understood the lesson.

After teaching the lesson, James asked some questions to review the content that was taught. However, each time James asked a question, no one volunteered to respond. Eventually, James called on a student to stand up and answer. The student, however, refused to look James in the eye and was simply silent. James called on another student, but that student also did not look at James or say anything. James, getting more and more upset, then asked directly, "Do you understand my question? Yes or no?" The students simply sat silent and did not look at James, who was now growing very frustrated.

Finally, the bell rang and the students left. James felt both angry and upset. He thought to himself, "None of my students respect me. None of my students even want to learn English. And since they couldn't even answer my questions, I must be a terrible teacher."

Reflection

1. How did James expect his students to act in class? How does this reflect American culture?

2. Was James right about why the students acted the way they did? Why did they act like they did? How do their actions reflect Chinese culture?

3. What can James do to become a more effective English teacher in China? What can the students do to help him?

Case 2

Jay, a Chinese foreign exchange student in America, became very interested in a female American classmate in his class named Kelly. After a few months, he decided to ask her out on a date. Kelly agreed.

Jay thought for a long time about where to go on his first date with Kelly, and he finally decided to have dinner together at a fancy restaurant. However, when he told Kelly his plans, she

Unit 3 Cultural Value Orientation

became quite uncomfortable. "How about we just go walking in the park instead," she suggested. Jay agreed, even though he was quite disappointed that she rejected his idea.

When they finally met at the park, Jay surprised Kelly by giving her a small gift of some cookies. Kelly accepted the cookies, but she was noticeably uncomfortable. As they started walking through the park, Jay offered to carry Kelly's purse for her. However, once again, Kelly was noticeably uncomfortable and refused. "I can carry it myself. Thank you, though."

As they walked, they talked about the weather, school, and future dreams. After a while, it was time for them to leave. Jay didn't say much when he left. He just told Kelly, "See you later!"

Afterward, Jay felt very upset because Kelly didn't seem to like him. Kelly, however, also felt quite upset. She thought Jay didn't seem to like her.

Reflection

1. How did Kelly's actions on the date reflect the value orientations of Americans toward human nature, human activity, and social relations? Why didn't she think Jay liked her?

   _____

2. How did Jay's actions on the date reflect the value orientations of Chinese toward human nature, human activity, and social relations? Why didn't he think Kelly liked him?

   _____

3. If your Chinese friend was going to date an American, what advice would you give him/her?

   _____

Case 3 Watch the following clip from the movie *"The Joy Luck Club "* and try to analyze the cultural phenomenon in an intercultural context.

Reflection

1. Why does Jun have a quarrel with her mother at the end of the clip?

   _____

2. What are the differences in education methods between Western and Eastern cultures?

   _____

III. Task-based Activities

Exercises

Choose the best choice according to the cultural context.

(   ) 1. Your American friend tells you that his dog just died and that he is very sad. You

Intercultural Communication in Movies

should say:

    a. "I can't imagine how you must feel."

    b. "I know how you feel."

( ) 2. You are waiting in line at the store to buy something when an American standing in front of you sneezes. You should say:

    a. You should not say anything.

    b. "Bless you."

( ) 3. While you are sitting on the bus with your American friend, a large woman with blonde hair gets on the bus. You tell your friend that you really like the glasses she is wearing, but your friend does not know who you are talking about. In order to point her out, you should say:

    a. "That fat woman over there."

    b. "That woman with blonde hair over there."

( ) 4. You are watching basketball with your American friend. Suddenly, one basketball player makes an amazing play. You want to express your surprise. You should say:

    a. "Oh my gosh!"

    b. "Oh my God!"

( ) 5. Your American friend just got a job, and you want to know how much money he makes. You should say:

    a. "How much money do you make?"

    b. You should not ask.

Group Work

Discussion 1

Ask students to discuss the following example in groups: Many 18-year-old Chinese students are accompanied to their standardized college test by their parents. The parents wait outside until they are finished. Why does this occur? Would you let you parents do this? Does it happen in the United States?

Discussion 2

Where did you learn your cultural or personal values? Identify some influential sources. Recommend two or three constructive ways to be mindful of your own values or other people's values in order to cultivate cultural awareness.

Assignment

Presentation 1

1. What are Americans' value orientations? What are Chinese peoples' value orientations? Fill in the blanks and give some examples to illustrate. Make a brief presentation about this topic.

Unit 3 Cultural Value Orientation

orientation	Chinese values	American values
1. Human Nature		
2. Relationship of Man to Nature		
3. Sense of Time		
4. Human Activity		
5. Social Relationship		

Presentation 2

Comparing your Chinese culture with Western culture, do you find that Chinese value orientations are changing? Do you think China must adopt the Western value orientation toward time? What examples can you give to support your opinions? Make a brief presentation about this topic.

Men at their birth are naturally good.
人之初，性本善。
The highest good is like that of water.
上善若水。

– Lao Tze's saying

Unit 4　Cultural Diversity

I. Definition of Cultural Diversity

Hofstede's Dimensions of Cultural Diversity:
1. Power Distance
2. Uncertainty Avoidance
3. Individualism vs. Collectivism
4. Masculinity vs. Femininity
5. Long Term Orientation

Cultural diversity refers to the differences in culture. It includes the various different social structures, belief systems, religions and customs in various parts of the world. In every culture, there are basic standards for social interaction. Hofstede, a Dutch cultural anthropologist, provides a definition of culture and a method for measuring it. This method assigns a score to each culture, ranging from 1 to 100. A score greater than seventy is considered high, and a score less than forty is considered low. His research shows that cultural differences matter. In the 1980s he took a different approach to analyzing cultural differences than did Kluckhohn and identified four pairs of contrasting values to describe social relationships. In the 1990s, he added a fifth one. According to his research, there are five value dimensions. His cultural dimensions are a framework for understanding intercultural communication. They emphasize national cultures rather than the layers of culture within a given country.

1. Power Distance (PD)

Hofstede (1984b, p83) defines power distance as the extent to which the members of a society accept that power in institutions and organizations is distributed unequally. People in large power distance societies accept a hierarchical order in which inequalities in power between people need no justification. People in low power distance societies strive for power equalization and demand justification for power inequalities among people when they occur.

A high PD score indicates that a given society accepts an unequal distribution of power and that people understand "their place" in the system. Its characteristics are strong hierarchies and large distances between those in authority and those under them. A low PD means that power is shared and that members of society view themselves as equals.

Power distance is determined by answers to a questionnaire filled out by business employees in each country. The United States scored a forty, which is considered low.

2. *Uncertainty Avoidance (UA)*

Uncertainty avoidance addresses a society's tolerance of ambiguity and uncertainty. Hofstede finds that it reflects the extent to which members of a society attempt to cope with anxiety by minimizing uncertainty. Hofstede notes that cultures that have a high tolerance of uncertainty "are more tolerant of behavior and opinions that differ from their own; they try to have as few rules as possible, and on the philosophical and religious level, they are relativist, allowing many currents to flow side by side" (Hofstede and Bond, 1988, p11).

Hofstede believes that uncertainty avoidance impacts the meaning of time and the desire for precision and punctuality. People in cultures with high uncertainty avoidance try to avoid ambiguous situations whenever possible. They are governed by rules and order, and they seek a collective truth. Cultures with a high UA have strong traditions and rituals and tend toward formal, bureaucratic structures and rules. Greece was rated as 1st, followed by Portugal and Guatemala. The US was 43rd. In contrast, people in cultures with low UA accept and feel comfortable in unstructured situations or changeable environments and try to have as few rules as possible. People in these cultures are encouraged to discover their own truth and to be more tolerant of change.

3. *Individualism (IDV) vs. Collectivism*

According to Hofstede (1984b, p83), individualism is a preference for a loosely knit social framework in society wherein individuals are supposed to take care of themselves and their immediate family only. Its opposite, collectivism, is a preference for a tightly knit social framework in which individuals can expect their relatives, clan, or other members of their group to look after them in exchange for unquestioning loyalty.

A high IDV score indicates loose connections. In countries with a high IDV score there is a lack of interpersonal connection and little sharing of responsibility beyond family and perhaps a few close friends. In an individualistic environment, the individual person and their rights are more important than the groups that they may belong to. A society with a low IDV score have strong group cohesion and a large amount of loyalty and respect for members of the group. The groups themselves are also larger, and people take more responsibility for each other's well-being.

Regarding the individualism index, North America and Europe can be considered as individualistic with relatively high scores. The US was number one here, closely followed by Australia and Great Britain. In contrast, Asia, Africa and Latin America have strong collectivistic values.

4. Masculinity (MAS) vs. Femininity

Masculinity versus Femininity refers to the distribution of emotional roles between the genders. Hofstede (2001, p297) explains, "Masculinity stands for a society in which social gender roles are clearly distinct: Men are supposed to be assertive, tough, and focused on material success; women are supposed to be more modest, tender, and concerned with the quality of life." He continues, "Femininity stands for a society in which social gender roles overlap: Both men and women are supposed to be modest, tender, and concerned with the quality of life."

This dimension addresses not only which gender's characteristics will be most valued but also the differences between the sexes. Some masculine societies strive for maximum social differentiation between the sexes. Other societies strive for minimal social differentiation between the sexes. High MAS scores are found in countries where men are expected to be "tough", to be the provider, and to be assertive. If women work outside the home, they tend to have separate professions from men. Low MAS scores do not reverse gender roles; rather, roles are simply blurred. Women and men work together equally across many professions. Men are allowed to be sensitive, and women can work hard for professional success. Japan led the list of the highest MAS scores, followed by Austria and Venezuela. The U.S. was 15th.

5. Long Term Orientation (LTO)

In the mid-eighties, a detailed survey called the Chinese Value Survey was designed by Michael Bond. All the values are taken straight from the teachings of Confucius. It ranges from long term orientation to short term orientation. Long term orientation refers to how much a given society values traditions and values. Hofstede and Bond (see Hofstede & Bond, 1988) produced this dimension in the 1990s after finding that Asian countries with a strong link to Confucian philosophy acted differently than Western cultures. For this reason, this orientation is also called Confucian dynamism or time orientation. Hofstede and Bond (1988) point out that Confucian teachings enforce the honoring of unequal relationships and emphasize the needs of the group. This explains the strict hierarchy and collectivist behaviors of Asian countries. In countries with a high LTO score, it is very important to deliver social obligations and avoid loss of "face".

Hofstede says, "On the long-term side one finds values oriented towards the future, like thrifty (saving) and persistence." This means that long term orientation focuses on to what extent a group invests for the future, perseveres, and is patient in waiting for results. High LTO scores were typically found in East Asia, Japan and China. The US was 17th. Please see Table 4.1.

Unit 4　　Cultural Diversity

Table 4.1　Hofstede's Rank Ordering of 53 Nations on Five Cultural Dimensions, Going From 1 (Highest) to 53 (Lowest)

Nation	Power Distance	Indivi-dualism	Masc.	Uncertainty Avoidance	Time Horizon (1 is Long)
Germany	42-44	15	9-10	29	11-12
Sweden	47-48	0-11	52	49-50	10
England	42-44	3	9-10	47-48	15-16
Australia	41	2	16	37	11-12
U.S.	38	1	15	43	14
Italy	34	7	4-5	23	
India	10-11	21	20-21	45	6
Japan	33	22-23	1	7	3
Republic of Korea	27-28	43	41	16-17	4
Arab nations	7	26-27	23	27	

Questions

1. What is Confucian Dynamism?

___

2. What are the Five Cultural Value Dimensions?

___

3. What is cultural diversity?

___

4. What is a high power distance and a low power distance? What are their characteristics?

___

Cultural Comprehension

Decide whether the following statements are true or false according to what you read.

(　) 1. The power distance dimension expresses the degree to which the less powerful members of a society accept and expect that power is distributed unequally.

(　) 2. According to Hofstede, people either prefer a close knit network of people, or they prefer to be left alone to fend for themselves.

(　) 3. The uncertainty avoidance dimension expresses the degree to which the members of a society feel comfortable with uncertainty and ambiguity.

(　) 4. Hofstede's masculinity vs. femininity dimension examines the extent to which different cultures accept ambiguous situations and tolerate uncertainty.

( ) 5. Hofstede's cultural dimensions are a framework for understanding intercultural communication.

II. Content-based Activities

Section A Movie Clips

 Introduction to the movie *October Sky*

Directed by Joe Johnson, this movie is about the story of the rocket boys. In 1957 the Soviet Union launched Sputnik, which inspires Homer Hickam and his friends. Hickam, however, was born and raised in a coal mining town in west Virginia where most people spend their lives mining coal. Therefore, it is natural for the older generation to expect their children to follow in their footsteps. There is no exception for Hickam's father, who regards his son's devotion to rockets as a passing fad. However, his wife wants to do anything she can to support his son's dreams.

The four young men collect scraps and bits of metal and materials from their basements and garages to set out to build a rocket. After countless failures they finally succeed, even winning a national science fair.

Introduction to movie clip 1

In this clip, the launching of Sputnik fuels the imagination of Homer Hickam, who decides to build his own rocket instead of working in the coal mine in the future. This idea is unbelievable to many in the town; however, his mother encourages him to pursue his dreams. She does not discourage Homer, but she does give him one condition – "Just don't blow yourself up."

 Introduction to the movie *Dead Poets Society*

Welton Academy is a famous preparatory school that is proud of its principles – "tradition, honor, discipline and excellence". Mr. Keating is a new teacher in the school, with his unique style of teaching he encourages students to think in their own way and pursue their own dreams. Inspired by him, a group of students secretly organize the Dead Poets Society to "suck the marrow of life". Neil, one of the students, has a dream of becoming an actor, but his father, Mr. Perry, does not agree. Encouraged by Mr. Keating, Neil secretly joins a play and has a successful performance. Although his father asks him to quit, he does not. Eventually, Neil commits suicide. Mr. Perry asks the school to investigate the case and under the pressure of the headmaster the students accuse Mr. Keating of misleading the students. Under such circumstances Mr. Keating has no choice but to leave. Although the students originally give into the pressure to blame Mr. Keating, eventually they regret their decision and respectfully bid farewell to their favorite teacher.

Introduction to movie clip 2

In this clip, Mr. Keating uses an unusual teaching method to cultivate individualism in his

Unit 4 Cultural Diversity

students. He asks them to walk in the courtyard; however, he encourages them not to mindlessly follow others but to create their own ways of walking.

Exercises

Task 1: Fill in the blanks to the following lines spoken in the movie clips you just watched.
1. I'm gonna build a rocket... Well, just don't_____ yourself_____.
2. I got it_____with the powder from 30 sky rockets.
3. I waited six months for the company carpenter to finally_____to puttin' up that fence.
4. Everyone started off with their own _____, their own pace.
5. I brought them up here to illustrate the point of _____, the difficulty in maintaining your own beliefs in the face of others. But you must trust that your beliefs are_____, your own.

Task 2: Watch the movie clips for a second time and decide whether the following statements are true or false.
(　) 1. Homer is a boy who believes in fate.
(　) 2. The Russian satellite Sputnik inspired Homer to build a rocket himself.
(　) 3. Homer is discouraged by his parents, who think he is too naïve.
(　) 4. Mr. Keating is a man of a conservative mind.
(　) 5. Students are encouraged to walk in their own way.
(　) 6. According to Mr. Keating, conformity is necessary to maintain harmony with others; therefore, everyone should conform.

Task 3: Discussion: Divide students into several groups to discuss the clips and the problems of intercultural communication.
1. Do you think America has a high uncertainty avoidance or a low uncertainty avoidance? Can you give an example from the movie clip?

___

2. Do you think China has a high uncertainty avoidance or a low uncertainty avoidance? Please give an example from your own experience.

___

3. In individualist cultures people tend to show their unique personality, which may seem odd to others. Do you think it is necessary to maintain conformity with others?

___

4. Chinese people attach great importance to harmony with others. Does this mean we all agree with each other? Explain.

___

Intercultural Communication in Movies
影视作品中的跨文化交际

Section B Intercultural Communication Reading

 Pre-reading Task

1. How does Hofstede's approach to cultural differences help people understand Asian culture? Do you think his approach is reasonable and valid?
2. Have you thought about the term individualism? Do you think it makes sense to you?
3. Why do Americans pay more attention to their privacy?

Passage 1
Hofstede's Asian Cultural Factors

In his original analysis of cultural factors, Geert Hofstede, a Dutch cultural anthropologist, identified five common cultural factors, but was surprised when they did not predict the Asian growth of the second half of the 20th century.

Confucian dynamism

Asian cultures replace the dimension of uncertainty avoidance by **Confucian dynamism**. Confucianism refers back to the teaching of **Confucius**, a Chinese teacher who lived at about 500 B.C. and was later added by Hofstede to his work about cultural differences. When he did research in Asian countries he discovered that his results are co-related with the theories of Confucius – Michael Bond called it Confucian dynamism. Confucianism is not a religion. It is a collection of pragmatic rules of daily life.

Hofstede said, "In practical terms Confucianism refers to a long-term versus a short-term orientation in life. It indicates the extent to which a society is more future or long-term orientated, or more past or short-term orientated." China and other Asian countries have an extraordinary long-term orientation. These values are **persistence**, which describes the **internationality** to pursue certain goals; ranking relationships by status, which reflects the deep sense of harmony and stable relationships; **thrift**, which is related to the **availability** of financial resources and saving money; and having a sense of shame, which emphasizes care for others, loyalty and **trustworthiness**. In particular, this was linked with the search for societal virtue rather than a search for truth. Within this dimension there are several sub-dimensions, which are explained below.

Persistence

There is a general perseverance and **tenacity** in pursuing a goal. Once something has been decided as requiring action, people will work through disappointment and difficult problems in order to reach the desired end.

Ordering relationships

Relationships are clearly defined, with strong **hierarchies** that people observe very carefully. With a clear power relationship, people do not spend time arguing and challenging orders – they move into the persistence that may be required to achieve the goals that have been set for them by their superiors.

Thrift

There is a general thrift and dislike of waste. This leads to creating of products that are economic in production and reliable in use. It also leads to careful economy with finances and consequent profitable firms and nations. A high level of savings and reduced borrowing leads to more financially stable institutions.

A sense of shame

If goals are not reached, then it is considered shameful – a fact which leads to persistence. Likewise, shame drives relationships, where to be seen to fail or otherwise lose face is highly undesirable. Thrift, also, is affected by shame, as a cultural thriftiness highlights individual overspending.

(438 words)

(This passage was edited to fit the format of this book. The original passage can be found at: http://changingminds.org/explanations/culture/hofstede_asian.htm)

Passage 2

The Values Americans Live by (II)

L. Robert Kohls

3. Equality

Equality is, for Americans, one of their most cherished values. This concept is so important for Americans that they have even given it a religious basis. They say all people have been "created equal." Most Americans believe that God views all humans alike without regard to intelligence, physical condition or economic status. In **secular** terms this belief is translated into the **assertion** that all people have an equal opportunity to succeed in life. Americans differ in opinion about how to make this ideal into a reality. Yet virtually all agree that equality is an important **civic** and social goal.

The equality concept often makes Americans seem strange to foreign visitors. Seven-eighths of the world feels quite differently. To them, rank and status and authority are seen as much more desirable considerations – even if they personally happen to find themselves near the bottom of the social order. Class and authority seem to give people in those other societies a sense of security and certainty. People outside the United States consider it reassuring to know, from birth, who they are and where they fit into the complex system called "society".

Many highly-placed foreign visitors to the United States are insulted by the way they are treated by service personnel (such as waiters in restaurants, clerks in stores, taxi drivers, etc.). Americans have an **aversion** to treating people of high position in a **deferential** manner, and, conversely, often treat lower class people as if they were very important. Newcomers to the United States should realize that no insult or personal indignity is intended by this lack of **deference** to rank or position in society. A foreigner should be prepared to be considered "just like anybody else" while in the country.

4. Individual and Privacy

Americans think they are more individualistic in their thoughts and actions than, in fact, they are. They resist being thought of as representatives of a **homogenous** group, whatever the group. They may, and do, join groups – in fact many groups – but somehow believe they're just a little different, just a little unique, just a little special, from other members of the same group. And they tend to leave groups as easily as they enter them.

Privacy, the ultimate result of individualism, is perhaps even more difficult for the foreigner to comprehend. The word "privacy" does not even exist in many languages. If it does, it is likely to have a strongly negative connotation, suggesting loneliness or isolation from the group. In the United States, privacy is not only seen as a very positive condition, but it is also viewed as a requirement that all humans would find equally necessary, desirable and satisfying. It is not uncommon for Americans to say – and believe – such statements as "If I don't have at least half an hour a day to myself, I will go **stark raving** mad".

Individualism, as it exists in the United States, does mean that you will find a much greater variety of opinions (along with the absolute freedom to express them anywhere and anytime) here. Yet, in spite of this wide range of personal opinions, almost all Americans will ultimately vote for one of the two major political parties. That is what was meant by the statement made earlier that Americans take pride in crediting themselves with claiming more individualism than, in fact, they really have.

5. Self-help Control

In the United States, a person can take credit only for what he or she has accomplished by himself or herself. Americans get no credit whatsoever for having been born into a rich family. Americans pride themselves in having been born poor and, through their own sacrifice and hard work, having climbed the difficult ladder of success to whatever level they have achieved – all by themselves. The American social system has, of course, made it possible for Americans to move, relatively easily, up the social ladder.

Take a look in an English-language dictionary at the composite words that have "self" as a prefix. In the average desk dictionary, there will be more than 100 such words, words like self-confidence, self-consciousness, self-control, self-criticism, self-deception, self-defeating, self-denial, self-discipline, self-esteem, self-expression, self-importance, self-improvement, self-interest, self-reliance, self-respect, self-restraint, self-sacrifice – the list goes on and on. The equivalent of these words cannot be found in most other languages. The list is perhaps the best indication of how seriously Americans take doing things for one's self. The "self-made man or women" is still very much the ideal in 20th-century America.

6. Competition and Free **Enterprise**

Americans believe that competition brings out the best in any individual. They assert that it challenges or forces each person to produce the very best that is humanly possible. Consequently, the foreign visitor will see competition being **fostered** in the American home and in the American classroom, even at the youngest age level. Very young children, for instance, are encouraged to answer questions for which their classmates do not know the answer.

You may find the competitive value disagreeable, especially if you come from a society that promotes cooperation rather than competition. But many U.S. Peace Corps volunteers teaching in Third World countries found the lack of competitiveness in a classroom situation equally **distressing**. They soon learned that what they thought to be one of the universal human characteristics represented only a peculiarly American (or Western) value.

Americans, valuing competition, have devised an economic system to go with it – free enterprise. Americans feel strongly that a highly competitive economy will bring out the best in its people and, ultimately, that the society that fosters competition will progress most rapidly. If you look for it, you will see evidence in all areas – even in fields as diverse as medicine, the arts, education, and sports – that free enterprise is the approach most often preferred in America.

(To be continued)

(975 words)

(The above passage is only the second portion of the entire work, the third portion is in Unit 5)

 After-reading Task

1. According to passage 1, what are Asian people's characteristics?

_____

2. According to passage 1, what plays a very important role in Asian culture?

_____

3. According to passage 2, why is self-help control very significant in American life?

_____

4. According to passage 2, what is the definition of equality?

_____

 WORDS LIST

Passage 1

Confucian /kən'fju:ʃən/ *a.* 孔子的，儒家的
dynamism /'daɪnəmɪzəm/ *n.* 活力；精力
Confucius /kən'fju:ʃəs/ *n.* 孔子（公元前551—前479，中国哲学家与教育家）
pragmatic /præg'mætɪk/ *a.* 实际的；实用的
persistence /pə'sɪstəns/ *n.* 坚持不懈
internationality /ˌɪntə'næʃnələtɪ/ *n.* 国际性
thrift /θrɪft/ *n.* 节俭，节约
availability /əˌveɪlə'bɪlətɪ/ *n.* 可利用性
trustworthiness /'trʌstwɜːðɪnəs/ *n.* 可信赖，确实性；信誉

Intercultural Communication in Movies
影视作品中的跨文化交际

tenacity /tə'næsətɪ/ *n.* 坚毅；不屈不挠
hierarchy /'haɪərɑːkɪ/ *n.* 层次；等级制度

Passage 2
secular /'sekjələ(r)/ *a.* 世俗的；长期的，长久的
assertion /ə'sɜːʃn/ *n.* 声称；明确肯定
civic /'sɪvɪk/ *a.* 城市的；公民的
aversion /ə'vɜːʃn/ *n.* 厌恶；讨厌的人或东西
deferential /ˌdefə'renʃl/ *a.* 恭敬的
deference /'defərəns/ *n.* 顺从；依从；尊重（尤指对位重者）
homogenous /hə'mɒdʒənəs/ *a.* 同质的，纯系的
stark /stɑːk/ *a.* 完全的；令人不快的
raving /'reɪvɪŋ/ *n.* 胡话；疯话
enterprise /'entəpraɪz/ *n.* 企（事）业单位
foster /'fɒstə(r)/ *v.* 培养；抚育
distress /dɪ'stres/ *v.* 使痛苦，使忧伤

Section C Case Studies

 Case 1

Mr. Wang, a Chinese CEO, was invited to an American university to give a lecture to graduate students about entrepreneurship. After the lecture, some students invited him to have dinner together to discuss business. After dinner, he called a colleague in China to discuss his experiences.

Colleague: "So, Mr. Wang, how was your lecture?"

Mr. Wang: "The lecture was fine; however, afterward some students took me to a restaurant to have dinner, and I don't think I have ever been treated more disrespectfully in my life! First of all, the waitress treated me just like the students, even though she knew I was a businessman and they were only students. She smiled and greeted them just like she did me. When she sat us down, she actually made me sit at the corner of the table while a student sat at the head. Since we were in America, we each had to order our own dish, but she took two students' orders first before she took mine. And when she brought out the food for us, she gave half of the students their food before she gave me mine. When she refilled our drinks, she never refilled mine first. I just can't believe how rude American waitresses are!"

Reflection

1. How does the above scenario reflect the differences in power distance in American and Chinese cultures?

Unit 4   Cultural Diversity

2. Was the waitress really being disrespectful? What might the waitress say if she was accused of disrespecting her customers?

Case 2

Tom, an American manager, works in a joint-venture company in China. Although he is glad to work with his Chinese colleagues he is always confused about what occurred at the meetings. For example, at one meeting he proposed a plan concerning the new market strategy and hoped other people would render some advice, but all of them kept silent. So he took it for granted that his new plan would be quite satisfactory. But to his great disappointment, after the meeting, his Chinese assistant came to his office and informed that the plan might not work properly and other Chinese colleagues held the same opinion. However, to his Chinese assistant's surprise, Tom seemed annoyed with it.

Reflection

1. What would Tom expect from his Chinese colleagues at the meeting?

2. Could you analyze the response of Chinese colleagues to Tom's proposal?

3. If you are on the Chinese staff, what you will do? Or suppose you know both of their cultures quite well, could you please give them some advice in order to help them understand each other well?

Case 3   Watch the following clip from the movie *"Anna and the King"* and try to analyze the cultural phenomenon in an intercultural context.

Reflection

1. Why does Anna feel uncomfortable about the King?

2. Discuss the differences between Western and Eastern value orientations by using the power distance theory.

Intercultural Communication in Movies
影视作品中的跨文化交际

III. Task-based Activities

Exercises

Choose the best choice according to the cultural context.

( ) 1. While you are studying abroad in America, you attend a math class. In class, the teacher is explaining how to do a problem. However, you think he made a mistake. You should:

   a. Remain quiet out of respect and approach him after class.

   b. Raise your hand and tell him you think he made a mistake.

( ) 2. Your American friend invites you to her house to have dinner with her family. You should:

   a. Not bring anything.

   b. Bring a small gift for the family.

( ) 3. When you visit the home of your American friend, as soon as you enter the home you should:

   a. Take off your shoes and put on house slippers if available.

   b. Keep your shoes on.

( ) 4. Your American friend calls you and tells you that he is sick, and you want to comfort him. You should:

   a. Tell him on the phone that you hope he gets better soon.

   b. Visit him and bring him some fruit.

( ) 5. You run into your American colleague while she is playing with her little daughter in the park. You think her daughter is very cute. You should:

   a. Pat her daughter on the head and tell her she is cute.

   b. Tell your colleague that her daughter is cute, but do not touch her.

Group Work

Discussion 1

Divide students into several groups and have them think about the concept of individualism vs. collectivism, and ask them to provide one or two specific example of both. Then offer them the following examples to further discuss the issue:

1. There is no word for "privacy" in many cultures. Do you think it has a negative connotation or not? Why?

2. "I" in the Chinese language is associated with words having negative meanings because it is bad when individuals make decisions without considering or being influenced by group norms.

Discussion 2

Work in pairs to match these statements with the cultural term. Check your answers and then

Unit 4 Cultural Diversity

write out statements of your own. Have your classmates guess the right answers.

a. *High power distance / Low power distance.*

b. *High masculine / Low masculine.*

c. *High uncertainty avoidance / Low uncertainty avoidance.*

d. *High long-term orientation / Low long-term orientation.*

e. *Individual / Collective.*

(   ) 1. "My boss's door is always open. I know that I can ask him questions or go to his office when I have good ideas."

(   ) 2. "We have to finish the timeline for our next work. It is really important to plan our deadlines and schedules very carefully so that we can finish everything on time."

(   ) 3. "Parents and elderly people have more authority than young men and women."

(   ) 4. "I can't imagine having a female boss. Men are much better at managing teams because they are better leaders and more assertive."

(   ) 5. "In our class we value good relationships among the students and treat each other with respect. I think that being in harmony with other students is important."

Assignment

Presentation 1

Divide students into several groups to describe the five dimensions of culture as identified by Geert Hofstede. Make a brief presentation about this topic.

Presentation 2

A. In groups, make a brief presentation about the main characteristics of individualism and collectivism. You must list at least three or four characteristics for each.

Characteristics of Individualism and Collectivism

Individualism	Collectivism

B. Complete the following sentences as soon as possible, each sentence begins with "I am...". Then try to analyze the differences between individualism and collectivism.

If you always give answers like this kind, such as "I am a student, I am a engineer...", you have to change your mind to make your answers specific and characteristic.

1. I am_____.

2. I am_____.

3. I am_____.

4. I am_____.

5. I am _____.
6. I am _____.
7. I am _____.
8. I am _____.
9. I am _____.
10. I am _____.
11. I am _____.
12. I am _____.
13. I am _____.
14. I am _____.
15. I am _____.
16. I am _____.
17. I am _____.
18. I am _____.
19. I am _____.
20. I am _____.

> *Beforehand preparation leads to success; improperness results in failure.* — Chinese Proverb
>
> 凡事预则立，不预则废。
>
> *To worry before the common people worries; to enjoy only after the people can enjoy.* — Chinese verse
>
> 先天下之忧而忧，后天下之乐而乐。

Unit 5   Context and Social Norms

I. Definition of Context and Social Norms

1. Edward T. Hall's High-context and Low-context Culture
2. Social Norms

1. Edward T. Hall's High-context and Low-context Culture

In order to help people better understand the powerful effect of culture in intercultural communication, the American anthropologist and cross-cultural researcher Edward T. Hall introduced a number of new concepts, including proxemics, polychronic and monochronic time, as well as high-context and low-context culture.

In this unit we will discuss his high and low context theory, which was published in his book *Beyond Culture* (1976). A key factor in this theory is context. What is context? Context is defined as the information that surrounds an event, and it is inextricably bound up with the meaning of that event. Context, therefore, affects how people effectively communicate. This relates to the framework, background, and surrounding circumstances in which communication or an event takes place.

Hall suggests that cultures can be divided into categories of high context and low context in order to understand their basic differences in communication style. As Hall explains, in a high-context culture "most of the information is either in the physical context or initialized in the person, while very little is in the coded, explicit, transmitted part of the message." (Hall, 1976, p79). In contrast, low-context communication is opposite. In low-context communication, "the mass of information is vested in the explicit code" (p70).

High context refers to societies or groups where people have close connections over a long period of time. These cultures are typically relational, collectivist, intuitive, contemplative, and less verbally explicit. Moreover, they do not tend to emphasize written or formal communication. This means that people in these cultures emphasize interpersonal relationships, preferring group harmony and consensus to individual achievement. In these cultures, backgrounds are common and shared, and "we" is emphasized over "I". These cultures include much of the Middle East, Asia, Africa, and South America.

Low context, however, refers to societies where people tend to have many connections but for shorter durations of time or for specific reasons. These cultures are typically logical, linear, individualistic, and action-oriented. They transmit information in explicit code to make up for the lack of shared meanings. Meanings are determined by what is said, rather than how it is said. Low context communication is used in cultures where backgrounds, meanings, and experiences are diverse. Low context cultures include North America and much of Western Europe.

The major difference between high and low context cultures is the amount of information that a person can comfortably manage. In a high context culture, background information tends to be implicit. In a low context culture, much of the background information needs to be made explicit in the communication. However, these are just tendencies. No culture uses low-context communication styles or high-context communication styles exclusively. Please see Table 5.1.

Table 5.1 Characteristics of Hall's High- and Low-context Cultures

High-context culture	Low-context culture
Many covert and implicit messages	Many overt and explicit messages
Internalized messages	Plainly-coded messages
Much nonverbal coding	Verbalized details
Reserved reactions	Reactions on the surface
Distinct in-groups and out-groups	Flexible in-groups and out-groups
Strong relationship bonds	Fragile relationship bonds
High commitment	Low commitment
Open and flexible time	Highly-organized time

Source: http://www.siu.edu/~ekachai/dimensions.html.

High contexts can be difficult to enter if a person is an outsider and can't instantly create close relationships. In contrast, low contexts are relatively easy to enter, and people can form relationships fairly quickly because accomplishing tasks is valued more than creating relationships.

One specific difference between high and low context cultures is worth discussing in detail, namely directness and indirectness. Edward Hall (1976) suggests that cultures in the East (such as China, Japan and Southeast Asian nations) tend to be high context, valuing politeness and indirectness, while cultures in the West (such as Britain, the U.S., and Australia) tend to be low context, valuing transparency and directness. Because high context culture is indirect, westerners see easterners as too ambiguous, whereas easterners see westerners as having less sense of face. The linguist Deborah Tannen (1994) states that "indirectness is a fundamental element in human communication". It is "one of the elements that varies the most from one culture to another, and one that can cause confusion and misunderstanding" (p79). In Table 5.2 we can clearly see the differences between direct and indirect forms of communication.

Table 5.2 Characteristics of Directness and Indirectness

Direct Communication Style	Indirect Communication Style
The message is to be sought within the words used not in the surrounding context. Speakers say what they mean and mean what they say.	The message is to be sought outside the words used in the surrounding contexts, such as proverbs, metaphors, and silence that indirectly deals with the problem. Speakers tend to give priority to relationships and harmony.
Speakers are frank and speak honestly. Honesty is the best policy. Communication is efficient and practical.	Speakers use a "go-between" policy. Being polite is more important than being honest. Focusing on relationships is wise in the long term.
It's okay to say no.	Avoid saying no; say "maybe" or "possibly", even if speakers mean "no."
Speakers feel that indirect communicators are not honest or are trying to avoid saying what they really think.	Speakers sometimes feel that direct communicators are rude or insensitive.

In evaluating these two communication methods, however, we must be aware that directness is not necessarily logical or effective, and indirectness is not necessarily manipulative or insecure; everything depends on one's cultural context.

2. Social Norms

Social Norms are beliefs about what is acceptable in a social context. They are socially accepted rules of behavior and conduct that are prescribed by society and expected of an individual by that society. Social norms are based on traditions, beliefs and values of a society, and they may change from one society to another. These rules may be explicit or implicit. Human behavior is influenced by a perceived group norm. Individuals who do not conform to these rules are said to have deviated from social norms.

Social norms, like many other social phenomena, are the unplanned, unexpected result of individuals' interactions. It has been argued that social norms ought to be understood as a kind of grammar of social interactions (Bicchieri, 2006). Like grammar, a system of norms specifies what is acceptable and what is not in a society or group. For this reason, adherence to social norms means obeying the old proverb: "When in Rome, do as the Romans do."

Questions

1. What are high context and low context cultures?

2. What are the characteristics of high context and low context communication? Please provide examples.

Intercultural Communication in Movies
影视作品中的跨文化交际

3. What are social norms? Can you give some examples?

_____

4. How are indirectness and directness related to high context and low context?

_____

Cultural Comprehension

Decide whether the following statements are true or false according to what you read.

( ) 1. Social Norms are based on traditions, beliefs and values of a society, and they may change from one society to another.

( ) 2. Cultural differences between Asian countries and the U.S. can be divided into high context culture and low context culture.

( ) 3. In high-context cultures, messages are indirect and are delivered in an abstract, implicit manner because the message is highly dependent on the context. In contrast, in low-context cultures, communication is direct and explicit.

( ) 4. Indirect communication means that people feel that indirect communicators are not honest or that they avoid saying what they really think.

( ) 5. The Middle East, Asia, Africa, and North America belong to high-context cultures. In these countries, backgrounds are common and shared and "we" is emphasized over "I".

II. Content-based Activities

Section A   Movie Clips

 Introduction to the movie *Outsourced*

The main character Todd is a 32-year-old manager of a Seattle customer call center and he receives the news that his entire Order Fulfillment department is about to be outsourced to India to reduce the company's cost. Even though he is unwilling to go to Mumbai to train the local manager as his replacement, he has no choice. During his short stay in Mumbai, Todd comes across enormous culture shock in the completely new environment. Puro (Asif Basra) is his likeable replacement and Asha (Ayesha Dharker) is his colleague. With the help of these two Indians Todd quickly adapts to the local customs, which improves his work efficiency. An overnight business trip eventually brings Todd and Asha together, but the result is beyond Todd's expectation.

Introduction to movie clip 1

In this clip, after Todd arrives in India he needs to take a train to Gharapuri. In the railway station he is greatly surprised by the crowds at the gates of the train. He even needs to jump in

Unit 5   Context and Social Norms

order to get on the train. After he arrives in Gharapuri he is placed in a private apartment, where the landlord is so hospitable that she asks such private questions as his age and marriage to show her warmth to Todd; however, this greatly upsets Todd. What is more, Todd is told that he should not use his left hand to eat food because Indian people regard the left hand as unclean.

 Introduction to the movie *The Joy Luck Club*

Culture differences are high lighted in this movie. The four Chinese women represent Chinese culture and their four daughters are deeply influenced by American culture. It is the maternal love that serve not only as a bridge between the daughters and mothers but also between the two cultures. For more details please refer to the movie introduction on page 18.

Introduction to movie clip 2

In this clip, when Li Na gets married she invites her mother to visit her house. Even though she tells her mother everything is OK, her mother is still worried about her, especially when she sees the bills that are split by the couple. Li Na is married to an American, who believes equal share in paying expenses means equal love between the two – even if the husband earns seven times more money than the wife does. Influenced by her mother, Li Na begins to feel that something is wrong with her marriage.

Exercises

Task 1: Fill in the blanks to the following lines spoken in the movie clips you just watched.

1. A kitsch is a garbage that people buy, and redneck_____means farmer.
2. You are a very good_____, strong and ready for anything and everything.
3. I did, but we_____a couple months ago.
4. At least that's what Harold calls it, _____ – everything fifty-fifty so our love is always equal.
5. With most everything we keep track of what we spend then_____it fifty-fifty.
6. You gave her to me as a birthday gift, and now you want me to pay to_____her fleas?

Task 2: Watch the movie clips for a second time and decide whether the following statements are true or false.

(   ) 1. Although it is very crowded on the train, Todd feels comfortable because a little boy offers his seat to him.

(   ) 2. Because of a misunderstanding, Puro does not meet Todd at the train station in Bombay.

(   ) 3. There are lots of cows wandering on the Indian streets, which has nothing to do with the Indian culture.

(   ) 4. Todd lives in a private apartment, and the landlord asks so many personal questions that it upsets him.

Intercultural Communication in Movies
影视作品中的跨文化交际

(　　) 5. Li Na likes eating ice cream very much, so she wants to share the expenses with her husband.

(　　) 6. Since Li Na's mother is a Chinese woman, she cannot understand Li Na's marriage – especially the way they share their money.

Task 3: Discussion: Divide students into several groups to discuss the clips and the problems of intercultural communication.

1. What kind of questions are considered "personal question" that cannot be asked when communicating with western people? Do Indian people have the same view?

_____

2. Why don't people in India use their left hands to eat? Can you figure out the underlying reason for this social norm?

_____

3. How do western people view couples sharing expenses?

_____

4. What is the most common way for Chinese couples to spend their money? Will they go Dutch or combine their money?

_____

Section B   Intercultural Communication Reading

 Pre-reading Task

1. Have you ever thought about the importance of understanding social norms in other countries? Why or why not?
2. How would you act in another culture if you weren't familiar with that culture? How would you tend to judge what is or is not appropriate?
3. Do you think it is necessary to learn the social norms of other countries? Why or why not?

Passage 1
American Culture & Social Life

Here you will find a brief guide to American culture and customs. Because the United States is so varied in its geography, ethnic backgrounds, and traditions, it is not possible to comment on every aspect of the culture or to say there is one acceptable or **prominent** set of social rules.

It is important to note that some people you meet will be more informed and accepting of cultural differences than others. Many people will be curious about your home culture and will ask numerous questions about the language, society, history, religion, and traditions of your country.

Basic Etiquette

Due to the friendly nature of most Americans, they are quick to use first names. Although this may make those who are accustomed to a more formal social environment somewhat uncomfortable, it is the norm for American culture. Formal titles (Mr., Ms., Mrs., Fr., Sr., Dr., etc.) are used together with the person's family name and should be used if you are speaking with the elderly or people in authority. They may later ask you to use their first name.

Punctuality is highly valued in the U.S. and is considered a sign of respect toward the person whom you are to meet. Punctuality for private parties and casual events is more flexible; however, always inform the host of a dinner or formal occasion if you will be late or must cancel. Students are expected to be on time for class and appointments with instructors. Your grade may be affected if you are late multiple times.

Many instructors and administrators welcome personal interactions with individual students. Students are encouraged to ask questions and express their opinions in the classroom. Observe the American students' actions to identify what is acceptable behavior.

Courtesy

Politeness and patience will serve you well in the United States. This includes remembering to say "please" and "thank you". This common form of respect is not reserved for those in a position of authority, but for each and every person that you meet in a store, on the street, in class, or in an office. If you need a favor or have a simple request, saying "please" will be much more effective than if you are simply demanding. Provided that you are kind, the person with whom you are speaking will likely return your kindness.

Personal Space

Americans prefer to maintain about 18 inches (46 cm) of space between themselves and the person with whom they are speaking. This personal space is very important and, if limited, the individual may become uncomfortable.

Typically, Americans do not hug or kiss an acquaintance upon greeting, but rather shake hands or nod their heads. They also do not touch while speaking, although a brief touch on the arm or shoulder might indicate sympathy or concern to someone they know well. Once a friendship has developed, women may greet each other with a hug or embrace.

Privacy

Privacy and personal possessions are important to Americans. People work hard to have a car, house, clothes, and other belongings. Be sure to ask how someone feels about sharing his or her space and belongings.

Apparel

Formal dress is seldom worn on university campuses. Students typically wear jeans, shorts, skirts, T-shirts, sweatshirts, and sweaters. For class presentations, job interviews, and other occasions, students may be asked to dress more formally. When attending a special event, you should ask the host of the event about appropriate **attire**.

Dining

The formality of meals in the U.S. varies considerably. To be safe, follow the lead of the host and other American guests. Here are some general etiquette guidelines:

- Food is generally eaten in small bites.

- It is not polite to pick up the plate from which you are eating.
- Do not **slurp** soup or beverages.
- It is polite to converse during a meal unless you are attending a lecture or a toast is being made.
- Always chew with your mouth closed.
- Wait until everybody is seated at the table before you start eating.

Language

The English Language can be difficult to learn. Speaking, reading, writing, and using grammar in another language is challenging.

One area of the English language that can be especially difficult for non-native speakers is the use of idioms. Idioms are a group of words that have a figurative meaning that is separate from the literal meaning. For example, take the phrase, "It is raining cats and dogs." When somebody says this they do not mean cats and dogs are falling from the sky! What they are actually saying is, "It is raining heavily."

Degrees of Friendship

Americans are generally very friendly people. They will often say, "Hi, how are you?" or "How is it going?" but do not wait for you to respond. These are friendly expressions, which are not always a question but rather another version of "Hello". If an American seems friendly, it does not necessarily mean that he/she has developed a friendship (a close relationship) with you. As is probably true in your culture, friendships are developed over a period of time. Although Americans may refer to classmates as "friends", often they are acquaintances rather than true friends. Finding true friends will take time; however, it is well worth the effort.

Dating and Sexual Relationships

A "date" is simply an agreement to meet at a certain time and place and to spend some time together. You should not interpret or expect a date to be anything more. It is common that someone you have met only briefly will ask you on a date. Generally, the male will pay for the date; however, many (especially students) "**go Dutch**", where each pays for him or herself.

In the U.S., dating is more casual and informal than in other cultures. Relationships between men and women of college age range from friendship to a strong emotional and physical relationship. As your friendships develop beyond acquaintance, you may not always understand what your partner expects of you. Be honest regarding your concerns and feelings as that can avoid misunderstandings and even greater discomfort. If your date appears interested in a sexual relationship and you are not, it is very important that you say "No" clearly. And if someone is saying "No" to you, listen. Unwanted sexual attention is a very serious matter in the U.S.; do not mistake an American's friendliness for **promiscuity**.

Practicing Your Religion

The United States is a multicultural society founded on tolerance and mutual respect; you should not hesitate to seek out opportunities to practice your religious beliefs. Organized religious groups of many **denominations** can be found here, and others exist in the surrounding community.

Unit 5 Context and Social Norms

Although America has a higher rate of church attendance than most other western societies, many Americans may be uncomfortable discussing religion. Others will want to share their religious views with you. Most people are sincere and straightforward, but some may try to take advantage of you or convert you to their religious beliefs by offering you their friendship. If you begin to feel uncomfortable in such a situation, politely but firmly explain that you are not interested.

Alcohol and Smoking

In the United States, it is illegal for any person under the age of 21 to purchase, attempt to purchase, or be in possession of alcohol or other intoxicating substances. Therefore, no alcoholic beverage may be served or sold to anyone under 21 years of age. Students must present two forms of valid photo identification in order to purchase alcohol. Students found presenting false identification or taking other steps to acquire alcohol as a minor will be subject to **disciplinary sanction**.

Smoking is prohibited within all non-residential, university-owned and -leased buildings and on all university grounds. This includes, but is not necessarily limited to, restrooms, lunch/break rooms, private offices, workstations, **hallways**, waiting rooms, conference rooms, and **vestibules**.

(1308 words)

(Portions taken from *International Student and Scholar Services Handbook* from the Office of International Student and Scholar Services, University of Missouri-St. Louis)

Passage 2

The Values Americans Live by (III)
L. Robert Kohls

7. Time and Its Control

Time is, for the average American, of utmost importance. To the foreign visitor, Americans seem to be more concerned with getting things accomplished on time (according to a **predetermined** schedule) than they are with developing deep interpersonal relations. Schedules, for the American, are meant to be planned and then followed in the smallest detail.

It may seem to you that most Americans are completely controlled by the little machines they wear on their wrists, cutting their discussions off **abruptly** to make it to their next appointment on time.

Americans' language is filled with references to time, giving a clear indication of how much it is valued. Time is something to be "on", to be "kept", "filled", "saved", "used", "spent", "wasted", "lost", "gained", "planned", "given", "made the most of", even "killed".

The international visitor soon learns that it is considered very rude to be late – even by 10 minutes – for an appointment in the United States. (Whenever it is absolutely impossible to be on time, you should phone ahead and tell the person you have been unavoidably **detained** and will be a half hour – or whatever – late.)

Time is so valued in America, because by considering time to be important one can clearly accomplish more than if one "wastes" time and does not keep busy. This philosophy has proven its worth. It has enabled Americans to be extremely productive, and productivity itself is highly valued in the United States. Many American proverbs stress the value in guarding our time, using it wisely, setting and working toward specific goals, and even expending our time and energy today so that the fruits of our labor may be enjoyed at a later time. (This latter concept is called "delayed **gratification**".)

8. Future Orientation

Valuing the future and the improvements Americans are sure the future will bring means that they **devalue** the past and are, to a large extent, unconscious of the present. Even a happy present goes largely unnoticed because, happy as it may be, Americans have traditionally been hopeful that the future would bring even greater happiness. Almost all energy is directed toward realizing that better future. At best, the present condition is seen as preparatory to a latter and greater event, which will eventually **culminate** in something even more worthwhile.

Since Americans have been taught to believe that Man, and not Fate, can and should be the one who controls the environment, this has made them very good at planning and executing short-term projects. This ability, in turn, has caused Americans to be invited to all corners of the earth to plan and achieve the miracles that their goal-setting can produce.

9. Action/Work Orientation

"Don't just stand there," goes a typical bit of American advice, "do something!" This expression is normally used in a crisis situation, yet, in a sense, it describes most Americans' entire waking life, where action – any action – is seen to be superior to inaction.

Americans **routinely** plan and schedule an extremely active day. Any relaxation must be limited in time, pre-planned, and aimed at "recreating" their ability to work harder and more productively once the recreation is over. Americans believe leisure activities should assume a relatively small portion of one's total life. People think that it is "sinful" to "waste one's time", "to sit around doing nothing", or just to "daydream".

Such a "no nonsense" attitude toward life has created many people who have come to be known as "workaholics", or people who are addicted to their work, who think constantly about their jobs and who are frustrated if they are kept away from them, even during their evening hours and weekends.

The workaholic **syndrome**, in turn, causes Americans to identify themselves wholly with their professions. The first question one American will ask another American when meeting for the first time is related to his or her work: "Where do you work?" or "Who (what company) are you with?"

And when such a person finally goes on vacation, even the vacation will be carefully planned, very busy and active. America may be one of the few countries in the world where it seems reasonable to speak about the "dignity of human labor", meaning by that, hard, physical labor. In America, even corporation presidents will engage in physical labor from time to time and gain, rather than lose, respect from others for such action.

10. Directness, Openness and Honesty

Many other countries have developed subtle, sometimes highly **ritualistic**, ways of informing other people of unpleasant information. Americans, however, have always preferred the first approach. They are likely to be completely honest in delivering their negative evaluations. If you come from a society that uses the indirect manner of conveying bad news or **uncomplimentary** evaluations, you will be shocked at Americans' **bluntness**.

If you come from a country where saving face is important, be assured that Americans are not trying to make you lose face with their directness. It is important to realize that an American would not, in such a case, lose face. The burden of adjustment, in all cases while you are in this country, will be on you. There is no way to soften the blow of such directness and openness if you are not used to it except to tell you that the rules have changed while you are here. Indeed, Americans are trying to urge their fellow countrymen to become even more open and direct.

Americans consider anything other than the most direct and open approach to be dishonest and insincere and will quickly lose confidence in and distrust anyone who hints at what is intended rather than saying it outright.

Anyone who, in the United States, chooses to use an **intermediary** to deliver that message will also be considered **manipulative** and untrustworthy.

(972 words)

(Adopted from http://www.claremontmckenna.edu/pages/faculty/alee/extra/American_values.html)

 After-reading Task

1. According to passage 1, what are some basic etiquettes in America?

___

2. According to passage 1, is it easy for people to make friends in the U.S? How can people make true friends?

___

3. According to passage 2, what does American future orientation mean?

___

4. According to passage 2, do you think American directness tends to make you lose face?

___

 WORDS LIST

Passage 1

prominent /'prɒmɪnənt/ *a.* 突出的，杰出的
courtesy /'kɜːtəsɪ/ *n.* 谦恭有礼，礼貌
apparel /ə'pær(ə)l/ *n.* 衣服；服装（尤指正装）

Intercultural Communication in Movies
影视作品中的跨文化交际

attire /ə'taɪə(r)/ *n.* 服装，衣服
slurp /slɜːp/ *v.* 出声地吃或喝
go Dutch 各自付账；平摊费用
promiscuity /ˌprɒmɪsk'juːətɪ/ *n.* 滥交
denomination /dɪˌnɒmɪ'neɪʃn/ *n.* 宗派；教派
disciplinary /'dɪsɪplɪnərɪ/ *a.* 纪律的；惩罚的
sanction /'sæŋkʃn/ *n.* 制裁，处罚
hallway /'hɔːlweɪ/ *n.* 走廊，过道；门厅
vestibule /'vestɪbjuːl/ *n.* (美)火车车厢末端的连廊

Passage 2

predetermine /ˌpriːdɪ'tɜːmɪn/ *v.* 预先裁定；预先确定
abruptly /ə'brʌptlɪ/ *ad.* 突然地；（言谈举止）唐突地
detain /dɪ'teɪn/ *v.* 留住；耽搁
gratification /ˌgrætɪfɪ'keɪʃn/ *n.* 满足；喜悦
devalue /ˌdiː'væljuː/ *v.* 使（货币）贬值；降低……价值
culminate /'kʌlmɪneɪt/ *v.* 达到极点
routinely /ruː'tiːnlɪ/ *ad.* 例行公事地；常规地
syndrome /'sɪndrəʊm/ *n.* 综合征；典型表现
ritualistic /ˌrɪtʃʊə'lɪstɪk/ *a.* 固守仪式的；惯例的
uncomplimentary /ʌnˌkɒmplɪ'mentrɪ/ *a.* 贬降的
bluntness /'blʌntnəs/ *n.* 率直
intermediary /ˌɪntə'miːdɪərɪ/ *a.* 中间的；调解的
manipulative /mə'nɪpjələtɪv/ *a.* 巧妙处理的

Section C Case Studies

Case 1

John, an American, was visiting his Chinese friend Wang Peng in China during the summer holiday. Wang Peng was very excited to show John around his hometown, hoping it would leave John with a lasting impression.

The first evening they were together, Wang Peng took John to the other side of the city – a part of the city Wang Peng was not very familiar with. He wanted to take John to a famous Chinese restaurant he heard about. However, when they arrived in that part of the city, Wang Peng could not remember where the restaurant was located. After walking with John for over half an hour, he still could not find the restaurant, but he didn't tell John that he was lost.

John: "Wang Peng, do you know where the restaurant is?"

Wang Peng: "Yeah, we're almost there."

John: "We've been walking for a long time. Are you sure you know where it is? Maybe you should ask for directions."

Unit 5 Context and Social Norms

Wang Peng: "Don't worry about it. It's right over there."

However, after another fifteen minutes of walking, John finally asked a stranger on the street for directions to the restaurant. When they finally found the restaurant, John was very frustrated with Wang Peng and felt very disrespected. He also felt like he could not trust Wang Peng anymore.

John: "Why didn't you tell me we were lost? We could have asked for directions and arrived much earlier!"

Reflection

1. Do John and Wang Peng come from high or low context cultures?

2. How do John's actions and reactions reflect his high or low context culture? Why did he want Wang Peng to ask for directions? Why did he feel disrespected by Wang Peng and feel like he lost his trust?

3. How do Wang Peng's actions and reactions reflect his high or low context culture? Why did he refuse to ask for directions? How was he trying to show respect toward John?

Case 2

One day April, an American girl, was talking to her Chinese roommate, Xiao Li, about an American guy, James, who was interested in dating Xiao Li. The week before, James had sat next to Xiao Li in the school cafeteria and had what he thought to be a great conversation. Later that evening, Xiao Li received an email from James saying that he wanted to date her and asking Xiao Li if she would date him. Xiao Li, however, was not interested in James. She hoped if she just ignored the email that he would understand. But over the next week she received three more emails from him. She knew that April was good friends with James, and she hoped April could tell James for her that she was not interested in him.

April: "So, Xiao Li, do you like James? Are you going to date him?"

Xiao Li: "He's a nice guy, but I am not really interested in him."

April: "Well, did you tell him that?"

Xiao Li: "No, I did not tell him. In fact, since you are his friend, I was hoping you could tell him for me."

April: "What do you mean? Why don't you tell him?"

Xiao Li: "I'm just not comfortable telling him. Why don't you tell him for me?"

April: "This isn't my problem. It's your responsibility to tell him. Even if you aren't interested in him, you should at least show him some respect."

Intercultural Communication in Movies
影视作品中的跨文化交际

Reflection

1. How does Xiao Li reflect a high context culture in how she handles the situation with James?

2. How do James and April reflect a low context culture in how they handle the situation?

3. Give an example of something Xiao Li could say to James that would clearly communicate to him that she does not want to date him but that would not make him feel disrespected.

Case 3 Watch the following clip from the movie "*Go Lala Go*" and try to analyze the cultural phenomenon in an intercultural context.

Reflection

1. Why does Rose say she needs an operation?

2. How do the staff members respond to Lester's questions?

3. Can you see any examples of high-context culture in the clip?

III. Task-based Activities

Exercises

Choose the best choice according to the cultural context.

(   ) 1. You are in an American restaurant and you want to call the waiter over to refill your glass of water. You should:
   a. Raise your hand toward the waiter and say, "Excuse me."
   b. Yell "Waiter!" in the direction of the person.

(   ) 2. An American friend of yours invites you to dinner at a very fancy restaurant one evening for no apparent reason. It is not a special day, and you cannot think of any reason why he would do that. Your friend is likely doing this because:
   a. He later wants to ask you to do a favor for him.
   b. He just wants to treat you to a nice meal because you are his friend. He has no special motive.

(   ) 3. You are a Chinese guy, and while you are walking next to your best American friend

Unit 5   Context and Social Norms

on campus, you want to express your friendship to him. You should:

    a. Put your arm around his shoulder as you walk with him.

    b. Tell him, "I'm really glad I've gotten to know you here."

( ) 4. You are celebrating your friend's birthday at an American restaurant with a group of friends. You should make sure to:

    a. Be quiet in the restaurant.

    b. Be loud in the restaurant (to express excitement and joy).

( ) 5. As you are celebrating your friend's birthday with a group of American friends, you want to offer a toast to your friend. You should:

    a. Pour beer into others' glasses and pressure them to toast with it.

    b. Let each person toast with whatever beverage they want to use, and do not pressure them to drink alcohol.

Group Work

Discussion 1

Do you believe Hall is correct in his assumptions? If so, what examples can you give to demonstrate high- and low-context cultures? How would context help explain miscommunication and misunderstanding between North Americans and Chinese?

Discussion 2

Read the following two conversations and try to distinguish which one comes from low-context culture and which one comes from high-context culture.

A

Man: Hi, how are you?

Woman: I'm fine, thank you. And you?

Man: Fine. We haven't seen each other for a while. How about going to see a movie this afternoon?

Woman: I'm sorry. I don't really want to see a movie, but I would love to go to a café.

Man: Hmm, I really want to see this movie. Can we go to the café another day?

Woman: I really don't like that movie, but why don't we go to the movie theater first and then go to a café?

Man: OK, that sounds good.

B

Man: Good evening. How are you?

Woman: I'm fine, thank you. How is your family?

Man: Fine, thank you. How about your family?

Woman: They are all very fine, thanks a lot.

Man: Do you have an idea for something we could do this evening?

Woman: What would you like to do?

Intercultural Communication in Movies
影视作品中的跨文化交际

Man: Oh, I don't know. Do you have any ideas?

Woman: I don't know, either. Hmm, how about going to see a movie?

Man: Hmm, is that what you want to do?

Woman: What about you, what do you think about it?

Man: OK, it sounds interesting.

Assignment

Presentation 1

Please make a presentation to your classmates about indirectness in Chinese culture and try to give some examples to illustrate the point. As Chinese, what main social norms should people know?

Presentation 2

Look at the table below and add some examples under each heading. Please make a presentation to your classmates to explain your examples.

Low context vs. High-context Communication

Low context/ U.S., Germany	High-context/ China, Japan
Meaning is reliant on verbal message	Meaning can be derived from context
Nonverbal communication is low importance	Nonverbal communication is high importance
Silence is avoided	Silence is normal

Source: E. McDanied, "Crossing Cultural Borders: Intercultural Communication from the Interpretation and Translation Perspective", Journal of Interpreting and Translation Studies, 2011, 14(2): 359.

> *Human beings draw close to one another by their common nature, but habits and customs keep them apart.* – Three-character Canon
> 性相近，习相远。
>
> *In the application of the rituals it is harmony that is prized.* – Confucian saying
> 礼之用，和为贵。

Unit 6　Time and Space across Culture

I. Definition of Time and Space across Culture

1. Time: Monochronic Time vs. Polychronic Time
2. Proxemics

In this unit we will introduce another two of Edward T. Hall's cultural theories: monochronic/polychronic time and proxemics. In human relationships, "silent language" plays a very important role. Hall analyzed the many ways in which people "talk" to one another without the use of words. In his books *The Silent Language* (1959) and *The Hidden Dimension* (1966), he defined nonverbal communication as communication that does not involve the exchange of words. According to Hall, the concepts of space and time are tools with which all humans beings may transmit messages and communicate.

1. Time: Monochronic Time vs. Polychronic Time

Hall (1959) believes that "time talks". He explains, "It speaks more plainly than words. The message it conveys comes through loud and clear. Because it is manipulated less consciously, it is subject to less distortion than the spoken language. It can shout the truth where words lie." (p1)

Time is one of the fundamental bases on which all cultures rest and around which all activities revolve. Because cultures differ in how they conceive of time, they schedule, organize and plan differently. Hall puts forth the two paradigms of polychronic time and monochronic time to describe how cultures structure their time.

Monochronic time (M-time) means "doing one thing at a time". It assumes careful planning and scheduling and it is a familiar Western approach that appears in disciplines such as time management (p6). People of low context tend to be monochronic. In polychronic time (P-time), human interaction is valued over time and material things, leading to a lesser concern for getting things done. People of high context tend to be polychronic.

Contrasting the two concepts, we can see that monochronic time follows the principle of "one thing at a time", while polychronic time focuses on multiple tasks being handled at one time, and time being subordinate to interpersonal relations. Below (Table 6.1) is a more complete comparison of both concepts.

Table 6.1 A more complete comparison of M-Time and P-Time

M-Time	P-time
One thing at a time	Multitasking
Time is limited; precisely segmented, schedule driven	Time is viewed as being flexible, less tangible and multidimensional
Punctuality	Poor punctuality
Respect of commitment and given word	Respect of delays
Tight schedules	Loose schedules

Because time orientation is different in many cultures, people deal with things in different ways. Polychronic time prevails in Mediterranean, Latin American, Indian and especially Arab cultures, while monochronic time prevails in Anglo-Saxon, German, North European and North American cultures.

2. Proxemics

In *The Hidden Dimension* (1966), Hall develops his theory of proxemics, discussing the human perceptions of space. He claims that different frameworks for defining and organizing space, which are internalized in all people at an unconscious level, may lead to serious failures of communication and understanding in cross-cultural settings. Hall believes that "the patterning of perceptual worlds is a function not only of culture but of relationship, activity and emotion. Therefore, people from different cultures, when interpreting each other's behavior, often misinterpret the relationship, the activity, or the emotions. This leads to alienation in encounters or distorted communications" (p181).

Proxemics can be defined as "the interrelated observations and theories of man's use of space as a specialized elaboration of culture" (p1). Hall analyzes both the personal spaces that people form around their bodies as well as macro-level surroundings, such as the organizing of offices, streets, neighborhoods and cities. He divides proxemics into two categories: personal space and territory. Personal space describes the immediate space surrounding a person, while territory refers to the area which a person may "lay claim to" and defend against others. Personal space includes intimate distance for embracing, touching or whispering; personal distance for interactions among good friends or family members; social distance for interactions among acquaintances; and public distance used for public speaking. The four kinds of human territory in proxemics are public territory, which is a place where one may freely enter; interactional territory, which is a place where people congregate informally; home territory, which is a place where people claim as their individual territory; and body territory, which is the space immediately surrounding a person. This sense of personal space can include an area or physical object that has come to be considered that individual's "territory". It not only includes visual space (things seen) but also aural space (things heard), thermal space (skin), kinesthetic space (muscles) and olfactory space (scent). If people come too close, they may intrude on the other person's privacy. The following picture (Figure 6.1) demonstrates the proper distance in communication.

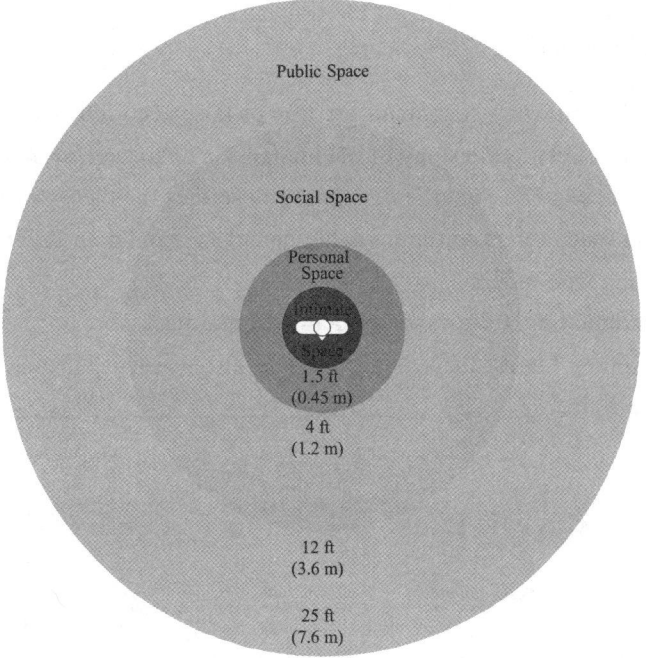

Figure 6.1 Proxemics in Personal, Social and Public Distance
(source: adapted from the Wikimedia Commons by Libb Thims)

From the picture above, we can see that there are different spatial zones that cultures will use for communication. For example, among those of Anglo-Saxon heritage, such as the United States, there is an intimate zone that extends from 0 to 18 inches from a person. Only close relations will communicate this closely. The next zone is the comfort zone, which extends from 1.5 feet to 4 feet. Communication in this zone reflects friendship and closeness. The next zone extends from 4 feet to 12 feet and is reserved for impersonal communication. Anything outside of 12 feet is the public zone, where an individual may greet others but is unlikely to converse with them. However, some cultures prefer much closer contact. For example, in many Arab cultures contact is so close that individuals frequently can smell each other's breath.

Questions

1. What is Proxemics? How many zones are there?

_____

2. What are the characteristics of monochronic and polychronic time?

_____

3. When and in which book does Hall put forth his space theory? What significance does it have?

_____

4. According to Hall's theory, how do people from different cultures perceive time?

_____

Cultural Comprehension

Decide whether the following statements are true or false according to what you read.

( ) 1. Proxemics refers to the study of the human use of space within the context of culture.

( ) 2. In Hall's books *The Silent Language*, he describes the theory of proxemics.

( ) 3. Personal space refers to the invisible boundary around an individual that is used for interacting with others.

( ) 4. Monochronic time follows the principle of multitasking.

( ) 5. In the United States, there is an intimate distance that extends from 0 to 18 inches from a person.

II. Content-based Activities

Section A   Movie Clips

 Introduction to the movie *Outsourced*

Being sent to India to train his replacement, Todd is surprised by the sight of the Indian culture. Soon he experiences a great culture shock. For more details please refer to the movie introduction on page 62.

Introduction to movie clip 1

In this clip, Todd tries to deal with the slow working pace of Indian people while trying to cut down customer service time. Indian people do not think it is necessary to work fast, which is an obstacle for Todd. The average customer service time is 12 minutes. In order to solve the problem, he decides to learn from the Indian people and use an incentive program that allows employees to work in Indian ways. After a while, he succeeds in greatly shortening the customer service time.

 Introduction to the movie *Pushing Hands*

Pushing Hands is part of Ang Lee's trilogy *My Father Knows Best*. It is a story about an elderly Chinese tai chi professor, Lao Zhu, who emigrates from China to America after his retirement to live with his son Alex, American daughter-in-law Martha, and grandson in New York. Because of cultural differences between Lao Zhu and Martha, Lao Zhu eventually decides to leave the house and earn money to support himself.

Introduction to movie clip 2

In this clip, Lao Zhu moves to live in his son's house in America. Since he is neither familiar with the environment nor good at speaking English, he can do nothing but practice tai

Unit 6 Time and Space across Culture

chi in the house, which is shared by Martha. Martha becomes very frustrated because she cannot concentrate on her writing. One of her friends comes to try to sell a house to her, but Alex will not let her buy it.

Task 1: Fill in the blanks to the following lines spoken in the movie clips you just watched.

1. If we don't get it down to six minutes I'll be_____India for the rest of my life.
2. What would make your workday a more_____experience?
3. Your_____program is a very good idea, sir.
4. Where's grandpa? He's so_____with the headphones on.
5. You'll have your own room to write in. Grandpa could be out in the back_____bricks or whatever he does out there.
6. From the way Alex has acted for the last seven years you_____he didn't have a father and then boom.

Task 2: Watch the movie clips for a second time and decide whether the following statements are true or false.

(   ) 1. At the beginning Todd is very unhappy about his work because his colleagues don't respect him.
(   ) 2. With Todd's permission the Indian employees decorate the office in their own way. Some bring family pictures and some put idols on the work desks.
(   ) 3. Even though Purohit doubts Asha's ability, she gets promoted by Todd.
(   ) 4. At first Martha thinks Alex doesn't have a father.
(   ) 5. Martha can't concentrate on her writing since her father-in-law has come to live with them.
(   ) 6. Alex plans to buy a larger house for his wife and send his father to a nursing home.

Task 3: Discussion: Divide students into several groups to discuss the clips and the problems of intercultural communication.

1. In the movie clip, Indian people work with low efficiency. What do you think is the reason for this? Do you think it is related to their time orientation?

_____

2. How does Todd succeed in reducing the customer service time? How does he apply intercultural communication methods we have discussed so far?

_____

3. From the movie *Pushing Hands*, how can we see the differences between the use of space in Western and Eastern cultures?

_____

4. Do you think Alex will send his father to a nursing home? How do older people view happiness?

_____

Intercultural Communication in Movies

Section B Intercultural Communication Reading

 Pre-reading Task

1. Are you a polychron or a monochron? Have you ever asked yourself this question?
2. Do you typically make plans or schedules for your day? Do you think scheduling your time is important and necessary?
3. Do you have an awkward experience of a stranger invading your personal distance? If so, explain.

Passage 1
Time Sense: Polychronicity and Monochronicity

Are you a **polychron** or a **monochron**?

My guess is you have no idea what I am talking about. And yet, this is one of the most important questions you can ever ask yourself. Knowing if you are a polychron or a monochron will help you understand a lot about yourself, including how you fit into the world and how you get along with others.

The terms monochron and polychron have to do with our time sense: how we perceive and manage time. To a polychron, time is continuous, with no particular structure. Polychrons see time as a never-ending river, flowing from the infinite past, through the present, into the infinite future.

In the workplace, polychrons prefer to keep their time unstructured, changing from one activity to another as the mood takes them. Although polychrons can meet deadlines, they need to do so in their own way. A polychron does not want detailed plans imposed upon him, nor does he want to make his own detailed plans. Polychrons prefer to work as they see fit without a strict schedule, following their internal mental processes from one minute to the next.

Monochrons see time as being divided into fixed elements that can be organized, quantified and scheduled. Monochrons relate to time differently: to them, time is **discrete**, not continuous. Monochrons see time as being divided into fixed elements – seconds, minutes, hours, days, weeks, and so on – temporal blocks that can be organized, quantified and scheduled. Monochrons love to plan in detail, making lists, keeping track of their activities, and organizing their time into a daily routine. Monochrons prefer to do one thing at a time, working on a task until it is finished, then, and only then, moving on to the next task. To a monochron, switching back and forth from one activity to another is not only wasteful and distracting – it is uncomfortable.

Polychrons are different. They love to work on more than one thing at a time. To a polychron, switching from one activity to another is both stimulating and productive and, hence, the most desirable way to work.

Can you see yourself in here somewhere?

I bet you can and, once you do, you can see how easy it would be for a monochron and a polychron who live or work together to **butt** heads frequently, driving each other crazy without even knowing what is happening.

Here is a common example. Because of the way polychrons see time, they are often late. This only makes sense because, to a polychron, exact times (and even exact dates) are not really meaningful and, hence, are not all that important. Try telling this to the monochron who is kept waiting for that polychron. While the polychron was finishing a couple of last-minute **chores** at home, the monochron was at the appointed place five minutes early, anxiously looking at his watch. To a monochron, time is exact and, as he sees it, being late is both rude and disrespectful. To a polychron, any time – even an exact time – is just an **approximation**. If someone keeps him waiting, he doesn't really care. He just figures that something must have happened to hold up the other person, and it's not that big of a deal.

In order to keep the peace, polychrons do learn to be on time when they really need to be. However, if you can get them to talk truthfully, they will tell you that they don't really understand why so many people feel that punctuality is a virtue.

The important lesson here is that, when it comes to organizing time, we all think that how we do it makes the most sense. The hidden assumption is that there is only one right way to understand time (our way). The truth is there is more than one way to think about time, and neither extreme is right or wrong; they are just different.

Of course, this is not to say that, in a particular society, it won't be more advantageous to be either **polychronic** or **monochronic**. Indeed, the terms "polychronic" and "monochronic" were first used to describe whole cultures and not individuals (by the anthropologist Edward Hall in his book The Silent Language, 1959).

According to Hall, some cultures are traditionally monochronic. In such a culture, time is thought of as being **linear**. People are expected to do one thing at a time, and they will not tolerate lateness or interruptions. In polychronic cultures, time is thought of as being **cyclical**. In such cultures, it is not important to be punctual, and it is acceptable to interrupt someone who is busy.

If you live in the United States, Canada, or Northern Europe, you live in a monochronic culture. If you live in Latin America, the Arab part of the Middle East, or sub-Sahara Africa, you live in a polychronic culture.

If you are a monochron living in a monochronic culture, you fit in without knowing it. But what if you are a polychron (as I am) living in, say, the United States? You will find yourself at **odds** with the work habits of most of the people around you, perhaps even disagreeing regularly with family members or spouses.

I have already mentioned that, to a polychron, it is acceptable (and even desirable) to be late, but there is a lot more. Polychrons consider a schedule to be less important than interpersonal relations. So they will, for example, be glad to stop what they are doing to talk to someone, or take a phone call, or to send email. Although polychrons like to handle more than one task at a time, they won't care if someone interrupts them during their work time or even during their break time. To a polychron, all time is the same, and they tend not to separate their work time from their personal time.

Although I live in a monochronic country, I know many polychrons. To my eye, they seem to enjoy their lives a lot more than the majority of monochrons, who live in a highly demanding world that rarely seems to let them relax and just be who they really are.

Perhaps being a polychron in a monochronic country isn't all that bad. You get to watch all the busy bees around you, planning, scheduling, and working hard, making sure that the many things that need to be done are done and done on time, which means that you get all the advantages (and there are many) of living in a monochronic society.

Moreover, as long as you can finesse your way around the demands of punctuality and **mandatory** deadlines, you can work when you want to, on whatever it is that interests you at that moment. Since you don't need to make an artificial **distinction** between your work and the rest of your life, you have no need to separate what you think from what you feel. Thus, you can live your life with a great deal of **passion**, much of which will find its way into your work.

No wonder I feel as if I am always on vacation!

(1191 words)

(This article was edited to fit the format of this book. For the original article, please visit: http://www.harley.com/writing/time-sense.html)

Passage 2
How to Use Proxemics in the Corporate Classroom
Jeff Welch

Skilled classroom **facilitators** always make an extra effort to effectively practice both their verbal and non-verbal communication skills. Verbally, it's important that we use proper grammar, minimize speech **fillers**, and clearly **articulate** our words and syllables. Non-verbally, it's critical that we incorporate gestures, facial expressions, and movement to help convey our message.

There's another aspect of non-verbal communication that we, as facilitators, need to **be mindful of**; it's an aspect called proxemics.

Proxemics is the theory of using measurable distance and space to make people feel comfortable or more relaxed while interacting with them. The term was **coined** by the late anthropologist, Edward T. Hall, Jr. during the early 1960s. Proxemics is usually categorized by personal **territory** and physical territory.

Personal territory proxemics is that safe distance of space that we keep between us and the person we're standing behind while waiting in line at a ticket counter. Another example of personal territory proxemics is the space or area that we comfortably settle into when we enter an elevator with other people.

Proxemics as it relates to physical territory involves the use of furniture and seating arrangements. Think about how the seats in movie theaters and on public transit usually consist of individual chairs, often with an arm rest or divider, as opposed to a long, singular bench. Designers of these public spaces often consider proxemics.

Unit 6 Time and Space across Culture

As classroom facilitators the awareness and practice of proxemics can be used to our advantage. Let's first explore personal territory proxemics.

Dr. Hall separated personal territory proxemics into four distinct zones: intimate, personal, social, and public. There have been countless studies conducted to determine what is considered a comfortable distance in each zone.

In North America, the "comfort zones" between individuals are usually as follows:

- Intimate – Ranges from one foot or less of space, and usually involves some sort or touching, such as whispering or embracing.
- Personal – Ranges from 2-4 feet of space, and is usually practiced among friends and family members.
- Social – Ranges from 4-10 feet of space, and is typically exercised when business associates and strangers communicate with each other.
- Public – Ranges from 12-25 feet of space, and is often the distance between a public speaker and his/her audience.

In the classroom, practicing social distance or proximity is usually most advantageous when interacting with your learners. It's not necessary to actually consult a tape measure to determine the suggested 4-10 feet of space; however, I feel it's important to be mindful of a learner's personal space. I try to practice this habit when I'm conversing with a learner and giving feedback.

I often have **flashbacks** of a time where I was made to feel very uncomfortable by an instructor who didn't practice this proximity guideline. I was being trained for a job in a call center which required heavy usage of a desktop computer. During training, if I had difficulty using my computer or entering data, the trainer would assist by **hovering over** me and invading my personal space. I'm not even sure she realized how uneasy I felt as we were both virtually cheek to cheek while looking at the computer screen. I never want to make my learners feel uncomfortable like this in any of my training classes.

Public distance or **proximity** should be considered as you set up your classroom. The 12-25-foot range gives you a safe distance from your learners when you present in front of your audience. It also creates an **ample** and **unobstructed** area, which is good for movement during your presentation.

You may have noticed I made specific reference to North America when explaining the "comfort zone" proximities. Not all cultures practice the same **protocol** as it relates to personal space. I have read that certain Middle Eastern, Latin American, and African cultures are considered "high contact" cultures because close proximity is the cultural norm for them.

I experienced this first hand on a trip to South Africa. While waiting in line at a South African fast food chain, the person standing behind me was so close, I actually felt him breathing on my neck. Feeling uncomfortable, I immediately got out of line and went to the restroom. As I waited "in queue" (as they say in South Africa) for a second time, I realized the next person who came behind me stood just as close. I remember looking around to see if a large crowd of people had suddenly arrived at the restaurant. Because the restaurant was not crowded, I was left to assume that standing in such close proximity was simply a cultural difference; however, as an American, it made me feel a bit uneasy.

In regard to training, if your audience is comprised mostly of North Americans or other members of "low contact" cultures, it's probably best to practice personal territory proxemics and keep what's considered a safe or appropriate distance.

I also recommend practicing physical territory proxemics in the corporate classroom. As mentioned earlier, physical territory proxemics involves the use of furniture and seating arrangements.

As you arrange your classroom tables and chairs, be mindful of the learners' personal space. Typically they will be seated for extended periods of time next to other individuals during a course. At Langevin, we recommend 30-35 square feet of space per person while seated. If your learners are required to write, we recommend providing tables with 4-6 square feet of table space per person so they have adequate "elbow room".

On the flip side, research shows that too much distance between learners can actually reduce interaction and participation. Still keeping the "elbow room" concept in mind, I recommend using seating arrangements such as the "**Bistro**" style at round tables. Or, you might consider using the "**U**" or "**Horseshoe**" style set-up. These seating arrangements have a tendency to promote comfortable interaction and participation, rather than limit it.

Perhaps proxemics are already part of your presentation skills **toolkit**; if not, I encourage you to incorporate this powerful tool to help you better connect with your learners by making them feel comfortable and relaxed in your classroom.

(1023 words)

 After-reading Task

1. According to passage 1, what are the characteristics of monochronic time and polychronic time? Which one do you think is better?

2. According to passage 1, if you are a polychron, how will you fit in to society in America?

3. According to passage 2, what is proxemics? How many different zones are there?

4. According to passage 2, how many feet is the "comfort zone" proximity for North America? How do teachers keep a safe distance from students?

 WORDS LIST

Passage 1
polychronicity /ˈpɒlɪˌkrəˈnɪsɪtɪ/ *n.* 多向记时制

monochronicity /ˌmɒnəˌkrə'nɪsɪtɪ/ *n.* 单向记时制
polychron /'pɒlɪkrən/ *n.* 多向记时制的人
monochron /'mɒnəkrən/ *n.* 单向记时制的人
discrete /dɪ'skriːt/ *a.* 分离的；不相关联的
butt /bʌt/ *n.* 烟蒂；（武器或工具的）粗大的一端
approximation /əˌprɒksɪ'meɪʃn/ *n.* 接近；近似
polychronic /ˌpɒlɪ'krɒnɪk/ *a.* 多向记时制的
monochronic /ˌmɒnəʊ'krɒnɪk/ *a.* 单向记时制的
linear /'lɪniə(r)/ *a.* （过程）线性的；直线的
cyclical /'sɪklɪkəl/ *a.* 循环的；周期的
at odds 争执（不一致）
mandatory /'mændətərɪ/ *a.* 强制的；命令的
distinction /dɪ'stɪŋkʃn/ *n.* 差别；不同
passion /'pæʃn/ *n.* 激情，热情

Passage 2
proxemics /prɒk'siːmɪks/ *n.* 空间关系学；人际距离学
filler /'fɪlə(r)/ *n.* 填装物，填塞物
articulate /ɑː'tɪkjʊleɪt/ *vt.* 清晰地发（音）；言语表达
be mindful of 注意，留心
coin /kɔɪn/ *v.* 杜撰；创造
territory /'terɪt(ə)rɪ/ *n.* 领域，范围
flashback /'flæʃbæk/ *n.* 倒叙；（往事的）突然重现
hover over 在……盘旋
proximity /prɒk'sɪmɪtɪ/ *n.* 邻近；接近度；距离
ample /'æmpl/ *a.* 足够的；充足的，丰富的
unobstructed /'ʌnəb'strʌktɪd/ *a.* 不被阻塞的，畅通无阻的
protocol /'prəʊtəkɒl/ *n.* 礼仪；社交礼节
on the flip side 另一方面
bistro /'biːstrəʊ/ *n.* 小酒馆，酒吧
horseshoe /'hɔːsʃuː/ *n.* 马蹄铁；马蹄形
toolkit /'tuːlkɪt/ *n.* 工具包，工具箱

Section C Case Studies

Case 1

Susie, an American living in China, brought her four-year-old son to a park one afternoon to let him play. As he was playing beside her, however, she looked around and noticed many people staring at her child. She started to become quite upset. Then, suddenly, one man took out his phone and started to take a photo of the boy. Susie confronted the man, "What are you doing? You have

Intercultural Communication in Movies
影视作品中的跨文化交际

no right to photograph my boy!" She angrily took her boy and moved to another part of the park.

After a few minutes, Susie started to calm down. However, just as she was comfortable again, an elderly Chinese woman walked up with a big smile and reached down and patted the boy's head. "He's so cute!" she said. She then proceeded to rub his cheeks with her hand.

As the woman was touching his face, however, Susie quickly reached down and picked the boy up. "How dare you touch my son!" she yelled at the woman angrily. Before the woman had a chance to respond, Susie stormed off with her boy and never returned to that park.

Reflection

1. Why does Susie get so upset at the people staring, the man taking the photo, and the woman touching her son?

   _____

2. How does this reflect American proxemics?

   _____

3. How should the Chinese people have acted when they saw her boy playing?

   _____

Case 2

Michael, an American international student, was good friends with his Chinese classmate, Zhang Peng. Final exams were almost over and Zhang Peng found out that Michael did not have any plans to celebrate Spring Festival. So, he decided to ask Michael if he wanted to travel home with him and spend the holiday with his family.

Zhang Peng: "Hey Michael, if you aren't doing anything for Spring Festival, I would love to have you visit my home for a couple weeks."

Michael: "That sounds great! Though, a couple weeks sounds like a long time. What kind of things do you have planned to do?"

Zhang Peng: "I don't know yet, but I will plan something. So, do you want to come?"

Michael felt quite uneasy since two weeks was a long time, but he trusted that Zhang Peng would plan many exciting activities to do. So, Michael agreed, and a few weeks later he went to Zhang Peng's home.

On the first day he arrived, Zhang Peng's family made Michael a delicious feast. Michael was very happy and excited for what else Zhang Peng had planned.

Michael: "So, Zhang Peng, what are we going to do tomorrow?"

Zhang Peng: "I don't know. What do you want to do?"

Michael: "I thought you said you would make some plans. I'm not familiar with your hometown."

Zhang Peng: "That's OK. Let's just wait until tomorrow, and we'll do whatever we feel like doing."

Unit 6 Time and Space across Culture

Every day for the next two weeks, Zhang Peng asked Michael what he felt like doing. Since Michael was not familiar with the town, he rarely had any ideas. Zhang Peng would sometimes think of some interesting places to go, but often times they would just stay at home and talk or watch movies.

Although Michael was happy his friend invited him to his home, he soon regretted going. He grew more and more upset and even began to feel like Zhang Peng did not respect him.

Reflection

1. Why do you think Michael is upset and feels disrespected?

2. How do Michael and Zhang Peng's actions reflect the Western and Eastern orientations toward monochronic and polychronic time?

3. What do you think Zhang Peng should have done?

Case 3 Watch the following clip from the movie *"Every Move You Make"* and try to analyze the cultural phenomenon in an intercultural context.

Reflection

1. How many distance zones in American culture are mentioned by the head policeman?

2. How does the head policeman come to the conclusion that Lin Weisheng knows about the woman who has been murdered?

III. Task-based Activities

Exercises

Choose the best choice according to the cultural context.

(   ) 1. You go to a convenience store in America to buy a pack of candy. After you pay for the candy, the cashier gives it to you. You should say:
   a. "Thank you!"
   b. You should not say anything. Americans do not thank cashiers for simply doing business.

(   ) 2. You are eating a meal with your American friend, and you think that the potatoes you are eating are really delicious. You want your friend to try some. You should:

a. Put a spoonful of your potatoes on his plate and encourage him to try them.

b. Ask him if he wants to try any.

(   ) 3. You are leading a business meeting between executives from your Chinese company and executives of a partner American company. You said the meeting would start at 9:00 a.m., but you suddenly find out that one of your colleagues will be ten minutes late. All of the Americans are present and it is 9:00 a.m. You should:

a. Start the meeting.

b. Tell them that you are going to wait until your colleague arrives at 9:10 a.m.

(   ) 4. You have studied in America for three years, and you just returned again after visiting your family in China. Your America friends are all eager to see you again. You should:

a. Visit your closest American friends first, since they are most important.

b. Visit your least closest friends first, since you know your best friends will most understand the pressure you are facing to see so many people.

(   ) 5. You are having a meal in an American restaurant with a group of business colleagues. You have no leadership position but are just an office worker. The table you are sitting at is square. You should:

a. Sit at the end of the table closest to the door.

b. It doesn't matter where you sit.

Group Work

Discussion 1

Divide students into several groups and discuss proper Chinese personal distance and public distance.

Discussion 2

Make student share their personal experiences about times their personal space has been violated by strangers. Alternatively, the teacher can have a volunteer come to the front and violate their personal space. The discussion can focus on the students' reactions and feelings.

Assignment

Presentation 1

Anthropologist Hall makes a useful distinction between monochronic time and polychronic time. Now think about the following question: Do you make plans for the future, such as studying, activities, or holidays? Use this information to determine which type of time orientation you belong to. Give a presentation to your classmates to explain your findings.

Presentation 2

You may choose to invade the comfort zones of three to five people. Get close enough to them

Unit 6 Time and Space across Culture

to make them wonder what is going on, but DO NOT touch them. You will see the importance of the personal space boundaries we draw and how much we depend on them. It could be eye contact on an elevator with strangers or sitting next to strangers in a classroom or cafeteria. Write down important details, like exactly where you were, what time each invasion started and ended, and verbal and nonverbal reactions (describe specifically and briefly what the person said, did, or both). Fill in the table and give a brief presentation to your classmates.

Items	(verbal and nonverbal) reaction
when	
where	
who	
what	
notes	

Time and tide waits no man.
时不我待。
Never put off what you can do today until tomorrow.
今日事今日毕。

Unit 7　Verbal and Nonverbal Communication

I. Definition of Verbal and Nonverbal Communication

1. Verbal Communication

2. Nonverbal Communication

Communication consists of two types: verbal and nonverbal communication. It is frequently asserted that approximately 35% of communication between individuals is transmitted by the words they use, while the other 65% is transmitted without words.

1. Verbal Communication

Verbal communication refers to the use of sound and language to relay a message and acts as the primary tool for expression between two or more people. It can be very beneficial to communication when carried out successfully, but it can also be harmful when used incorrectly. The words people use are important, but equally important is the way people express them, especially when communicating with people from different cultures.

1) What is the relationship between language and culture?

The Sapir-Whorf hypothesis made by Edward Sapir and Benjamin Lee Whorf (1929; 1940; 1956) brings attention to the relationship among language, thought and culture. The hypothesis theorizes that thoughts and behavior are determined (or are at least partially influenced) by language. Culture influences the structure and functions of a group's language, which in turn influences the individual's interpretation of reality. Both Sapir and Whorf agree that it is human culture that determines language, which in turn determines the way that people categorize their thoughts about the world and experiences in it. Therefore, language is a carrier of culture, and culture is a reflection of language.

2) Intercultural lexical meaning

Words have both denotations (literal meanings) and connotations (suggestive meanings). These are two principal methods of describing the meanings of words. Denotation refers to the literal meaning of a word, the "dictionary definition". Connotation, on the other hand, refers to the associations that are connected to a certain word or the emotional suggestions related to that word. The connotative meanings of a word exist together with the denotative meanings. Understanding both the denotation and connotation of words can help people convey their meanings more clearly.

In different cultures the denotations of words are similar, but their connotations are often different. Connotation in language involves the semantic or deep-structure of words, expressions and texts and is, therefore, strongly related to culture. For example, if the Chinese battery brand *White Elephant* (白象牌) were to be exported to the United States, what would happen? Nobody would buy it because the cultural connotation of the phrase *white elephant* in English means *a useless item*. Another example is the translation of some Chinese holidays, such as Spring Festival (春节). The word *spring* in English denotation refers to the season where the weather is warm and flowers bloom. Thus, Westerners are often confused when they hear that Spring Festival is celebrated in January or February, which are considered winter months. A third example has to do with dogs. The word *dog* has the same meaning in Chinese and Western denotations, but its connotation is completely different. A dog is often regarded as a *man's best friend* and loyal companion in Western culture. However, in Chinese culture, the word *dog* often has a bad connotation, such as 狗仗人势, 狼心狗肺 and 鸡鸣狗盗. Therefore, while the phrase *you are a lucky dog* has a good meaning in American culture, the Chinese translation of the phrase would be insulting to someone in China. A fourth example is colors, which each have different denotations and connotations in Eastern and Western cultures. In Chinese, the phrase 红白喜事 refers to weddings and funerals, but an American would not know what *red and white happy things* means. Another example of this is the word 眼红 or *red-eyed* in Chinese, which is actually translated as *green-eyed* or *jealous* in English. A fifth example of verbal communication is that situations, occasions and objects should be taken into account. Chinese people have to pay attention to avoid mentioning the word "那个" in Chinese in the specific context, especially in the presence of African-American in the U S. Because the pronunciation of this Chinese word is very similar with the pronunciation of English word "nigger", and this word has the meaning of racial discrimination. A final example of how connotations in different cultures affect communication is in regards to characters in history, classic literature and movies. The names of these people often have specific connotations within a culture that people from other cultures may not understand.

3) Verbal communication style

From the intercultural perspective of high and low contexts, verbal communication style can be categorized into 4 dimensions (Ting-Toomey, 1996, p100): direct vs. indirect style, person-oriented vs. status-oriented verbal style, self-enhancement and self-effacement verbal style, and beliefs expressed in talk vs. silence.

- Direct vs. indirect style

Direct-indirect style refers to the way a speaker expresses his intentions in terms of his needs, wants and desires. Members of individualistic, low-context cultures tend to use a direct style, which corresponds best to the value orientations (honesty, openness and individual worth) of such cultures. However, members of collectivistic, high-context cultures prefer to use an indirect verbal style, which emphasizes the need to save face and preserve harmony within the group – something low-context cultures do not particularly value.

• Person-oriented vs. status-oriented verbal style

Person-oriented verbal style is individual-centered and emphasizes the importance of respecting unique, personal identities throughout the interaction. It is marked by informality and symmetrical power relationships. Status-oriented verbal style, however, is role-centered and stresses the importance of honoring prescribed power-based membership identities. (Ting-Toomey, 1996, p106)

According to Gudykunst and Ting-Toomey, people of low-context cultures tend to see every individual as equal, which is also reflected in their language. North Americans prefer a first-name basis and direct address. Using titles, honorifics and so on is often avoided. Differences in age, status and sex are no reasons to use different language styles. Therefore, they use a person-oriented style of communication that reflects an egalitarian social order where both the speaker and the listener have the same rights and use the same language patterns. This can be found in all places, including workplaces, classrooms and meetings.

In contrast, members of high-context cultures use a status-oriented style in verbal communication. This style is heavily based on a hierarchical social order and stresses formality and asymmetrical power relationships.

• Self-enhancement and Self-effacement Verbal Style

The self-enhancement verbal style emphasizes the importance of boasting about one's accomplishments and abilities, whereas the self-effacement verbal style stresses the importance of humbling oneself via restraints, modest talk, and use of self-deprecation concerning one's efforts or performance (Ting-Toomey, 1996, p107).

• Beliefs Expressed in Talk vs. Silence

Ting-Toomey (1996, p110) believes that while people in low context cultures tend to express their ideas and beliefs openly and directly, those in high-context cultures often utilize silence, which is most common between asymmetrical power relationships such as teacher-student, male-female, and expert-client. In these cultures, being quiet is often a sign of respect for the wisdom and expertise of others. This silence can have both positive and negative effects. Although silence may hold strong, contextual meanings in high-context cultures, prolonged silence is often viewed as "empty pause" in low-context cultures. If both parties are not aware of these cultural differences, intercultural miscommunication may occur.

2. Nonverbal Communication

We use nonverbal communication as much as we use verbal communication. There are as many forms of nonverbal communication as there are cultures in the world. Certain forms of eye contact, facial expressions, or body language may be acceptable in one culture but offensive in another.

Non-verbal communication refers to communication effected by means other than words, assuming words are the verbal element (Knapp, 1978, p5). It is a silent infiltrator, having broad influence over our social environment. It provides us with a mode for conveying messages without the use of verbal language (Dunn 1999, p1). Nonverbal communication can be categorized into several different types. These mainly include body language (kinesics), paralanguage, environmental language and object language.

1) Body Language /Kinesics

Body language refers to all nonverbal codes that are associated with body movements. According to Ekman and Friesen (1969), kinesics refers to the study of gestures, facial expressions, postures and body movements.

Gestures are messages sent through the movement of the body and arms. There are five types of gesture:

• Emblems (象征性动作): Direct replacements for words (e.g., the peace sign).

• Illustrators (说明性动作): Acting out what is being said (e.g., a circular hand movement to describe a circle).

• Affection displays (情绪表露动作): Expressions of emotion (e.g., hugging to express love, smiling to express happiness, etc.).

• Regulators (调节性动作): Expressions for controlling the flow of conversation (e.g., raising your hand when you want to speak).

• Adaptors (适应性动作): Self-oriented tension relievers (e.g., chewing your fingernails or twirling your hair, indicating nervousness).

Eye contact is an especially important type of nonverbal communication. The way a person looks at someone can communicate many things, including interest, affection, hostility, or attraction. Eye contact is also important in maintaining the flow of conversation and for measuring the other person's response. In the United States, using direct eye contact is accepted and considered to be a sign of attentiveness, honesty, confidence, and respect for what the other is saying. However, in Asian cultures it is the opposite. Direct eye contact is considered to be rude, confrontational, and aggressive.

Facial expression is universal. The human face is extremely expressive, able to express countless emotions without saying a word. The facial expressions for happiness, sadness, anger, surprise, fear, and disgust are the same across cultures.

Posture has great significance in interpreting body language. Postulating (adopting a posture) is a universal approach for adjusting to, relating with and defending ourselves from various physical environments, social situations, objects and persons. Posture speaks loudly. Unlike facial expressions or voice, posture can be observed or sensed from long distances; therefore it is a very powerful form of communication.

Touch is a vital form of nonverbal communication – especially for conveying physical intimacy in interpersonal relationships. Touch is also the most misunderstood and carries the most potential problems if it is ill-used. For example, in China people can touch babies whom they don't know, while in America this is considered very offensive and even threatening to do without the parent's permission. Chinese people also show more affection to the same gender than do Westerners. For example, a male might put his arm over another male's shoulder, and two females might hold each other's hands. These gestures express friendship in China, but in Western cultures they may carry a sexual connotation.

2) Paralanguage

Paralanguage is vocal characteristics of speech. It refers to the nonverbal elements of speech such as vocal pitch, intonation, rate and silence, all of which can be used to communicate attitudes, convey emotion, or modify meaning. In simple terms, paralanguage can be thought of as how something is said rather than what is said. The study of paralanguage is known as "paralinguistics". Humans often use paralanguage purposefully, though they may use it subconsciously, as well.

In low context cultures, individuals who speak fast are generally viewed as competent and eager, while those who speak slowly can potentially convey dim-wittedness, caution, or lack of interest. People who consistently speak too loudly are perceived as aggressive or overbearing, while people who speak too softly are believed to be shy and timid.

3) Environmental language

Environmental language includes proxemics/space and chronemics/time. Proxemics is the study of how people use and perceive the physical space around them. The space between the sender and the receiver of a message influences the way the message is interpreted. Chronemics is the study of the use of time in nonverbal communication. The way people perceive time, structure time and react to time are all important characteristics of communication.

One example of the relationship of time to communication was already addressed by Hall's theory in Unit 6. People in polychronic cultures may answer the phone, drink coffee, transmit sign language to their colleagues, listen to presentations, and think about lunch all at the same time. They get bored and restless if only one thing is happening. Those in monochronic cultures, however, respect timetables and carefully plan activities.

4) Object language

Object language comprises all intentional and non-intentional displays of material things, such as machines, art objects, and architectural structures, as well as the human body and whatever clothes cover it. The design and structure of letters as they occur in books and on signs has a material substance, and as a result these are also considered forms of object language. (Jurgen R., 1969, p139)

Questions

1. What is environmental language?

2. What is paralanguage?

3. Explain the role and importance of nonverbal communication.

4. What is verbal communication? How does lexical meaning play an important role in intercultural communication?

Cultural Comprehension

Decide whether the following statements are true or false according to what you read.
(   ) 1. The voice not only reveals our thoughts and emotions, but also reflects to others our self-confidence and knowledge.
(   ) 2. Eye contact in American society is very similar to that of Chinese society.
(   ) 3. Illustrators refer to gestures that accompany and illustrate verbal messages and provide meaning.
(   ) 4. The denotation and connotation of a word is completely different between cultures.
(   ) 5. The way we touch depends on many variables, particularly on one's family experience and cultural background.

II. Content-based Activities

Section A   Movie Clips

 Introduction to the movie *My Fair Lady*

The musical *My Fair Lady* was adapted by Alan Jay Lerner and Frederick Loewe from the George Bernard Shaw's comedy *Pygmalion*. It tells the story of a language expert named Henry Higgins (Rex Harrison) succeeding in transforming a flower girl named Eliza Doolittle (Audrey Hepburn) into a fair lady by teaching her proper English. At first, Eliza is a disheveled cockney flower girl. But after six months of rigorous training, her English improves greatly. While attending a ball held by Greek ambassadors, Eliza is even mistaken for a member of a royal family – no one suspecting that she is a flower girl.

Introduction to movie clip 1

These three clips show the three different stages of Eliza's transformation. The first clip reveals the original state of the poor flower girl, who has broken English and vulgar manners. The second clip mainly focuses on the training process. The last clip shows the outcome of the training and presents Eliza as a graceful woman who can speak proper English.

Intercultural Communication in Movies
影视作品中的跨文化交际

 Introduction to the TV series *Lie to Me*

This TV series is based on the real-life experiences of psychologist Paul Ekman. In the series, Dr. Cal Lightman (Tim Roth) is an expert in how facial expressions and body languages betray emotions. He owns a private investigation company that provides assistance for governments, police departments, the FBI, law firms and big corporations if they have trouble with an investigation. Psychologist Dr. Gillian Foster is Lightman's professional partner, who is responsible for analyzing the motions of suspects. Eli Locker and Ria Torres are the other two members of their team.

Introduction to movie clip 2

In this clip, a high-school teacher named Mrs. McCartney is murdered, and one of her students, James, is caught running from her house. Lightman and Dr. Gillian Foster ask some questions about the incident. By observing the facial expressions and eye contact of James, as well as the tones and other kinds of paralanguage used by him, they think James may not have intentionally murdered his teacher, even though he does tell a few lies during the interrogation.

Exercises

Task 1: Fill in the blanks to the following lines spoken in the movie clips you just watched.
1. Shut up! Shut up! Do I look like a_____?
2. Remember, you are a human being with a soul... and the divine gift of_____speech.
3. Every time you_____the letter "H" correctly, the flame will waver.
4. Mrs. McCartney thought that you should be_____a year because she felt you were having some problems with your classmates.
5. But I thought most people avoid_____when they're lying.
6. It's possible he didn't_____kill his teacher.

Task 2: Watch the movie clips for a second time and decide whether the following statements are true or false.
(   ) 1. In the first scene, Eliza becomes very scared because she's afraid somebody will hurt her.
(   ) 2. Linguistic expert Higgins makes great efforts to train Eliza since her English is very poor.
(   ) 3. Eliza's language training proves to be fruitful and effective, enabling her to speak standard English eloquently.
(   ) 4. James denies the fact that he has been to his teacher's house before.
(   ) 5. Dr. Cal Lightman thinks that people try to avoid eye contact with others when they are lying.
(   ) 6. James shows a kind of sadness when being asked about his teacher's death.

Task 3: Discussion: Divide students into several groups to discuss the clips and the problems of intercultural communication.

Unit 7   Verbal and Nonverbal Communication

1. To what extent do you think language is related to communication?

2. What is the relationship between one's language and one's family background, social status or profession?

3. Do you think it is reliable to solve cases by analyzing suspects' facial expressions and eye movements? Why?

4. How can we interpret verbal and non-verbal communication so that we understand what others really feel and think?

Section B   Intercultural Communication Reading

 Pre-reading Task

1. Have you ever noticed the importance of paralanguage? How do you use it in your daily life?
2. How often do you employ silence in the classroom? What are the main reasons? What do you want to express?
3. Do you think humor is an important aspect of introducing yourself to others? Why or why not?

Passage 1
Nonverbal Aspects of Language (Paralinguistics) I

Introduction

What we communicate consists not only of the words we speak. Just as we can "read between the lines" in written text, there is also a lot of meaning between the words or sentences in speech. Tone, **pitch** and **intonation** convey emotions, politeness or sexuality, for example, pauses and stress aid understanding and indicate importance. But there are linguistic differences in all of these that can alter the messages sent and received. The social implications of these messages are also subject to cultural interpretation.

Stress, tone and pitch

Stress, tone or changes in pitch vary a great deal between languages. Some Asian languages, for example, have a fairly **flat profile** reflecting a respect for self-control. In contrast, Latin languages have a "lively" profile with many changes in pitch reflecting a more emotional culture. English lies somewhere in between. Someone speaking English using an Asian profile sounds disinterested, boring or remote while a Latin profile sounds exaggerated and over-emotional.

97

Stress not only conveys emotion but also meaning. There's more stress in German and in English Germans can sound forceful.

Pitch has linguistic and social meanings. In English it's used primarily to express emotion. In tonal languages such as Chinese, Thai and Vietnamese, it determines meaning with similar words or symbols differentiated by tone. In other languages it differentiates statements and questions, such as: "He is going to school today?" Concepts of masculinity and femininity also affect pitch. In a New Zealand TV advertisement only men with deep voices get a 4WD – a real man's car! Equally, some cultures favour a light, high pitch in women.

Pauses and **tempo** changes

Every language has patterns of pauses and tempo changes. Most English speakers pause **fractionally** every few words, and vary the tempo of their speech. Formal speeches demand even greater expression. A good speaker varies pace to maintain listeners' interests and pauses to add emphasis. In contrast, in some Asian languages people pause only at the ends of sentences and too many changes in tempo indicate a lack of control and over-emotional expression.

The pauses between dialogue partners are very important. In some languages, including English, you can begin speaking as soon as the other person finishes. In others such as Japanese it's polite to add a "thinking" pause in between. In Spanish and Italian, speakers can start speaking before the other person has finished, without sounding rude. So while a Japanese student politely waits to say something, a Spaniard has long jumped in with their reply.

Silence

Silence is golden, but only nine **carats** in some cultures and twenty-four in others. In most Western countries, silence is considered a failure of dialogue to be filled as quickly as possible, even with a **facile** reply. However, in many Eastern cultures silence has traditionally been highly valued as a sign of respect for the previous speaker, and a person who says little is considered respectful, deep-thinking or calm. In contrast, a person who says little in an English-speaking environment is considered shy, **taciturn** or uncommunicative.

In the classroom silence reflects several aspects of culture. In western classrooms, for example, "having a go" is encouraged, but in other cultures you shouldn't answer a question unless you really know the answer. Students are punished, or publicly **humiliated** for giving a wrong answer. In most **Anglo-Saxon** cultures, speaking up is actively encouraged. In contrast, in Sweden students are less likely to **initiate** communication even though there are no sanctions for making mistakes.

Turn-taking

In multicultural classes "turn-taking" is an issue. Some students politely wait their turn and don't get to say anything, while others dominate the conversation, jumping in at every opportunity or interrupting. Although this is an issue in any classroom, cultural differences **exacerbate** the problem. Differing speech patterns are an issue. In some cultures it is also assumed that everyone should have an opportunity to say something, while in others it's assumed that if someone has something to say, they'll say it. Status may also determine who speaks.

Unit 7   Verbal and Nonverbal Communication

Directness/indirectness

In some languages people say what they mean while in others they can only imply it. Even UK English is indirect relative to American and is loaded with phrases such as, "Would it be all right if…?" East Europeans are also relatively indirect and messages are communicated by what is NOT said as well as what is said. Direct communicators perceive indirect communicators as **evasive** or even dishonest. Indirect communicators experience the direct are rude and insensitive.

Differences in communication styles can cause **friction** in the classroom. Those who speak as briefly as possible are frustrated by classmates who never seem to get to the point. Students who openly state their opinions offend classmates from cultures in which courtesy demands more tact. Indirect styles of communication are difficult for EFL students to understand. "Would you mind closing the door?" for example, is more difficult to understand than "Please close the door."

English communication patterns are linear. In formal situations, we usually start with the most important points and add details. In other languages the details come first with the punch line at the end or speakers circle in on or hint at the main point, perhaps never mentioning it. Others express themselves in a "stream of consciousness" manner, saying whatever comes into their minds. The potential for missing the most important points when someone from another culture is speaking is obvious.

Yes and no

Yes and No don't always mean yes and no. In many Asian countries, for example, "No" is considered rude and people will avoid using it, or "Yes" means "I heard you" rather than "I agree." This can lead to a lot of confusion if Yes/No cultures interpret a "Yes" to mean agreement. Agreeing with a suggestion, for example, may be the best way to save face for both sides. Of course, it is then unlikely that any action will follow.

In English you say "Yes" to agree with a positive statement. "You like him, don't you?" "Yes, I do." And you say "No" to agree with a negative statement. "You don't like him, do you?" "No, I don't." In many languages you use "Yes" in all cases of agreement.

(1034 words)

(This article has been edited to fit the format of this book. The original article can be viewed at: http://www.culturesintheclassroom.com/5_paralinguistics.shtml)

Passage 2
Nonverbal Aspects of Language (Paralinguistics) II

Understatement/overstatement

People from some cultures tend to exaggerate or overstate, while others understate. This is true even within English speaking cultures. The English usually understate, for example: "My son isn't bad at football." Americans, however, are more likely to overstate, such as: "My son is a great football player." Neither of these statements is dishonest or meant to deceive. Within their respective cultures, the message is clear. Other cultures have similar patterns. The Japanese tend towards understatement while the Spanish are comfortable with **extravagant** statements.

Conversation

In English conversations good listeners respond verbally from time to time. They say "Yes", "Sure", "Really?" or use tag questions like "Does he?" and "Is it?" to show they're listening. However, in other cultures saying anything may register as an interruption, so attention is indicated in other ways. The Japanese tend to show they're listening by nodding from time to time, for example, and they may even close their eyes to show they're listening carefully.

Interruptions

Interruptions are part of conversation. They're an irritating part of dialogue, but the level of rudeness they're considered to display varies from culture to culture. What constitutes an interruption also depends on the language group. In **hierarchical** societies, it depends on the status of the conversation partners. The reasons for interrupting also vary.

Students from other cultures have **internalized** different sets of "interruption rules." In some countries students interrupt teachers with questions or to challenge something that's been said, but in others it's very rude to interrupt – even if the class has gone overtime, the teacher's made a mistake, or students haven't understood. Teachers in some countries interrupt students to end activities while in others students expect time to fit the activities rather than vice-versa. Other rules govern student-student behavior. Can students interrupt each other in a discussion, for example, or **contradict** or challenge each other in class?

Giving opinions

When asking for opinions, teachers expect ideas and reasons. However, Japanese students may simply state whether they agree or not. If asked for a reason they will often give a brief answer, such as: "Because he's friendly." Russian students, in contrast, can spend time explaining their thoughts on a subject without saying whether they agree or disagree.

In many educational systems students aren't encouraged to form opinions. They therefore find it difficult to develop and express opinions, especially on educational topics. However, most hold opinions on personal topics such as likes and dislikes, and this is a good place to learn to express opinions. These students should have a good grasp of material and **terminology** before being expected to discuss it.

For many students holding an opinion doesn't include considering other points of view. This is true of some students in all cultures, but particularly among those who have never been expected to **weigh pros and cons**. In addition, they may not be used to justifying their opinion.

Making mistakes

Every aspect of error correction is cultural. Different beliefs about the nature of knowledge and diverse educational philosophies mean that schools and teachers in different cultures and countries have different ideas as to what constitutes a mistake and how to deal with these errors. This affects the way students learn and the difficulties they face when changing countries and educational systems.

What's considered a mistake depends on beliefs about knowledge. If knowledge is thought to be absolute and unchanging there can only be one right answer to any question. In this case answers that don't accurately replicate this knowledge are wrong. However, if knowledge is thought to be constantly changing and is considered only a matter of perspective, there may be a variety of answers. The correctness of an answer then depends on the reasoning or the process of finding the answer.

Our beliefs about knowledge affect teachers' behaviour in the classroom. When teachers are the keepers of knowledge rather than **facilitators** in students' learning, their responsibility for producing the correct answer is high. So, too, is their desire to defend this knowledge. However, if students are expected to discover information themselves, teachers' responsibility for producing the correct answer is lessened, and they're open to alternative answers. This is confusing for students from "keeper of knowledge" cultures. They may mistrust a teacher who doesn't produce an absolute answer or who is prepared to discuss an answer.

Forms of address

Certain aspects of culture affect forms of address, such as formality, power distance, hierarchies, and relationships. English, unlike most languages, doesn't distinguish between familiar and formal forms of "you" and distinguishes male and female only in the singular – "he" and "she." They don't distinguish cousins by sex, nor do they distinguish aunts and uncles by their mother's and father's families. All of these features exist in other languages.

English is fairly informal, especially American English. People frequently use first names even with relative strangers or business colleagues, which would be unthinkable in some cultures. This may sound too impersonal to many people, but it is respectful in many languages. Although most Westerners address strangers and colleagues by their first names, it is still most common for teachers to be addressed by their last names (i.e. Mrs. Smith).

Humour

Humour in the classroom lightens things up, but it takes care and practice to get it right. Most people like things that make them laugh, but nothing is more cultural than humour. A **hilarious** joke in one culture is insulting, **puerile** or **inane** in another. While some cultures find jokes about body parts and functions funny, others find them disgusting. Comedy and tragedy are **juxtaposed** in some cultures; therefore, a disastrous event may have people in fits in one country but in tears in another.

Word-play based humor relies on linguistic skills. While situational humor translates well, word plays often use a high level of language. These include using words with more than one meaning, playing with **homophone**s or complex constructions. Additionally, some word play is based on social or political events that may be **incomprehensible** to newcomers.

Many jokes are about other cultures or nationalities. The English make jokes about the Scots and Irish. Austrians bear the **brunt** of Swiss jokes. In cross-cultural situations such humour has no place, as it's often perceived as deliberately offensive. Cultures also differ in their willingness and

Intercultural Communication in Movies
影视作品中的跨文化交际

ability to laugh at themselves. Taboo subjects also vary. In Western cultures very little is **sacrosanct**, while religion may be off limits in other cultures.

(1073 words)

(This article has been edited to fit the format of this book. The original article can be viewed at: http://www.culturesintheclassroom.com/5_paralinguistics.shtml)

  After-reading Task

1. According to passage 1, why can't you say "No" easily in many Asian countries compared with Western countries?

_____

2. According to passage 1, how does silence reflect culture?

_____

3. According to passage 2, how should you address your teachers in America? How should you address your teachers in China?

_____

4. According to passage 2, how do Chinese and Japanese people evaluate their achievements? Why?

_____

 WORDS LIST

Passage 1

pitch /pɪtʃ/ *n.* 音高；音调
intonation /ˌɪntə'neɪʃn/ *n.* 语调，声调
flat profile   平铺直叙的语调
tempo /'tempəʊ/ *n.* [乐]速度，拍子
fractionally /'frækʃənəlɪ/ *ad.* 部分地，略微地
carat /'kærət/ *n.*（宝石、金子的重量单位）克拉；开
facile /'fæsaɪl/ *a.* 轻率做出的；肤浅的
taciturn /'tæsɪtɜːn/ *n.* 沉默寡言的
humiliate /hjuː'mɪlɪeɪt/ *v.* 使蒙羞，使丢脸
Anglo-Saxon /'æŋɡləʊ'sæksən/ *a.* 盎格鲁−撒克逊人（语）的
initiate /ɪ'nɪʃɪeɪt/ *n.* 开始，发起
turn-taking   话轮转换
exacerbate /ɪɡ'zæsəbeɪt/ *v.* 使恶化；使加重
evasive /ɪ'veɪsɪv/ *a.* 回避的；避而不谈的
friction /'frɪkʃn/ *n.* 摩擦；冲突

Passage 2

extravagant /ɪk'strævəgənt/ *a.* 奢侈的；铺张的
hierarchical /ˌhaɪə'rɑːkɪkl/ *a.* 等级制度的
internalize /ɪn'tɜːnəlaɪz/ *v.* 使内在化；吸收
contradict /ˌkɒntrə'dɪkt/ *v.* 反驳；否认；与……矛盾
terminology /ˌtɜːmɪ'nɒlədʒɪ/ *n.* 术语；用词
weigh pros and cons   权衡利弊
facilitator /fə'sɪlɪteɪtə(r)/ *n.* 促进者，帮助者
hilarious /hɪ'leərɪəs/ *a.* 非常滑稽的；令人捧腹的
puerile /'pjʊəraɪl/ *a.* 幼稚的；孩子气的；愚蠢的
inane /ɪ'neɪn/ *a.* 无意义的；无比愚蠢的
juxtapose /ˌdʒʌkstə'pəʊz/ *v.* 把……并列，把……并置
homophone /'hɒməfəʊn/ *n.* 同音异义词
incomprehensible /ɪnˌkɒmprɪ'hensəbl/ *a.* 难理解的
brunt /brʌnt/ *n.* 承受主要压力；首当其冲
sacrosanct /'sækrəʊsæŋkt/ *a.* 极神圣的；不可侵犯的

Section C   Case Studies

Case 1

Wang Gang, a Chinese Ph.D. foreign exchange student, was always interested in the military affairs. One day, a military base near his school in America held an "open house" where anyone could come and tour the military base for free. Wang Gang was ecstatic and eagerly asked his American friend John if John could take Wang Gang and his wife and child to the open house. John agreed and drove them there later that afternoon.

When they arrived, a lieutenant named Mark greeted them and acted as their tour guide. Lieutenant Mark first took them to see a tank. The lieutenant stood by the tank and talked about the history of tanks, as well as the specific details about the tank next to him. As Lieutenant Mark talked, neither Wang Gang nor his family looked at him. Sometimes they looked at the tank, and other times they just looked at the ground. Only John maintained eye contact with the lieutenant as he spoke. The lieutenant grew increasingly anxious and upset. After he was done talking, he walked next to John and whispered somewhat angrily, "I never knew Chinese people disliked soldiers so much." John didn't know how to respond.

Just then, Wang Gang's wife pulled out her camera and began taking pictures of her husband and son standing by the tank. As they were posing for the camera, Wang Gang and his son both held up their hands, raising two fingers with each hand. As soon as Lieutenant Mark saw them posing like that by the tank, he sternly told Wang Gang and his family to leave the military base. Wang Gang and his family were very surprised and left disappointed. "Why was he so angry?" they thought.

As they were walking back to the car, John felt very bad for Wang Gang because he knew Wang

Intercultural Communication in Movies
影视作品中的跨文化交际

Gang wanted to look at more of the military base. So, John ran back inside to buy Wang Gang a little gift. He bought a green hat that soldiers wear in the army. When he returned to his car, he gave Wang Gang the green hat to try to cheer him up. "Put it on!" he said excitedly. Wang Gang and his wife, however, looked at John both angered and embarrassed. He refused to put on the hat and remained silent all the way back home. John couldn't understand why Wang Gang and his wife were so upset.

Reflection

1. How did misunderstandings about eye contact lead to cultural conflict between the lieutenant and Wang Gang? What was Wang Gang trying to communicate? How did Lieutenant Mark interpret it?

2. How did misunderstandings about gestures lead to cultural conflict between the lieutenant and Wang Gang? What was Wang Gang trying to communicate by his gestures? How did Lieutenant Mark interpret it?

3. How did misunderstandings about object language lead to cultural conflict between Wang Gang, his wife and John? What was John trying to communicate? How did Wang Gang and his wife interpret it?

Case 2

William, an American, and his Chinese friend Zhang Tao went to a Chinese restaurant one day to have dinner together. When they arrived, Zhang Tao opened the front door for William and directed him to enter the building. As he did so, William replied, "Thank you!" Zhang Tao, however, was surprised and a little disappointed when he heard William. Nevertheless, he remained silent and sat down at a table with William.

After they sat down, Zhang Tao yelled, "Waiter!" A young woman came to their table and gave them a menu. William, however, did not look at the menu. Instead, he was glaring at Zhang Tao with a look of disapproval. Zhang Tao, however, could not understand why William was upset. Still, they remained silent and ordered their food.

After the food came, they began eating and talking. After a while, Zhang Tao used his chopsticks to take some of the beef and peppers off of his plate and put them on William's plate. "You have to try this. It's so good!" William, however, was noticeably uncomfortable and irritated. He did not touch the beef and peppers but instead continued eating his own food.

When they were finished eating, William still had some rice left in his bowl. He placed both of his chopsticks vertically in the rice and got up to leave. Zhang Tao, however, reached over and removed the chopsticks from the rice and laid them beside the bowl. William, once again, was noticeably irritated when he saw Zhang Tao's actions. He quickly paid for their meal and both of them left the restaurant silent and upset.

Unit 7   Verbal and Nonverbal Communication

Reflection

1. What kind of misunderstandings occurred between William and Zhang Tao in their verbal communication? What meanings are given to the phrases "Thank you!" and "Waiter!" in their respective cultures?

_____

2. How do Eastern and Western understandings of proxemics (space) account for William's being irritated by Zhang Tao when he places food on his plate and removes the chopsticks from his rice?

_____

3. How does object language account for Zhang Tao's removing William's chopsticks from his rice? What was William communicating to others in the Chinese restaurant by placing his chopsticks in his rice?

_____

Case 3   Watch the following clip from the movie *"Rush Hour 3"* and try to analyze the cultural phenomenon in intercultural context.

Reflection

1. Why is Carter so confused about the master's words, especially "You" and "Me"?

_____

2. What does this clip show us about the nature of verbal language and the importance of understanding culture?

_____

III. Task-based Activities

Exercises

Choose the best choice according to the cultural context.

(   ) 1. A Chinese brand of dumplings called 狗不理 wants to sell dumplings in the US. What is the better translation of their product in an American context?

　　　a. Dogs Ignore Dumplings

　　　b. Gobble Down Dumplings

(   ) 2. You are a man and your American friend sees you talking with a girl in your class. After she leaves, your American friend asks you, "Who is your friend?" But when he says the word "friend", he raises two fingers in each hand and bends them up and down quickly two or three times. What is he communicating with this gesture?

105

Intercultural Communication in Movies
影视作品中的跨文化交际

  a. He is assuming that this girl is not an ordinary friend but a friend whom you want to date.

  b. He is communicating that he thinks the girl is very pretty.

(   ) 3. You are sitting next to your American friend listening to a CEO's lecture at your school. As the man is talking, your American friend looks at you, points with one finger at the CEO, and points his other finger at his own ear while making a circular motion with it. What is he communicating with this gesture?

  a. He thinks the CEO is saying nonsense.

  b. He cannot hear the CEO very clearly.

(   ) 4. An American asks you how you usually discipline your child when they misbehave. You should say:

  a. "I beat him."

  b. "I spank him."

(   ) 5. As you are walking through a grocery store in the U.S., a stranger walks pass you and smiles at you. What is he communicating by this facial expression?

  a. He thinks something is funny or different about you.

  b. He thinks he has seen you before and wants to talk.

  c. He is just being friendly and does not want to talk.

Group Work

Discussion 1

Imagine that you have a new foreign English teacher, but she knows little about Chinese culture. One day after she finishes her class, she is very upset because nobody answered her questions during class. But you know all students prepared well for her class. What could you do to help her understand the cultural differences? What does silence mean in Chinese culture? Additionally, discuss whether or not non-Western students should adopt the western style of communication in the classroom if their teacher is a westerner. Why or why not?

Discussion 2

Do colors have any cultural meaning? Some colors seem to convey the feelings and beliefs of a culture. For example, red, white and blue seem to effectively convey the positive and patriotic feelings of the American culture. Also, white in China represents death or a funeral, but it represents the complete opposite in America. Divide students into several groups to think of any other colors that have cultural meaning.

Assignment

Presentation 1

Go to your dormitory room or your room where you are currently living. List the personal artifacts that you have put there. Do not list any that were given to you that you didn't choose. Beside each item on the list, explain its significance to you and what it communicates about your

Unit 7   Verbal and Nonverbal Communication

identity (This exercise is taken from North & Wood, 2006).

Example: Artifact – Photograph of me and my sister in England. *This picture makes me think of my family and how I love traveling.*

A. _____

B. _____

C. _____

D. _____

Presentation 2

Your body posture, movements, facial expressions and gestures all contribute to your non-verbal communication. What aspects of American nonverbal communication surprise you? Why? Select two gestures and explain how those gestures differ in China. Then, fill in the table with appropriate words by means of the brief description. Finally, record a video demonstrating body language and present it to the class.

Form of Body Language	Meaning (some cultures)
open hands, palms up, hands on waist	
shrug	
glancing at exit, rigid, unmoving posture with fixed stare, yawning	
nail biting, finger movement, sighing, hand wringing rapidly, twitchy movements, clearing throat	
hand raised	
head shake	
eye movements	
folded arms, moving away from another, rubbing nose, lack of eye contact, scratching head	
raised fist, change in skin color, hostile stare	
hand-shake	
taking a different posture than others in a group, especially with hands behind head; standing or walking with hands behind back and chin up	

> *Silence is sometimes the severest criticism.*
> 缄默有时就是最严厉的批评。
> *A word spoken is an arrow let fly.*
> 一言既出，驷马难追。

Unit 8　Culture Shock and Adaptation

I. Definition of Culture Shock and Adaptation

1. What Is Culture Shock?
2. Intercultural U-Curve and W-Curve Adjustment Model
3. Intercultural Competence

Nowadays it is all too common for people from different cultures to interact with each other. However, when people move to a new culture, they tend to be unaware of cultural norms. They project their own culture onto the new culture and act as if they are still living in their own culture. They do not consider how the beliefs that influence their own culture might be different from those that influence another culture. And the bigger the differences between cultures are, the more apparent one's own cultural distinctives become. As a result, cultural conflicts caused by differences in rules, meanings, and values are inevitable.

1. What Is Culture Shock?

Culture shock was studied by Canadian anthropologist Kalervo Oberg in 1954. He lays out the basics of culture shock and says it is caused by "the anxiety that results from losing all our familiar signs and symbols of social intercourse" (1954, p1). Oberg calls culture shock "an occupational disease of people who have been suddenly transplanted abroad" (1960, p185). Other researchers later developed Oberg's ideas about culture shock. One of them, P. S. Adler, defined culture shock as "a set of emotional reactions to the loss of perceptual reinforcements from one's own culture, to new cultural stimuli which have little or no meaning, and to the misunderstanding of new and diverse experiences" (1975, p13).

2. Intercultural U-Curve and W-Curve Adjustment Model

We know that culture shock is the feeling of disorientation or confusion that occurs when a person leaves a familiar place and moves to an unfamiliar one. The Oberg-based U- and W-curve models were developed to display the different stages of culture shock and adaptation.

S. Lysgaard (1955) first observed that the sequence of adjustment over time could be generalized to a curvilinear trend, that is a U-curve. The U-Curve model utilizes the form of the letter "U" to describe the emotional ups and downs that occur during intercultural exploration. It suggests that a sojourner begins his/her intercultural experience with high spirits, but later drops to a more negative state after the initial "honeymoon" period ends, eventually regaining a positive perspective as he or she becomes more comfortable in the host culture. Cultural shock can be diagrammed as a U-curve with three main stages often described as the honeymoon stage, the crisis stage, and the adaptation stage (see Figure 8.1 below). These stages often blend and overlap and vary in length for different people:

(1) Honeymoon stage: initial adjustment, optimistic or elation phase.

(2) Crisis stage: stressful phase, overwhelmed by one's own incompetence.

(3) Adaptation stage: regained adjustment, settling-in phase, effective coping.

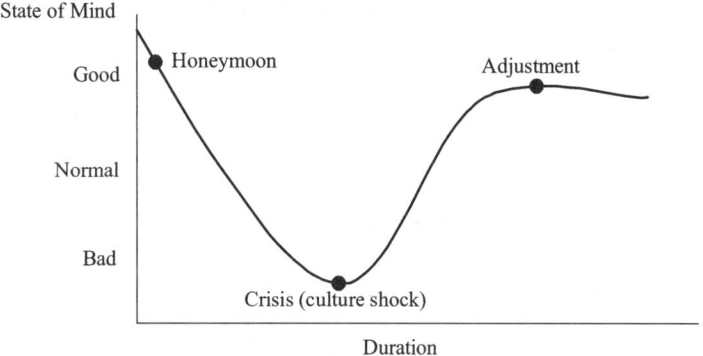

Figure 8.1 The U-Curve Adjustment Model

The W-Curve (see Figure 8.2 below), created by Gullahorn & Gullahorn (1963, 1966), simply adds another "U" to the U-Curve model. This second U depicts the sojourner's experience upon his/her return home. It suggests that, once home, he or she again experiences a negative emotional drop during the re-entry process, but regains a positive outlook as time passes. The U- and W-Curves are a helpful way to show general emotional ups and downs that occur while experiencing a new culture; however, they are not applicable to everyone's experience. The seven phases of the W-curve can be seen below:

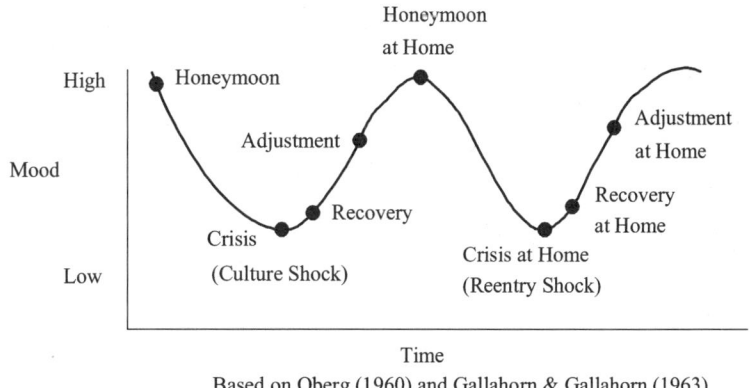

Based on Oberg (1960) and Gallahorn & Gallahorn (1963)

Figure 8.2 The Revised W-Shaped Adjustment Model

(1) Honeymoon: excited, curious about new environment.

(2) Hostility: major emotional upheavals (loss of self-esteem, self-confidence); 3 types of "culture shockers".

(3) Humorous: learn to laugh at their cultural embarrassment.

(4) In-sync (同步) adjustment: "at home" experience, identity security.

(5) Ambivalence (矛盾情绪): grief, nostalgia, pride, relief at going home.

(6) Reentry culture shock: not anticipating reentry shock (usually feel more depressed and stressed than during entry shock).

(7) Resocialization: adjustment at home.

Intercultural adaptation is gradual and requires time and patience. People eventually start to develop a social network and feel less isolated. They find a balance between the values of their home countries and those of the host country as they become more familiar with societal practices and customs.

3. Intercultural Communication Competence

Ting-Toomey says, "Communication skills refers to our operational abilities to interact appropriately, effectively, and satisfactorily in a given situation." (2007, p269) The acquisition of intercultural competence allows one to avoid a number of conflicts and increases the effectiveness of intercultural cooperation. So what is intercultural competence? It refers to "the ability to communicate effectively in cross-cultural situations and to relate appropriately in a variety of cultural contexts" (Bennett and Bennett, 2004, p149). Ting-Toomey defines it as "a wealth of interaction skills that permit individuals to cross cultural boundaries flexibly and adaptively" (2007, p271). Cultural competence is marked by a number of attributes that aid in intercultural communication, as seen in Table 8.1 according to Ting-Toomey.

Table 8.1 Transcultural Competence: Attributes and Abilities

Attributes	Abilities
Tolerance for Ambiguity	To meet new situations with mindfulness
Open-mindedness	To respond in non-evaluative ways
Flexibility	To shift frame of reference
Respectfulness	To show respect & positive regard for others
Adaptability	To adapt appropriately to particular situations
Sensitivity	To convey empathy verbally & nonverbally
Creativity	To engage in divergent thinking

In short, any national culture is not necessarily homogeneous. It is not uniform throughout, and culture may not be the same everywhere in the country. Moreover, an individual's personal traits are not all determined by their culture. The dimensions of cultural values describe general tendencies rather than absolute and eternal truths. So it's best to obtain some basic information about intercultural communication. With the help of intercultural learning one can acquire knowledge, attitudes or behavior that is connected with the interaction of different cultures. It can also denote a concept of how people with different cultural backgrounds can live together peacefully.

In this book we have discussed different value orientations, many intercultural theories, and a variety of cases from real life and movies that illustrate these concepts. We have seen how the many varied cultures around the world require us to develop effective intercultural communication skills and competence in order to minimize misunderstanding and maximize understanding and cooperation. Only with an appropriate framework can we effectively work with one another across cultures and maintain healthy relationships that foster mutual growth and understanding, as well as permit individuals to cross cultural boundaries flexibly and adaptively.

Questions

1. What is culture shock? How many stages are there according to Lysgaard?

2. What is the U-curve?

3. What is the W-curve?

4. Why is developing intercultural competence important?

Cultural Comprehension

Decide whether the following statements are true or false according to what you read.

( ) 1. Culture shock is a term used to describe the anxiety and feelings of surprise, disorientation and confusion felt by an individual coming into contact with an entirely different environment, such as a different country.

( ) 2. The bigger the differences between cultures are, the less apparent one's own cultural distinctives become.

( ) 3. Kalervo Oberg was the first anthropologist to use the expression "culture shock" to describe the stress and disorientation experienced by individuals adjusting to a new culture.

( ) 4. The W-Curve mainly depicts the sojourner's experience upon his/her return home.

( ) 5. The U-Curve model utilizes the form of the letter "U" to describe the emotional ups and downs that occur during intercultural sojourns.

Intercultural Communication in Movies

II. Content-based Activities

Section A   Movie Clips

 Introduction to the movie *Gung Ho*

Starring Michael Keaton, *Gung Ho* tells the story of an American who hopes to save a failing Pennsylvania automobile-assembly factory from having to close its doors. Keaton tries hard to persuade a Japanese auto company to reopen the factory, retrain its staff, and streamline its operation. However, because of culture differences the American-born workers become resentful of the disciplinary demands of their new Japanese bosses very soon. Thanks to the strange sense of humor of the poker-faced owner of the company, all ends well, though.

Introduction to movie clip 1

In this clip, Stevenson and his wife Audrey are having dinner with his Japanese colleagues and their wives. When they begin to talk about the business in the factory all the Japanese wives choose to leave. Audrey, however, stays – which leads to conflict between Stevenson and her.

 Introduction to the movie *English Vinglish*

In India, there are three important standards for judging a person: money, fame and one's knowledge of English. This movie is about the transformation of Shashi, an Indian housewife. Since she knows no English, she feels very insecure. However, a trip to New York later provides her with an opportunity to learn the language. Eventually, she learns the language and becomes more confident and self-assured.

Introduction to movie clip 2

This clip is about the different stages of Shashi's transformation. When she goes to a café in New York, she can't understand the waitress, which causes her great distress. Later, she is determined to learn English and attends a class, where she makes many friends. In the end, she makes an excellent speech at a wedding, earning her much respect.

Exercises

Task 1: Fill in the blanks to the following lines spoken in the movie clips you just watched.

1. Actually, I'm kind of_____what's going on at the plant.
2. See, you're stateside now. But you're still_____a bunch of Yokohama mamas. No offence.
3. I'm_____a delicate situation.
4. Lady, do you see? You are_____my line. This is not rocket science.
5. We have an entrepreneur in the class! Entrepreneur: It's a person who runs his or her_____.
6. That is the time you have to_____. Nobody can help you better than you.

Unit 8　Culture Shock and Adaptation

Task 2: Watch the movie clips for a second time and decide whether the following statements are true or false.

( ) 1. The Japanese men don't mind Audrey's staying while they discuss business.
( ) 2. In Japan, workers work overtime for the company for no pay.
( ) 3. Audrey becomes very angry because Stevenson makes her lose face before his business partners, who think women are inferior to men.
( ) 4. At the café, Shashi is embarrassed because she cannot order food.
( ) 5. In the English training class, the teacher and the classmates look down on Shashi because she can only make snacks at home.
( ) 6. Shashi is too nervous to make a speech at the wedding.

Task 3: Discussion: Divide students into several groups to discuss the clips and the problems of intercultural communication.

1. How does Audrey experience culture shock in clip 1?

_____

2. What are the differences between gender roles in Japan and the U.S.A.?

_____

3. How does Shashi succeed in adapting herself to a world where English plays a very important role?

_____

4. List several things that people need to overcome when learning a language.

_____

Section B　Intercultural Communication Reading

 Pre-reading Task

1. Do you agree with the following statement: culture shock is the biggest difficulty when studying abroad? Why or why not?
2. How can people overcome intercultural conflicts and misunderstandings with the development of globalization?
3. What is the purpose of studying intercultural communication?

Passage 1

Cultural Adjustment

Berkeley is one of the more culturally diverse cities in the U S. Here you will find students and visitors alike from different origins, **ethnicities**, and cultures. Despite this **cosmopolitan** orientation, if you are new in town, you may still feel like a stranger in a strange land, whether you come from a different country or a different American city.

113

Cultural Adaptation

Adapting to a new environment takes time and the pace of **transition** varies from person to person. The typical pattern of cultural adjustment often consists of distinct phases: Honeymoon, Crisis, Recovery, and Adjustment. Notice that this cycle is then repeated upon re-entry to one's home country or culture of origin.

The Honeymoon Phase

This phase is best described by feelings of excitement, optimism and wonder often experienced when you enter into a new environment or culture. While differences are observed, students are more likely to focus on the positive aspects of the new environment.

The Crisis Phase

This is what is often termed as "culture shock." Culture shock has been defined in different ways by many social scientists. In general, it is a term used to describe the anxiety and feelings (of surprise, disorientation, confusion, etc.) felt when people have to operate within an entirely different cultural or social environment. It grows out of the difficulties in **assimilating** to the new culture, causing difficulty in knowing what is appropriate and what is not. Often this is combined with strong disgust (moral or **aesthetical**) about certain aspects of the new or different culture. Culture shock does not necessarily occur suddenly, but may gradually begin to affect a person's moods over time. The length of time a person experiences culture shock depends on how long they stay in the new environment, as well as their level of self-awareness.

The Recovery & Adjustment Phases

Recovering from culture shock is handled differently by everyone – we each have our unique circumstances, background, strengths and weaknesses that need to be taken into consideration. With time and patience, we can experience positive effects of cultural adjustment, like increasing self-confidence, improved self-motivation and cultural sensitivity. As you gradually begin to feel more comfortable in and adjusting to the new environment, you will feel more like expanding your social networks and exploring new ideas. You will feel increasingly flexible and objective about your experience, learning to accept and perhaps practice parts of the new culture, while holding onto your own cultural traditions.

Symptoms of Culture Shock

Culture shock manifests itself in different forms with different people but some symptoms may include the following: changes in eating habits and sleeping habits; acute homesickness; calling home much more often than usual; being hostile/complaining all the time about the host country; culture **irritability**; sadness; depression; frequent frustration; being easily angered; self doubts; sense of failure; recurrent illness; or withdrawing from friends or other people and/or activities.

Suggestions for easing the transition:

Realize that what you are going through is normal. Remember that the unpleasant feelings are temporary, natural and common to any transition that a person makes during their life. Be patient and give yourself time to work through the process. Keep in touch with your home country. Read newspapers from home, international magazines, etc. Watch international television channels or surf the internet. Call home regularly. Have familiar things around you that have personal meaning, such as photographs or **ornaments**. Find a supplier of familiar foods or visit restaurants that are similar to your home **cuisine**. Take care of yourself. Eat well, exercise, and get enough sleep. Talk to someone. Find friends who are going through a similar process, call your family back home, or see a **counselor**. In the US it is very common to talk with a counselor about problems or difficulties. Take advantage of the resources available to you at the university. Have fun and relax! Join student groups. Get out of your room and volunteer to help others. Take up a new sport. Participate in activities, clubs and student organizations of interest to you. Improve your English skills. Cultural adaptation is greatly enhanced by perfecting your English skills. Not being able to clearly communicate can create isolation and loneliness. Make a point to join activities that give you the opportunity to share in conversation and express your identity.

(713 words)

(This article has been edited to fit the format of this book. For the original article, please visit: http://internationaloffice.berkeley.edu/cultural_adjustment)

Passage 2
Cultivating Intercultural Communication Competence
Howard Schwartz

How can Intercultural Communication Competence (ICC) be built and achieved? Two main ways to build ICC are through experiential learning and reflective practices. We must first realize that competence isn't any one thing. Part of being competent means that you can assess new situations and adapt your existing knowledge to the new contexts. What it means to be competent will vary depending on your physical location, your role (personal, professional, etc.), and your life stage, among other things. Sometimes we will know or be able to figure out what is expected of us in a given situation, but sometimes we may need to act in unexpected ways to meet the needs of a situation. Competence enables us to better cope with the unexpected, adapt to new routines, and connect to uncommon frameworks. I have always told my students that ICC is less about a list of rules and more about a box of tools.

Three ways to cultivate ICC are to **foster** attitudes that motivate us, discover knowledge that informs us, and develop skills that enable us. Janet M. Bennett (2009) in her book "Cultivating Intercultural Competence" says that to foster attitudes that motivate us, we must develop a sense of wonder about culture. This sense of wonder can lead to feeling overwhelmed, **humbled**, or awed. Paul Martin Opdal (2001) points out that this sense of wonder may correlate to a high tolerance for uncertainty, which can help us turn potentially frustrating experiences we have into teachable moments.

I've had many such moments in my intercultural encounters at home and abroad. One such moment came the first time I tried to cook a frozen pizza in the oven in the shared kitchen of my apartment in Sweden. The information on the packaging was written in Swedish, but like many college students, I had a wealth of experience cooking frozen pizzas to draw from. As I went to set the oven dial to preheat, I noticed it was strange that the oven didn't go up to my usual 425-450 degrees. Not to be **deterred**, I **cranked** the dial up as far as it would go, waited a few minutes, put my pizza in, and walked down the hall to my room to wait for about fifteen minutes until the pizza was done. The smell of smoke drew me from my room before the fifteen minutes was up, and I walked into a corridor filled with smoke and the smell of burnt pizza. I pulled the pizza out and was puzzled for a few minutes while I tried to figure out why the pizza burned so quickly, when one of my corridor-mates gently pointed out that the oven temperatures in Sweden are listed in Celsius, not Fahrenheit! Despite almost burning the kitchen down, I learned a valuable lesson about assuming my map for temperatures and frozen pizzas was the same as everyone else's.

Discovering knowledge that informs us is another step that can build on our motivation. One tool involves learning more about our cognitive style, or how we learn. Our cognitive style consists of our preferred patterns for "gathering information, constructing meaning, and organizing and applying knowledge". As we explore **cognitive** styles, we discover that there are differences in how people attend to and perceive the world, explain events, organize the world, and use rules of logic. Some cultures have a cognitive style that focuses more on tasks, analytic and objective thinking, details and precision, inner direction, and independence, while others focus on relationships and people over tasks and things, concrete and **metaphorical** thinking, and a group consciousness and harmony.

Developing ICC is a complex learning process. At the basic level of learning, we accumulate knowledge and assimilate it into our existing frameworks. But accumulated knowledge doesn't necessarily help us in situations where we have to apply that knowledge. Transformative learning takes place at the highest levels and occurs when we encounter situations that challenge our accumulated knowledge and our ability to **accommodate** that knowledge to manage a real-world situation. The cognitive **dissonance** that results in these situations is often uncomfortable and can lead to a hesitance to repeat such an engagement. One tip for cultivating ICC that can help manage these challenges is to find a community of like-minded people who are also motivated to develop ICC. In my graduate program, I lived in the international dormitory in order to experience the cultural diversity that I had enjoyed so much studying abroad a few years earlier. I was surrounded by international students and US American students who were more or less interested in cultural diversity. This ended up being a tremendous learning experience, and I worked on research about identity and communication between international and American students.

Developing skills that enable us is another part of ICC. Some of the skills important to ICC are the ability to **empathize**, accumulate cultural information, listen, resolve conflict, and manage anxiety. Janet M. Bennett (2009) believes "again, you are already developing a foundation for these skills by reading this book, but you can expand those skills to intercultural settings with the motivation and knowledge already described. Contact alone does not increase intercultural skills; there must be more deliberate measures taken to fully capitalize on those encounters". While research now shows that intercultural contact does decrease prejudices, this is not enough to become interculturally competent. The ability to empathize and manage anxiety enhances prejudice reduction, and these two skills have been shown to enhance the overall impact of intercultural contact even more than acquiring cultural knowledge. There is intercultural training available for people who are interested. If you can't access training, you may choose to research intercultural training on your own, as there are many books, articles, and manuals written on the subject.

Reflective practices can also help us process through rewards and challenges associated with developing ICC. As we open ourselves to new experiences, we are likely to have both positive and negative reactions. It can be very useful to take note of negative or defensive reactions you have. This can help you identify certain triggers that may create barriers to effective intercultural interaction. Noting positive experiences can also help you identify **triggers** for learning that you could seek out or recreate to enhance the positive.

(1051 words)

(This article has been edited to fit the format of this book. For the original article, please see chapter 8 of "A Primer on Communication Studies" by Howard Schwartz.)

 After-reading Task

1. According to passage 1, what are the main symptoms of culture shock?

2. According to passage 1, what can people do to relieve the stress of culture shock?

3. According to passage 2, what are three ways to cultivate people's intercultural communication competence?

4. According to passage 2, what happened to the author when he once tried to cook pizza in Sweden?

 WORDS LIST

Passage 1

ethnicity /eθˈnɪsəti/ *n.* 种族特点；种族渊源

cosmopolitan /ˌkɒzməˈpɒlɪtən/ *a.* 世界性的；国际化的

transition /trænˈzɪʃn/ *n.* 过渡；转变

assimilate /əˈsɪməleɪt/ *v.* 吸收；同化

aesthetical /iːsˈθetɪkəl/ *a.* 美学的；审美的

manifest /ˈmænɪfest/ *v.* 显示，表明

irritability /ˌɪrɪtəˈbɪləti/ *n.* 易怒
ornament /ˈɔːnəmənt/ *n.* 装饰；装饰物
cuisine /kwɪˈziːn/ *v.* 烹饪；烹调法
counselor /ˈkaʊnsələ/ *n.* 顾问；咨询师

Passage 2

foster /ˈfɒstə(r)/ *v.* 培养；抚育
humbled /ˈhʌmbld/ *a.* 谦逊的；谦卑的
deter /dɪˈtɜː(r)/ *v.* 阻止；威慑
crank /kræŋk/ *v.* 转动曲柄移动
cognitive /ˈkɒɡnɪtɪv/ *a.* 认知的；认识的
metaphorical /ˌmetəˈfɒrɪkl/ *a.* 隐喻性的
accommodate /əˈkɒmədeɪt/ *v.* 容纳；使适应
dissonance /ˈdɪsənəns/ *n.* 不和谐；不一致
empathize /ˈempəθaɪz/ *v.* 有同感；移情
trigger /ˈtrɪɡə(r)/ *n.* （枪）扳机；诱因

Section C　Case Studies

Case 1

Claire, an American foreign exchange student, traveled to China to study abroad for two years. When she first arrived, she became friends with a Chinese student, Xiao Min. For the first few weeks, Xiao Min showed Claire around the city. Claire was ecstatic, often taking photos of all the interesting sights she saw. Claire often told Xiao Min how much she loved China – everything from KTV to roast duck to the warm hospitality. Claire always looked forward to spending time with her friend Xiao Min and exploring more of China with her.

After about two months, however, Xiao Min noticed that Claire did not want to spend time with her. She often made excuses that she had to stay in her dormitory to do homework. When Xiao Min did spend time with her, Claire almost seemed like a different person.

One day, when they were walking down the street, they passed a person selling purses. There was a speaker next to the purses that continually played a recording of the seller trying to attract customers. When Claire passed it, she yelled at the seller, "Do you have to play that so loud?! No one is going to buy a purse from you as long as that is playing!" She then turned to Xiao Min and said, "Sometimes I can't stand Chinese people. They are so rude!"

Another day, Xiao Min treated Claire to have lunch together. When Claire took a bite of some peppers and beef, she put down her chopsticks and exclaimed, "Chinese food is all the same! I can't stand it!"

A few days later, Xiao Min was trying to practice her English with Claire and Claire snapped at her, "Did you befriend me just so I could help you with your English?! I'm not here to teach English. I'm here to learn Chinese. Please stop taking advantage of me!"

Unit 8   Culture Shock and Adaptation

Xiao Min didn't know what to think. She couldn't understand why Claire changed so much. Claire used to like China and used to like being around Xiao Min, but now she wanted to be alone in her dorm room. Xiao Min thought she must have done or said something wrong to Claire, but she could not remember what it was.

Reflection

1. Is Xiao Min right in assuming that Claire is upset because she did or said something wrong to her? Why has Claire changed so much?

2. Using the U-curve, analyze what stages of culture shock Claire has experienced.

3. What are some specific things Xiao Min can do to help Claire?

Case 2

Song Hao studied abroad in the U.S. for four years. Although he did experience a difficult time during his first year there, he later became quite accustomed to American life. He made many American friends and thrived in his studies. But, as graduation approached, he became very excited at the thought of returning home to China. Finally, he would have the opportunity to eat Chinese food again, speak in Chinese with store clerks, see his relatives, watch Chinese TV shows and movies, and walk the streets of his childhood. Even though he really enjoyed his time in the U.S., he was eager to return home.

A few weeks before his graduation and return to China, he talked with his mom on the phone.

"I have some wonderful plans for you when you get back," she told him. "First, we'll have a big party. Then we can take a few days visiting family members. They all want to hear about your experiences in the U.S. Every day I will cook some of your favorite Chinese food that you haven't had in a long time. Your high school classmates also want to spend time with you. You guys play together in the park and then have a party at KTV. I've also downloaded a couple really good Chinese movies that came out when you were in the U.S. We can watch them together! You've been away from home for so long, and I'm sure you will be so happy to experience real Chinese life again!"

When Song Hao heard all of this, he was excited, too. "I can't imagine how wonderful it will be to return home after four years of being away!"

Reflection

1. Do you think life back in China will be as wonderful as Song Hao and his mom believe it will be? Why or why not?

2. How might the W-curve give Song Hao and his mother a more realistic picture of what life for Song Hao will be like when he returns to China? What should they expect?

3. Using the W-curve and your knowledge of culture shock, give Song Hao's mother some suggestions about how best to help Song Hao transition back into life in China. How should she change her plans?

Case 3 Watch the following clip from the TV series "*Little Daddy*" and analyze the cultural phenomenon in an intercultural context.

Reflection

1. Why does the lawyer want to prove Yu Guo is somewhat addicted to beer or alcohol?

2. What role does spanking play in Chinese and Western families? Which do you think is better?

III. Task-based Activities

Exercises

Choose the best choice according to the cultural context.

( ) 1. You are eating a meal with an American. But when the waiter brings the food, you don't think it is enough for both of you. You ask your friend, "Is this enough?" Your friend responds, "You can order more if you want." What does your friend mean?
   a. He doesn't think there is enough food for both of you, and he wants you to order more.
   b. He has enough food for himself, but if you need more food for yourself you can order more.

( ) 2. You break your leg while studying in America and must stay in the hospital for a few days. However, although some of your friends call you or send you a text message wishing you fast recovery, no one visits you. Why?
   a. Your friends don't consider you a very close friend.
   b. Your friends assume you prefer privacy and don't want to bother you while you recover.

( ) 3. You meet an American who just arrived in China three days ago. You want to be his friend, so you invite him to lunch. Considering the U-curve, what kind of restaurant would he most likely prefer?
   a. Western

Unit 8 Culture Shock and Adaptation

    b. Chinese

( ) 4. You meet an American who has been living in China for four months. You want to be his friend, so you invite him to lunch. Considering the U-curve, what kind of restaurant would he most likely prefer?

    a. Western

    b. Chinese

( ) 5. An American friend of yours gives you a hat for your birthday. Which of the following are appropriate responses?

    a. "Where did you get it?"

    b. "How much did it cost?"

    c. Neither of these are appropriate responses.

Group Work

Discussion 1

Imagine you are planning to study abroad or work in a joint venture company. What will you do to avoid culture shock and to develop intercultural competence?

Discussion 2

Watch the movie "Outsourced" and discuss the culture shock and cultural adaptation that Todd Anderson experienced. Then write an essay titled "How to overcome cultural barriers in intercultural communication".

Assignment

Presentation 1

In groups, discuss anything else you might have previously learned about culture shock and intercultural competence. Do you think it is necessary to study other cultures? Find some movie clips related to culture shock and present them to your class.

Presentation 2

Divide into several groups and interview foreigners or overseas students to find out what kinds of intercultural obstacles they have faced. How is this culture different from their own? Make a video about your interviews and present it to the class.

Do in Rome as the Romans do. – English proverb
入乡随俗。
Do not do toward others anything you would not want to be done to you. – Confucius saying
己所不欲，勿施于人。

Appendixes

Appendix I　Cultural Terms

1. 什么是交际（Communication）？

（1）Samovar & Porter 认为：交际是指人类在相互交往中使用符号创造意义和反射意义的动态和系统过程。

（2）David Pinto 认为：交际是指信息传播的多种方式，它包括信息发出者、信息接收者和信息的过程。

交际的过程包括信息源、信息、编码、渠道、干扰、信息接收者、解码、信息接收者的反应、反馈以及语境十个要素。其基本特点：强调交际是动态变化的、不可逆转的过程；具有符号性、系统性；交际是交互式的过程；交际发生在特定的语境中。

　　a. 信息发出者/信息源（Sender/Source）：指传递信息的人。

　　b. 信息（Message）：引起信息接收者反应的任何信号。

　　c. 编码（Encoding）：信息发出者用言语或非言语的方式发出有目的信息的行为。

　　d. 渠道/媒介（Channel/Medium）：发送信息的方法、途径。

　　e. 信息接收者（Receiver）：接收到信息并且赋予信息某些含义的人。

　　f. 解码（Decoding）：指信息接收者给予接收到的信息或符号意义解读的行为。

　　g. 反馈（Feedback）：指信息接收者对信息发出者的信息所做出的反应。

　　h. 干扰（Noise）：指妨碍信息交际的各种因素，包括外界干扰、生理干扰、心理干扰和语义干扰。

　　i. 语境（Context）：指交际发生的环境，包括自然语境、社会语境和人际语境。

2. 什么是跨文化交际（Intercultural Communication or Cross-cultural Communication）？

（1）Samovar & Porter 认为：跨文化交际是指文化感知和符号系统的不同足够改变交际事件中人们之间的交际。

（2）David Pinto 认为：跨文化交际是指具有不同文化背景的人们之间的交际。既指本族语者与非本族语者之间的交际，也指任何在语言和文化背景方面有差异的人们之间的交际。

跨文化交际的形式包括跨种族交际、跨民族交际和同一文化群体之间的交际。

（3）Cross-cultural communication 和 Intercultural communication 的区别。

Gudykunst 认为：Intercultural communication 涵盖所有意义上或是任何层面上不同文化背景下人们之间交际的研究。Cross-cultural communication 是 intercultural communication 研究的一部分，主要侧重于对不同文化交际的语境和行为作对比研究。

（4）跨种族交际（Interracial communication）：跨种族交际是指信息交流的信息源和信息接收者来自不同的种族而进行的交际。

（5）跨民族交际（Interethnic communication）：跨民族交际是指交际发生在来自一个国家或文化内部的不同民族群体之间的人们中。

（6）文化内交际（Intercultural communication）：文化内交际是指同一文化内部成员之间的交际。

3. 什么是文化（Culture）？

（1）Kroeber and Kluckhohn 认为：文化是通过符号而获得，并通过符号而传播的行为模式，它具有显性和隐性特征；其符号也像人工制品一样体现了人类的成就；在历史中形成和选择的传统理念，特别是所代表的价值观，是文化的核心。文化体系可以看作是行动的产物，也可以看作是进一步行动的制约因素。

（2）Samovar & Porter 认为：从跨文化交际学角度定义文化，文化是指一群人通过个体或群体世代努力所获得的一切沉淀物，包括知识、经验、信仰、价值观、行动、态度、意义、等级制度、宗教、时间观、角色、空间关系、宇宙观和产品等。

文化定义的三个层次：a. 文化是行为模式；b. 文化符号是文化载体；c. 文化是历史发展的产物。

4. 文化冰山模式（Iceberg Model of Culture）

文化冰山模式主要研究组成文化的要素以及这些要素中显性和隐性的部分。这个理论把文化比喻成冰山：露出水面的可视部分只不过是冰山的一小部分，如：建筑、艺术、音乐、行为、语言等。但这部分需要隐藏在水下的不可视部分作支撑，如：代表某一群体文化的历史、风俗、价值观以及对于空间、自然和时间的态度等，而这一隐性部分则是文化的基础。因此，我们平时观察到的文化表象只是冰山一角，真正造成表象不同的部分都藏在水下，即影响各民族文化表面差异的隐含部分，包括信念、价值观和社会规范。

5. Lewis 文化模型（The Lewis Model of Culture）

Lewis 文化模型提供了不同文化的人们彼此理解和交际的实践框架。他把世界上的国家分为三类：

（1）Linear-actives（单任务型）：指那些做事会制订计划、时间表，组织并遵循任务链，一次只做一个任务的人。美国人、德国人和瑞士人属于这一类。其特点为：礼貌但直接；以工作为重；坚持事实；重视结果；坚守日程安排；重视书面文字；有限的肢体语言。

（2）Multi-actives（多任务型）：指那些活跃好说，会同时做许多事情，不根据时间表来计划，而根据事物的紧急性、重要性来安排的人。意大利人、拉丁美洲人、阿拉伯人属于这一类。其特点为：事情仅大概计划；情绪化；以人为中心；感觉先于事实；重视关系；徘徊不定；重视口头话语；过多的肢体语言。

（3）Reactives（反应型）：指那些把礼节、尊敬放在第一的文化，安静、仔细地聆听说话人，会认真对待其他人提议的人。中国人、日本人、芬兰人属于这一类。其特点为：遵循大的准则；礼貌含蓄；对话不直视；以人为重；重视和谐；经常要求重复；重视面对面交流；微妙的肢体语言。

6. 价值观（Value）

价值观是指一个人对周围的客观事物（包括人、事、物）的意义、重要性总的评价和标准。价值观通过人们的行为取向及对事物的评价、态度反映出来，是世界观的核心，是驱使人们行为的内部动力。

7. 文化价值观（Cultural Value）

文化价值观是指渗透于整个文化所共有的一整套价值理念，包括人道、本性和时间观，在各文化之间具有普遍性和差异性。

8. Kluckhohn & Strodtbeck 的价值取向理论（Kluckhohn and Strodtbeck's Value Orientation）

Kluckhohn & Strodtbeck（1961）在《价值取向的变奏》一书中提出了五个价值取向理论。他们认为：由于不同群体人们文化特征的不同，他们对待问题的观念、价值取向和解决方法都不相同。五个价值取向具体如下：

（1）人性的取向是什么？如：人性本善（Good）、人性本恶（Evil）或善恶兼有之（Mixed）。

（2）人与自然的关系取向是什么？如：征服（Mastery）、服从（Submissive）或和谐（Harmony）。

（3）人与他人之关系形态是什么？如：个体（Individualism）、团体（Group）或等级（Hierarchy）。

（4）人的活动导向是什么？如：存在（Being）、成为（Becoming）或做（Doing）。

（5）人的时间观是什么？如：过去（Past）、现在（Present）或将来（Future）。

9. Geert Hofstede 的文化维度（Hofstede's Dimensions of Cultural Diversity）

荷兰学者霍夫斯泰德在 1967—1973 年间对美国 IBM 公司分布在世界 50 多个国家的 11 600 名员工进行了价值观调查，在对数据进行统计分析的基础上，提出了自己的价值理论：文化主要体现在价值观上，也会通过一些表象化的事物显现出来。他采用定量分析方法提出了五个"文化维度"模型，指出所有的差异都可追溯到基本维度中的一个或几个。这在文化研究领域中得到了广泛应用。1980 年，他在《文化的后果》一书中发表了该研究的成果，并提出了四个跨文化维度：

（1）个体主义与集体主义：指着眼于个体还是集体的利益；

（2）权力距离：指人们对社会或组织中权力分配不平等的接受程度；

（3）不确定性回避：指对事物不确定性的容忍程度；

（4）男性特征和女性特征：一种文化所展示的传统男性价值观或女性价值观的程度。

霍夫斯泰德的第五个维度发表在 1991 年出版的《文化与组织》一书中，即：

（5）长期导向与短期导向：指做事时着眼于现在还是放眼于未来。

1）权力距离（Power Distance）

权力距离表明一个社会能够接受社会或组织的权力在各成员之间不平等分配的程度，权力距离与等级有关。每个社会在处理权力不平等问题上的方式、方法不同，形成了价值观上的差异。权力距离差异的强弱通过权力距离指数（Power distance index）体现。在权力差距大的社会，人们接受较强的等级制，安心于自己的位置。在权力差距小的社会，人们接受较弱的等级制。

例如，印度、韩国以家庭为背景安排婚姻就显示社会等级的重要性：重要的不是个人的成就，而是这个人所属的家庭。在中国、韩国和日本有着较强的权力距离，长幼、师生和上下级有严格的界限，应该服从。而美国则属于权力距离差异较弱的国家，你可以称呼老师名字，可以质疑老师或权威的话。

2）不确定性规避（Uncertainty Avoidance）

不确定性规避指的是一个社会感受到的不确定性和模糊情景的容忍程度。对不确定性规避程度较强的文化往往有明确的社会规范和原则来指导几乎所有情况下发生的行为，而不确定性规避程度较弱文化的社会规范和原则就不那么明确和严格。规避不确定性的强弱程度可以通过不确定性规避指数（Uncertainty Avoidance Index）来体现。

低度不确定性规避的文化容易接受不确定性，精神压力小，鼓励年轻人，更愿冒险，警惕权威，人们更容易接受从一个地方换到另一个地方生活、工作，如美国人则属于这个范畴。他们乐于创业、探险，喜欢去不同的地方和国家工作，具有很强的冒险精神。

高度不确定性规避的文化认为不确定性是威胁，精神压力大，怀疑年轻人，认为权威是必要的。更倾向于采取一些措施来防止不确定性，如寻找稳定的工作，防止由于更换工作带来的陌生环境、陌生人；对不符合常规的想法和行为表示怀疑和拒绝，因为不知道它们会带来怎样不确定的结果。如中国人更倾向于在某个固定的地方工作，买房子安家，对创业的风险充满忧虑，对工作模糊性的安排乐于接受，而美国人则完全相反。

3）个人主义和集体主义（Individualism vs. Collectivism）

个人主义和集体主义是指社会中个人与群体的关系。个人主义是指一种松散的社会组织结构，其中每个人重视自身的价值与需要，强调个人权利与自由，依靠个人的努力来为自己谋取利益。而集体主义则是一种紧密的社会结构和组织，其中所有的人往往以在群体之内（in-group）和在群体之外（out-group）来区分，他们期望得到群体之内人员的照顾，但同时也以对该群体保持绝对的忠诚作为回报。

个人主义者往往把个人价值、权利和隐私摆在首位，但喜欢高估自己的个人能力和个人在集体中的重要性。集体主义者非常重视和谐与责任，常常低估个体的能力，在集体中表现谦卑，个性和个人价值被淹没在群体之中。

美国是典型的以个人目标为主的文化，英语中特有的 self 一词就可以概括；中国、韩国和日本则是一个典型的以群体目标为主的文化，其文化特征可以用"枪打出头鸟"一言概之。

4）男性特征和女性特征/刚性与柔性（Masculinity vs. Femininity）

这个维度指一种文化展示传统男性特征或女性特征强弱的程度，以及维持性别差异的程度。在强调男性特征的文化中，社会中两性的社会性别角色差别鲜明。男性应该自信、坚强、有雄心，并且专注于物质的拥有和成功；而女性则应该重视家庭、谦卑、温柔，并且追求生活的质量。在强调女性特征的文化里，男性和女性的社会角色表现相同，即：无论男性还是女性都应该谦逊、温柔，并且关注于生活质量。

男性特征指数（Masculinity Index）则代表一个社会男性特征强弱的程度。根据霍夫斯泰德的研究，男性社会会以更加传统和保守的方式来定义性别角色，推崇坚决行为以及获取财富。而女性化社会对于男女双性在工作场所和家庭中扮演的大量角色则持较为开明的观点，关心他人，看重家庭生活与工作之间的平衡。中国是典型的男性特征国家，尤其在古代，男性具有较高的社会地位，"大男子主义"倾向很强，主张"男主外，女主内"，女人要遵从"三从四德"。

5）长期取向（Long Term Orientation）

学者麦克·邦德与一些中国研究者基于亚洲学者儒家价值观的观点，提出了一种新的调查方法。霍夫斯泰德在此基础上补充了他的学说。

长期取向的文化关注未来，重视节俭和毅力。他们强调固执、坚持来达到目标，节俭是重要的，对社会关系和等级关系敏感，愿意为将来投资，有耐心接受最终的结果。这种社会考虑人们的行为将会如何影响后代。

10. 社会规则/准则（Social Norms）

社会规则是文化上已根深蒂固的正确或不正确的，或社会习俗中包含的关于人们行为的准则、标准、规定等。一旦违背，会接受一种公开或非公开形式的惩罚。

11. Hall 的语境文化理论（Edward T. Hall's Context）

（1）语境（Context）：语境是使用语言的环境，包括一切主客观因素，即围绕一次事件的一系列相关因素，包括说话人所在的语言、社会文化背景、交流的环境与社会距离以及其他外部因素，以最深刻、微妙的方式影响着人们的跨文化交际。

美国文化人类学家爱德华.T.霍尔在1976年出版的《超越文化》一书中，提出文化具有语境性，并将语境分为两种类型：高语境（High Context，即 HC）和低语境（Low Context，即 LC）。

（2）高语境（High Context）：在信息传播时绝大部分信息或存在于物质语境中，或内化在个人身上，极少存在于编码清晰的被传递的信息中，也就是说意义没有包含在话语之中。特点是含蓄、隐晦、间接。高语境文化重视信息周围的语境，即促进因素，其次才是信息本身，通常交际的语言本身常常不涵盖所有的信息。在一个高语境的文化中，人们看重的是"体会言外之意"，即"重要的不是说了什么而是谁说的""不在于你说什么，而在于你如何说"等交流准则，中国、日本和韩国是典型的高语境文化。

（3）低语境（Low Context）：低语境则恰好相反，在信息传播时大部分信息必须处在传递的信息中，以便补充语境中丢失的部分，也就是说意义直接包含在话语之中。在低语境文化中，语义主要包含于进行交际的语言里，其字面意义就是最大化的含义，人们希望得到的是具体而不是抽象的意思，特点是直接、坦率。低语境文化将主要的意思放在客观交流的信息里，其次才是语境。人们看重交流中的速度、准确性和效率等交流准则，如"请告诉我事实""请告诉我事情的本质"。低语境文化很重视书面文字，倾向于拥有书面协议，德国、瑞士、美国是典型的低语境文化。

这两者之间的最大区别在于：在高语境文化中，说话者的言语或行为意义来源于或内在化于说话者当时所处的语境，他所表达的东西往往比他所说的东西要多；而在低语境文化中，人们强调的是双方交流的内容，而不是当时所处的语境。

12. Hall 的跨文化时间和空间理论（Edward T. Hall's Time and Space Theory）

1）单向记时制（Monochronic Time）和多向记时制（Polychronic Time）

霍尔根据文化的时间维度，把不同文化群体的时间概括为单向记时制（monochronic time）和多向记时制（polychronic time）。单向记时制的人们把时间看作是一条直线或缎带，可以切割成一段一段，倾向于做短期计划，同一时间内只做一件事情，强调时间表、日程和期限，强调事先安排；多向记时制的人们习惯于同一时间内同时处理几件事情，强调人们的参与和任务的完成，而不强调一切都按时间表进行。

美国人是典型的单向记时制者，他们认为时间就像重量和价值一样，是真实存在的，是可以测量和估价的。单向记时制者最大的特点是一个单位时间只做一件事情，讨厌被人打断。他们注重的是目标、任务和结果，而不是人际关系，强调一心专用。与此相反，多向记时制的人喜欢在同一时间做几件事情，被他人打断是常有的事情。中国人属于多向记时制，使用时间比较随意，灵活性强。在一定程度上，中国人是时间的主人，可以随意支配时间，可以一心多用。如最后期限（deadline）这个词，在美国，所有人都明白所说的时间是不可更改的，而在中国，如果老师告诉学生在最后期限之前交作业，学生可以找出各种理由来为自己的拖延找借口，因为他们没有把时间看作是真的，认为时间是可以灵活的。

2）空间关系学（Proxemics）

空间关系学研究空间（space）利用和支配空间利用的原则，指的是人们如何运用空间进行交流；而领土（territory）则描述了我们如何坚持要求某一区域。Hall 指出我们的周围空间有四个区域（distance），并且在交流中都有不同的意义，对个人空间的解释随着文化的不同而不同。

（1）公众距离（Public distance）：可以达到 360 cm 之远。

（2）社交距离（Social distance）：由 120 cm 到 360 cm。

（3）个人距离（Personal distance）：由 45 cm 到 120 cm（可以伸手碰到对方，虽然认识却没有特别关系）。

（4）亲密距离（Intimate distance）：由 45 cm 到零距离（通常是亲人、很熟的朋友、情侣或是夫妻）。

13. 言语交际（Verbal Communication）

言语交际指的是两人或以上的人们使用声音或语言传递信息或以其作为最基本工具进行交流。

换言之，当来自不同文化背景的人们用语言进行交流时，跨文化的言语交际就发生了。跨文化的言语交际形式有四种：直接与间接的言语交际方式（direct vs. indirect style）、以个人为导向和以身份为导向的言语交际方式（person-oriented vs. status-oriented verbal style）、自我增强和自我贬抑的言语交际方式（self-enhancement and self-effacement verbal style）、在交谈中表达观点和沉默的言语交际方式（beliefs expressed in talk vs. silence）。

1）沃尔夫–萨丕尔假说

沃尔夫–萨丕尔认为人类的思想是由语言所建构的，语言影响了人们的认知、经验和行为的方式。首先，语言支配着思维，是思想的塑造者，说不同语言的人对世界的看法不同；其次，语言通过影响思维模式影响文化，即语言是文化的载体，文化是语言的反映。

2）词义的内涵和外延

词语有其内涵和外延的概念。内涵（denotations）指的是一个词语字面的意思，也就是词典的定义；外延（connotations）指的是一个词语字面以外、与其内涵有关系的引申意思。

14. 非言语交际（Non-verbal Communication）

非言语交际指的是在一定的交际环境中，不借助于言语进行的交际。人类的交际体系在结构上可分为言语交际（verbal communication）和非言语交际（non-verbal communication）。调查显示，在人们的交际行为中，言语交际所传达的信息仅占 35%，而 65% 的信息则是通过非言语交际来传递的。从跨文化交际的角度出发，非言语交际分为以下四大类：

（1）体态语：指人们利用姿态和动作，包括身体动作、眼神接触、面部表情、手势和触碰来传达信息的非言语行为。

（2）副语言：副语言也称辅助语言，它包括发声系统的各个要素，如音质、音幅、音调、音色等。广义的副语言指无声而有形的现象，即与话语同时或单独使用的手势、身势、面部表情、对话时的位置和距离等所表达的某种意义，具有配合语言加强表达能力的作用。它包括沉默、话轮转换和各种非语义声音。

（3）环境语：环境语是指文化本身所造成的生理和心理环境，而不是人们居住的地理环境。不同的文化在空间距离和时间观上都存在差异。

（4）客体语：客体语指的是与人体有关的相貌、服装、饰品、气味等，以及艺术品、建筑物、家具和车辆所提供的交际信息等。这些东西在人际交往中有传递信息的功能，一般都具有实用性和交际性两个特点。

15. 文化冲击/文化休克（Culture Shock）

文化人类学家 Oberg 首先提出文化冲击这个理论，他认为文化冲击是指在非本民族文化环境中生活或学习的人，在失去自己熟悉的社会交往信息和符号时，在心理上经受的一种困惑、焦虑的状况。人类学家 Lysgaard 将其分为三个阶段：蜜月期、危机期和适应期。

16. 跨文化适应的 U 曲线和 W 曲线模型（Intercultural U-Curve and W-Curve Adjustment/Adaptation Model）

（1）跨文化适应（Intercultural adjustment/adaptation）：指人们在异文化的环境中，不断提高自己的适应能力，以期达到新文化环境的需要。

（2）U 曲线模型（U-Curve）：文化人类学家 Lysgaard 在 1955 年提出了 U 曲线模型。他认为：文化适应呈 U 字形发展，是一种动态的过程，从兴奋开始，逐渐出现危机，最后在新的文化环境中逐渐适应。

（3）W 曲线模型（W-Curve）：Gullahorn 在 1963 和 1966 年进一步发展了 U 曲线模型，提出了 W 曲线模型，主要指留学生或长期的旅居者回国后对家乡文化的再适应过程。

Appendix II List of Recommended Movies

1. *Anna and the King*《安娜与国王》，美国，1999
2. *Amelie*《天使爱美丽》，法国，2001
3. *Avatar*《阿凡达》，美国，2009
4. *Be There or Be Square*《不见不散》，中国，1998
5. *Crash*《撞车》，美国，2004
6. *Dances with Wolves*《与狼共舞》，美国，1990
7. *Dead Poets Society*《死亡诗社》，美国，1989
8. *East is East*《东方就是东方》，英国，1999
9. *Employee of the Month*《明星雇员》，美国，2006
10. *English Vinglish*《印式英语》，印度，2012
11. *Finding Mr. Right*《北京遇上西雅图》，中国，2013
12. *Go LA LA Go!*《杜拉拉升职记》，中国，2010
13. *Gung Ho*《打工好汉》，美国，1986
14. *I Not Stupid*《小孩不笨》，新加坡，2002
15. *Lie to Me*《别对我说谎》，美国，2009
16. *Little Daddy*《小爸爸》，中国，2013
17. *Little Miss Sunshine*《阳光小美女》，美国，2006
18. *Love Again*《烟台—莫里斯》，中国，2012
19. *My Big Fat Greek Wedding*《我的盛大希腊婚礼》，美国，2002
20. *My Fair Lady*《窈窕淑女》，美国，1964
21. *Monsoon Wedding*《雨季婚礼》，印度，2002
22. *October Sky*《十月的天空》，美国，1999
23. *On the Other Side of the Bridge*《芬妮的微笑》，中国，2002
24. *Outsourced*《世界是平的》，美国，2006
25. *Pushing Hands*《推手》，中国台湾，1991
26. *Rush Hour 3*《尖峰时刻3》，美国，2007
27. *Shanghai Calling*《纽约客@上海》，中国，2012
28. *Siao Yu*《少女小渔》，中国台湾，1995
29. *The Gua Sha Treatment*《刮痧》，中国，2001
30. *The Joy Luck Club*《喜福会》，美国，1993
31. *The Karate Kid*《功夫梦》，美国，2010

32. *The Mother PK Daughter-In-Law*《土婆婆 PK 洋媳妇》，中国，2009
33. *The Pursuit of Happyness*《当幸福来敲门》，美国，2006
34. *The Spanish maid*《西班牙女佣》，美国，2004
35. *The Terminal*《幸福终点站》，美国，2004
36. *The Wedding Banquet*《喜宴》，中国台湾，1993
37. *Up in the Wind*《等风来》，中国，2013

Appendix III   Scripts of Movie Clips

Unit 1 – Clip 1 (The Terminal)

Broadcaster 1: United Airlines announcing the arrival of Flight 9435 from Beijing, customer service representative, report to Gate C42.

Broadcaster 2: All visitors to the US should line up at booths one through 15. Please have your I-94 forms filled out.

The officer of Customs and Border Protection (CBP)

Inspector: What's the purpose of your visit?

Inspector: What is the purpose of your visit?

Inspector: What is the purpose of your visit? Business or pleasure?

Visitor: Just visiting. Shopping?

Customer: Au plaisir.

Visitor: Pleasure.

Visitor: Business.

Inspector: How long will you be staying?

Inspector: Could I see your return ticket?

Inspector: What's the purpose of your visit? Business or pleasure?

Inspector: Enjoy your stay. Next.

Broadcaster 2: Please have your passports, immigration forms, 1-94, and customs declarations ready to hand to the inspector.

CBP officer: Stand by. He's fishing.

CBP officer: Copy that.

Frank Dixon: See this bunch of Mickey Mouse sweatshirts?

CBP officer: That's the tour from China, connecting to Orlando.

Frank Dixon: When was the last time you saw Chinese tourists on their way to Disney World without any cameras?

CBP officer: Possible forged documents on 10 and 11.

Inspector: Sir. Sir. Passport. Thank you. Welcome, Mr. Navorski. Purpose of your visit? Business or pleasure? Sir, I have an IBIS hit on six.

Visitors: No!

CBP officer: Viktor, please follow me.

Broadcaster: ... flight number 746 from Montreal must proceed to US Immigration before claiming their luggage.

CBP officer: All right, Viktor, we'd like you to wait here, please.

Inspector: Next, please.

CBP officer: What are you doing in the United States, Mr. Navorski?

Viktor: (Thick Bulgarian accent) Yellow taxicab, please. Take me to Ramada Inn, 161 Lexington.

CBP officer: Staying at the Ramada Inn?

Viktor: Keep the change.

CBP officer: Do you know anyone in New York?

Viktor: Yes.

CBP officer: Who?

Viktor: Yes.

CBP officer: Who?

Viktor: Yes.

CBP officer: No, do you know anyone in New York?

Viktor: Yes.

CBP officer: Who?

Viktor: Yes. 161 Lexington.

CBP officer: OK, Viktor, I need to see your return ticket, please. No, your return ticket. Your...

Viktor: Oh... Yes.

CBP officer: Ah. This is just a standard procedure. I'm going to need the passport also.

Viktor: Oh... OK.

CBP officer: No, no.

Viktor: Thank you.

CBP officer: Mr. Navorsk. That. Passport. That.

Frank Dixon: Mr. Navorsk ? I'm Frank Dixon, Director of Customs and Border Protection here at JFK. I help people with their immigration problems. We're looking for an interpreter for you. How are we doing on that? Do we have an interpreter? But I understand that you speak a little English.

Viktor: Yes.

Frank Dixon: You do? I hope you don't mind if I eat while we talk. I've a bit of bad news. Your country has suspended all traveling privileges on passports issued by your government. And our State Department has revoked the visa that was going to allow you to enter the US. That's it in a nutshell, basically. While you were in the air there was a military coup in your country. Most of the dead were members of the Presidential Guard. They were attacked in the middle of the night. They got it all on GHN, I think. There were few civilian casualties. I'm sure your family's fine.

CBP officer: Mr. Navorsk, your country was annexed from the inside. The Republic of Krakozhia is under new leadership.

Viktor: Krakozhia. Krakozhia. Krakozhia.

Frank Dixon: Right. I don't think he gets it. Er... Let me... OK. Look. Imagine that these potato chips are Krakozhia.

Viktor: Kra-kozhia. Kra-kozhia.

Frank Dixon: Yes.

Viktor: Krakozhia.

Frank Dixon: OK. Er... So the potato chips are Krakozhia. And this apple...

Viktor: Big Apple. Big Apple.

Frank Dixon: ... Big Apple represents the Liberty Rebels. OK? No more Krakozhia! OK? New government. Revolution. You understand? All the flights in and out of your country have been suspended. The new government has sealed all borders, so your visa's no longer valid. So, currently you are a citizen of nowhere.

CBP officer: Now, we can't process you new papers until the US recognizes your country's new diplomatic reclassification.

Frank Dixon: You don't qualify for asylum, refugee status, temporary protective status, humanitarian parole, or non-immigration work travel. You don't qualify for any of these. You are at this time simply...unacceptable.

Viktor: Unacceptable.

Frank Dixon: Unacceptable.

Viktor: Unacceptable. Big Apple tour includes Brooklyn Bridge, Empire State, Broadway show Cats.

Frank Dixon: I got more bad news for you. Cats has closed.

Viktor: OK. OK. Now I go to New York City. Thank you.

Frank Dixon: No, Viktor. I cannot allow you to enter the United States at this time.

Viktor: Krakozhia.

CBP officer: We can't allow you to go home either.

Frank Dixon: You don't really have a home. Technically it doesn't exist. It's like a Twilight Zone.

Do you get that show over there? Talking Tina, Zanti Misfits.

CBP officer: Zanti Misfits was Outer Limits, sir.

Frank Dixon: Really? It's not important.

Viktor: Where do I buy the Nike shoes?

Frank Dixon: OK, Viktor, come here. Here's my dilemma, Viktor. You have no right to enter the US and I have no right to detain you. You have fallen through a crack in the system.

Viktor: I am crack.

Frank Dixon: Yes. Until we get this sorted out, I will allow you to enter the International Transit Lounge. I'm going to sign a release form that is going to make you a free man.

Viktor: Free?

Frank Dixon: Free. Free. Free to go anywhere you like in the International Transit Lounge. OK?

Viktor: OK.

Frank Dixon: OK.

Viktor: OK.

Frank Dixon: OK. Uncle Sam will have this sorted out by tomorrow, and welcome to the United States. Almost.

Viktor: Thank you.

Frank Dixon: OK. All right. Thanks, Judge.

Broadcaster 1: Announcing the arrival of flight 76 from Singapore Airlines.

CBP officer: Now, Viktor. Viktor. Viktor. This is the International Transit Lounge. You are free to wait here. These are food vouchers. You can use them in the Food Court. Your Krakozhian money is no good here. This is a 15-minute, prepaid calling card. You may call home, if you like. This, in case we need to contact you, is a pager. You must keep this with you at all times. Here is an ID badge for you to get into CBP. Beyond those doors... Viktor. I'm going to need you to look at me. Beyond those doors is American soil. Mr. Dixon wants me to make it clear that you are not to enter through those doors. You are not to leave this building. America is closed.

Viktor: America closed. What I do?

CBP officer: There's only one thing you can do here, Viktor. Shop.

Broadcaster 1: Passengers of flight 854 New York/Warsaw...

Unit 1 – Clip 2 (Gua Sha Treatment)

John Quinlan: Yes, he did. But...

Benton Davis: One look at the work Da tong Xu is engaged in day in and day out to see that this is a man steep in the culture of violence.

Da tong Xu: Culture violent?

Jian Ning: Da tong, no.

Da tong Xu: The character in my latest video is adapted from ancient Chinese story telling. Sun Wukong is a good-hearted, compassionate, righteous hero, he represents our traditional value and ethics.

Benton Davis: Oh, traditional value and ethics? Mr. Xu?

Female lawyer: We don't have to play hardball.

Benton Davis: We do, if we want to hit a homerun, sweet heart. Now, I've read *Journey to the West* in English, the book this character chosen from, values and ethics by this Chinese monkey, Sun Wukong. Ah, here is a story, where peaches that take nine thousand years harvest are entrusted to Sun Wukong, yet this ethical Chinese monkey appropriates this entire harvest for himself and when the poor farmer resist him he totally destroyed their orchard. Now here is another example of this creature's value system. A certain deity creates the pills of eternal use. Ah, well, Sun Wukong consumed all without the regard for life and wellbeing of anybody else, but he also overturns their furness and destroys the workshop that had taken a millennia to construct.

Da tong Xu: That's crazy.

Benton Davis: Now such a murderous, vulgar, devious Chinese monkey is what Mr. Da tong Xu refers to as an example of values and ethics. Well then I can see who...

Da tong Xu: Who the hell you think you are? You know nothing about Chinese culture, you are a liar, I love my son, and you know nothing.

Judge: That's enough! Stop it! This instant. Your theatrics are not appreciated in my court room Mr. Davis. Let him go. Mr. Xu, not only have you failed to prove that Guasha is a bona fide medical treatment, but your behavior in my court, provocations or not has show you to be a dangerous man. Hence, I order that Dennis Xu be kept under the supervision of CWA.

Unit 1 – Exercise (Anna and the King)

Prince: Gracious ladies, kind sirs, on behalf of 68 brothers and sisters, we thank you immeasurably and bid you most gracious evening.

Captain Blake: Your son bears a striking resemblance to his father, Mrs. Leonowens. I had the good fortune of serving with him a few years ago. He was a courageous soldier, ma'am.

Anna: I thank you, Captain Blake.

Princess: Father, may I please kiss good night?

King: If I may beg indulgence for not wishing to break family tradition. I will be there in your dreams as you will be in mine. Good night.

Princess: Good night.

Mycroft Kincaid: You have a remarkable family, King Mongkut. A remarkably large one. Hardly seems fair. All these women for one man. Makes me wish I was Siamese myself.

King: Mycroft Kincaid... of East India Trading Company. Correct?

Mycroft Kincaid: Guilty as charged, Your Majesty.

An English Trader: Mr. Kincaid's company is merely one of the ways we try to foster economic relations with other countries, Your Majesty.

King: Also, I think, to arrive at forefront of world in wealth and power. Yes? Still, progress through commerce is logic. King find most practical and excellent topic for discussion.

Mycroft Kincaid: With all due respect, Your Majesty, it is a little far-fetched to think that commerce alone will bring progress to your people. Especially when they're awash with superstition and fear. Like your lovely concubines here with their talismans, worn, no doubt, to protect them from us foreign devils.

King: A friend once said, Mr. Kincaid, English also have fantastical beliefs. Or am I mistaking your country for being land of Merlin and Camelot?

Mycroft Kincaid: Point taken, Your Majesty. However, there is no arguing the superiority of the English. And in the light of these dreadful massacres up and down your border, it's no wonder you're seeking our favor.

Anna: Superiority, Mr. Kincaid? I do not recall anyone being given the right to judge whose culture or customs are superior. Especially when those judging have frequently done so at the point of gun. Would you not agree, Your Majesty?

King: Quite.

Unit 2 – Clip 1 (The Joy Luck Club)

Waverly murmurs: Thank God I already prepped him on the Emily Post of Chinese manners. [Man Speaking Chinese]

Waverly murmurs: Actually, there were a few things I forgot to mention.

Richard: Let me make a toast. Here's to...

Waverly: He shouldn't have had that second glass... everyone in the family. When everyone else had had only half an inch just for taste.

Richard: Shrimp. My favorite.

Waverly: He should have taken only a small spoonful of the best dish... until everyone had had a helping.

Lindo: He has good appetite.

Waverly: He shouldn't have bragged he was a fast learner. But the worst... was when Rich criticized my mother's cooking, and he didn't even know what he had done. As is the Chinese cook's custom, my mother always insults her own cooking, but only with the dishes she serves with special pride.

Lindo: This dish is not salty enough. No flavor. It's too bad to eat. But... please.

Richard: Oh! Uh.

Waverly: That was our cue to eat some... and proclaim it the best she'd ever made.

Richard: You know, Lindo, all this needs is a little soy sauce.

Waverly's father: [Gasping] Oh!

Richard: So, how'd your mom react when you told her about the wedding?

Waverly: It never came up.

Richard: How come?

Waverly: She'd rather get rectal cancer.

Richard: Oh.

Waverly: Ma! Soft wave for body? What do you think?

Unit 2 – Clip 2 (Anna and the King)

Kralahome (Prime Minister): Cholera always in world but still hardly at all in Bangkok.

Anna: Is there nothing you can do?

Kralahome (Prime Minister): They have already begun. Listen, Phra Arahan. Reminding soul to go to heaven and not lose way. It is why men must not be heard weeping, as her soul will attach to sadness and remain to comfort living. His Majesty is grateful. The little one has made frequent mention of sir's name.

Appendixes

Unit 3 – Clip 1 (The Pursuit of Happiness)

Christopher: Are we there?

Chris Gardner: Yep.

Chris Gardner: Hey, you know what today is?

Christopher: Yeah.

Chris Gardner: What?

Christopher: Saturday.

Chris Gardner: You know what Saturday is, right?

Christopher: Yeah.

Chris Gardner: What?

Christopher: Basketball.

Chris Gardner: You wanna go play some basketball?

Christopher: Okay.

Chris Gardner: All right, then we're gonna go sell a bone-density scanner. How about that? Wanna do that?

Christopher: No.

Christopher: Hey, Dad. I'm going pro. I'm going pro.

Chris Gardner: Okay. Yeah, I don't know, you know. You'll probably be about as good as I was. That's kind of the way it works, you know. I was below average. You know, so you'll probably ultimately rank... somewhere around there, you know, so... I really... You'll excel at a lot of things, just not this. I don't want you shooting this ball all day and night. Right?

Christopher: All right.

Chris Gardner: Okay. All right, go ahead.

Chris Gardner: Hey. Don't ever let somebody tell you... you can't do something. Not even me. All right?

Christopher: All right.

Chris Gardner: You got a dream... you gotta protect it. People can't do something themselves... they wanna tell you you can't do it. If you want something, go get it. Period. Let's go.

Christopher: Dad, why did we move to a motel?

Chris Gardner: I told you. Because I'm getting a better job. You gotta trust me, all right?

Christopher: I trust you.

Chris Gardner: All right, here. Come on, come on. Keep up.

Christopher: Dad, when is Mom coming back? Dad, when is Mom coming back?

Chris Gardner: I don't know, Christopher.

Christopher: Dad, listen to this. One day, a man was drowning in the water.

Intercultural Communication in Movies
影视作品中的跨文化交际

Unit 3 – Clip 2 (Little Miss Sunshine)

TV DJ: And now, the moment we've all been waiting for: the talent competition. Miss Carly Nugent! Yodel-ay-hee-hoo, that was great! Wow! Funkylicious!

Richard: I'm going backstage.

Dwayne: Yeah. Right. See you.

Sheryl: Oh, look at you. Is that your costume?

Olive: OK, here.

Sheryl: What's going on?

Richard: I just came to wish Olive good luck. How are you doing, honey?

Olive: Good.

Sheryl: Nervous.

Richard: Yeah. You're gonna do great. I just know it. Can I talk to you for a second?

Sheryl: Yeah. What's up?

Richard: I don't want her to go on.

A staff member of the TV station: Are you authorized to be backstage?

Dwayne: No. Where are the dressing rooms?

Olive: Are you allowed to be here?

Dwayne: Just tell me where the dressing rooms are.

Richard: Listen, we're not in Albuquerque any more.

Sheryl: Hey, How are you feeling?

Dwayne: Better. Where's Olive?

Sheryl: Just there. What's up?

Dwayne: Mom, I don't want Olive doing this.

Sheryl: Oh, my God.

Dwayne: Look around. Mom, this place is fucked!

Richard: He's right!

Dwayne: Look, I don't want these people judging Olive. Fuck them!

Sheryl: It is too late.

Dwayne: It's not. You're the mom, and you're supposed to protect her. Everyone is gonna laugh at her, Mom. Please don't let her do this.

A staff member of the TV station: Olive Hoover, two minutes.

Dwayne: Look, she's not a beauty queen. She's just not. I'm gonna tell her.

Sheryl: No, you listen to me. Olive is who she is. She has worked so hard, she's poured everything into this. We can't just take it away from her. We can't. I know you want to protect her, I know, honey. But we've gotta let Olive be Olive.

A staff member of the TV station: Olive Hoover! Are you the family?

Sheryl: Yeah. OK? Olive, it's time. Are you OK?

Olive: Yeah.

A staff member of the TV station: We've gotta go. Now.

Sheryl: Hang on. Olive, look at me. If you don't wanna do this, that's OK. If you wanna sit this one out, it's totally fine by us. We're proud of you anyway.

A staff member of the TV station: We gotta go. It's time! Ready? Let's go.

Sheryl: Good luck, honey.

Unit 3 – Exercise (The Joy Luck Club)

June murmurs: When I was nine years old... my mother's version of believing in me... was believing that I could be anything... anything she wanted; the best piano prodigy this side of China. I never practiced. Lucky for me, old Mr. Chong couldn't tell the difference. He'd gone stone-deaf over the years.

Mr. Chong: Me and Beethoven, we both hear it in our head! Okey-dokey. Now, how many sharps... how many flats? What key are we in?

June : Z major.

Mr. Chong: What?

June: Z major!

Mr. Chong: Good. Now, for the recital... more feeling... more gusto!

A contestant: I'm a girl and by me that's only great I am proud that my silhouette is curvy.

June murmurs: When I was young, Auntie Lindo... was my mother's best friend and archenemy.

Their weapons of choice were comparing their children. Mom was sick of hearing Auntie Lindo brag... about her daughter Waverly, who was Chinatown's chess champion. That night Mom figured I'd redeem her... with my international piano debut.

Lindo: I ask my daughter... "Help me carry grocery." She think this too much ask. All day long she play chess. I dust off all her trophy. Appreciate me? No. You lucky you don't have the same problem.

Suyuan: My problem... worse than yours. If I tell June time to wash dish... she hear nothing but music. It's like you can't stop this natural talent.

A contestant: Being a girl

June murmurs: Until that night, I didn't believe I was a prodigy.

June: Twerp.

June murmurs: In fact, I used to go out of my way to prove my mother wrong... that I wasn't cut out to be the best anything... I could only be me. It was incredible. It was like my hands were possessed by Mozart. And everybody could see this, could hear this. I was a genius. I had been discovered. And then I heard it. Maybe they didn't notice.

Mr. Chong: Bravo! Bravo! Encore! Well done!

Music: Here we come walking down the street

June murmurs: After the talent show fiasco... I figured I never had to play the piano again.

Music: Everyone we meet

Suyuan: 4:00. Turn off TV.

Music: Hey, hey, we're the Monkees

Suyuan: Practice piano time.

Music: People say we monkey around

June murmurs: I couldn't believe what she was saying. Like I was... supposed to go through the same torture again. Forget it.

Music: But we're too busy singin' to put anybody down

Suyuan: What I say? 4:00.

Music: We're just tryin' to be friendly Come and watch us sing and play

June: I'm not going to play anymore. Why should I?

Music: We're the young generation

Suyuan: What did you say?

Music: And we've got something to say

June: I'm not your slave. This isn't China. You can't make me.

Suyuan: Get up!

June: No! No, I won't. No! No! No, I won't. You want me to be someone I'm not! I'll never be the kind of daughter that you want me to be!

Suyuan: There be two kinds of daughter: obedient or follow own mind. Only one kind of daughter

could live in this house: obedient kind.

June: Then I wish I wasn't your daughter! I wish you weren't my mom!

Suyuan: Too late to change this.

June murmurs: That's when I remembered what we could never talk about.

June: Then I wish I were dead... like them, the babies that you killed in China!

Unit 4 – Clip 1 (October Sky)

Coalminer 1: Sons of bitches gonna be droppin' bombs on us from up there.

Coalminer 2: Don't know why they'd drop a bomb on this place. Be a heck of a waste of a bomb.

TV broadcaster: The first game against Welch, that's the one that's gonna draw the scouts.

Jim: Yeah. Welch knows it, too. They're gonna be coming after us.

Elsie: Be careful, Jim. Last year, those two boys from Welch got their arms broken.

Jim: Well, they started it.

Elsie: It doesn't matter much who started it. I don't call that football.

John Hickam: You don't worry about Jim. Ain't nobody on the Welch team that can catch him. I wish the scouts could've seen that first game with Bluefield.

Homer: I'm gonna build a rocket. Like Sputnik. Well, I'm not sayin' it's gonna go up in space or anything... but I'm gonna do it. I'm gonna build a rocket.

Elsie: Just don't blow yourself up. More eggs, anybody?

Roy Lee Cook: Nice rocket, Homer.

Sherman O'Dell: How high do you think it will fly?

Homer: Well, I got it packed with the powder from 30 sky rockets. Three, four miles. You ready?

Roy Lee Cook: Yeah.

Homer: Ten, nine, eight, seven, six.

Sherman O'Dell: Should we get behind somethin'?

Elsie: What happened?

Homer: My rocket blew up.

Elsie: Are you okay?

Homer: I guess.

Elsie: My heart's poundin'. I thought the mine blew up. Oh, Homer. I waited six months for the company carpenter to put up that fence. Didn't I tell you not to blow yourself up?

Homer: Yes, ma'am.

Elsie: Then let's not.

Neighbor: Elsie.

Elsie: It's all right, Ms. Fields! It's all right.

Homer murmurs: Dear Dr. von Braun, my name is Homer Hickam. I'm 17 and I live in a small mining town in West Virginia.

TV broadcaster: Six, five, four, three – ignition.

Unit 4 – Clip 2 (Dead Poets Society)

John Keating: No grades at stake, gentlemen. Just take a stroll. There it is. I don't know, but I've been told.

Students: I don't know, but I've been told.

John Keating: Doing poetry is cold.

Students: Doing poetry is cold.

John Keating: Left. Left. Left, right, left. Left. Left. Left, right, left. Left. Halt! Thank you, gentlemen. If you noticed, everyone started off with their own stride, their own pace. Mr. Pitts taking his time. He knew he'll get there one day. Mr. Cameron, you could see him thinking, "Is this right? It might be right. It might be right. I know that. Maybe not. I don't know." Mr. Overstreet, driven by a deeper force. Yes. We know that. All right. Now, I didn't bring them up here to ridicule them. I brought them up here to illustrate the point of conformity, the difficulty in maintaining your own beliefs in the face of others. Now, I see the look in your eyes like, "I would have walked differently." Well, ask yourselves why you were clapping. Now we all have a great need for acceptance. But you must trust that your beliefs are unique, your own. Even though others may think them odd or unpopular. Even though the herd may go, "That's ba-a-a-a-ad." Robert Frost said, "Two roads diverged in the wood and I, I took the one less traveled by. And that has made all the difference." I want you to find your own walk right now, your own way of striding, pacing any direction. Anything you want, whether it's proud, whether it's silly, anything. Gentlemen, the courtyard is yours. You don't have to perform, just make it for yourself. Mr. Dalton, will you be joining us?

Dalton: Exercising the right not to walk.

John Keating: Thank you, Mr. Dalton. Just illustrated the point. Swim against the stream.

Unit 4 – Exercise (Anna and the King)

King: You articulate logical answer under pressure, Mem Leonowens.

Anna: That is very kind of you, Your Majesty.

King: But irritating superior attitude king find most unbeautiful. However, it will serve you well given decision I now make.

Anna: First impressions can often be misleading.

King: Along with my eldest son... you shall now teach all my children. Come. The royal family. 23 wives, 42 concubines, 58 offspring, and 10 more on the way. Each one unique. Each one my hope for the future. I understand your surprise. Not as many as Emperor of China, but he did not spend half of life in monastery. King making up for lost time.

Louise: Mother, what's a concubine?

King: Presenting original pupil and heir apparent. Prince Chulalongkorn. This, my son, is your new teacher.

Anna: It is a great honor, Your Highness.

Louise: He doesn't look too happy about it.

King: This is a necessary and practical gift I give to you and you must never forget to honor your renowned teacher Mem Anna Leonowens. Must not forget head wife, the Lady Thiang. It is my pleasure that you help make her a fine scholar also.

Anna: Lady Thiang.

Lady Thiang: Welcome, mem teacher.

King: Prince Thongkon Yai, Prince Suk Sawat, Princess Kannika Kaeo, and Princess Fa-Ying.

Princess Fa-Ying: I'm not princess. I'm monkey.

King: My deepest apologies. I study her in English myself.

Anna: Well, Your Majesty, I am most flattered by your welcome. And I find the opportunity to be in a school an exciting one. Such devotion to progress is to be commended.

King: Reform is vital for my country's survival. As tiny feet change, so too will Siam.

Anna: But being in a country with so many unique customs, if I am to raise my son to be like his father, which I very much hope he will be, then I must feel free to follow our own traditions.

King: As a father, I understand.

Anna: Good. Then His Majesty will appreciate why having a home outside the palace walls is of such great importance to us. A home which had been promised but so far has not been provided.

King: It is my pleasure that you live in the palace.

Anna: But it is not mine, Your Majesty.

King: You do not set conditions of your employment. And you shall obey!

Anna: May I respectfully remind His Majesty that I am not his servant but his guest!

King: A guest who is paid. Education begins tomorrow.

Unit 5 – Clip 1 (Outsourced)

An Indian person: Hi, you like it in India?

Todd: Well, it's interesting.

An Indian person: It is the best country... no problem. Hey... no problem, you've got to jump... jump.

Todd: What?

An Indian person: You jump... you must jump the train...

Todd: There's no room.

An Indian person: You must jump... jump. Jump... good.

Todd: I'll... I'll take one of those.

A vendor: No change, no change... impossible, no change.

Todd: Oh, that's okay, I'm dying of thirst. Keep the change.

A vendor: You're sure?

Todd: Yea, it's fine.

A vendor: You like?

Todd: Mm...

Puro: Are you Mr. Doad?

Todd: Mm, yes... no, I'm Todd, Todd Anderson. Western Novelty.

Puro: I sent a car, but you were not there.

Todd: I didn't see it. I had to take one of those taxi go-kart thingy.

Puro: So sorry for the inconvenience. I'm sorry, pleased to meet you, Mr. Doad. I'm Purohit Narsimacharaya Virajnarianan, but you can call me Puro.

Todd: Puro?

Puro: Puro, I'll take you to your hotel, please come.

vendor: Sir... Sir, please come back, I'm here. I'm waiting for you, good day, good night, good morning... please come.

Puro: You like India?

Todd: Bombay is a little crazy, but Gharapuri looks different... a little cleaner.

Puro: Bombay is terrible... terrible, Gharapuri is very clean. You have a business card, Mr. Doad?

Todd: It's Todd, please call me Todd.

Puro: Executive Vice-president of Marketing and Order fulfillment. Very impressive.

Todd: Not as impressive as it sound. What I really do, is to sell kitsch to rednecks. Now I train some other schmuck to do it.

Puro: May I ask a question?

Todd: Yea, go ahead.

Puro: Would you kindly be telling me, what is kitsch, and what is redneck, and what is schmuck?

Todd: Kitsch is garbage that people buy. And Redneck basically means farmer.

Puro: Farmer? And a schmuck?

Todd: That means like a nice guy... you're the person I'm gonna train? I'm sorry, I didn't realize that.

Puro: I'm so fortunate to be learning the way of American business from you, Mr. Doad.

Todd : Please... call me Todd.

Puro: Your first trip to India?

Todd: Yes

Puro: Some foreigners who come here, do not experience it well. But I can tell, you are of a different breed. A very good traveler. Strong, and ready for anything, and everything.

Todd: That's very kind of you. Why do you say that?

Puro: Most foreigners cannot eat cola without becoming very ill.

Todd: How far is the hotel?

Puro: Your reservation is for the Gharapuri Palace Hotel, but that place is very lonely. I'll take you to Aunt Ji's guesthouse. She will take care of you better, then your own real mother.

Todd: No, actually, I just like to go to my hotel, I'm tired, and I...

Puro: Please, I insist, we go to Aunt Ji. She has a very good garden, most excellent Indian cook... very hygienic. You won't be lonely there, I'm telling you.

Todd: OK, fine... I'll check it out, just make it quick.

Puro: Yes, schmuck.

Puro: There, please come, please come.

Aunt Ji: Welcome, welcome, welcome. You must be tired from your trip from Bombay.

Todd: No, no, no, we're just here to look.

Aunt Ji: Look, look... I have some tea freshly made, especially for you only. And what is your good name?

Todd: My good name?

Puro: This is Mr. Doad to you, fresh from America.

Aunt Ji: Oh... Mr. Doad, how sweet. Please come in, please... come in...

Puro: come In.

Todd: Thank you.

Aunt Ji: So... Mr. Doad. What does your father do? What is it you're selling? Are you married?

Todd: No, I'm not married.

Aunt Ji: Ah... you have a girlfriend, hmm?

Todd: No, I did, but we broke up a couple of months ago.

Aunt Ji: Why break up? You should be married.

Todd: Well er... she wanted to start a family and I wasn't quite ready yet.

Aunt Ji: Not yet? My god. You're old enough to be a grandfather. What're you waiting for, ha? Just eat. Very nice. Fresh.

Todd: That's good. What?

Puro: Sir, you should not place the hand that has been in your mouth, back in the food. And er... you should not eat with your left hand. In India, we eat with the right hand.

Aunt Ji: Left hand is considered to be... dirt.

Puro: Unclean.

Aunt Ji: Unclean, unclean, yes.

Todd: Why?

Puro: Why...

Todd: OK...

Unit 5 – Clip 2 (The Joy Luck Club)

Lena murmurs: Over the years Mom got better...although it seemed like all her fears turned into worries about me. So now that I'm married...and she's visiting our new house...I hope she can finally be happy for me.

Lena: Don't worry. Everything's fine. He's very nice to me.

Ying Ying: Nice. Nice. Very nice.

Lena: Oh, Mom? Mom –

Ying Ying: What's this?

Lena: Why don't you, uh, rest in the living room? I'll make you some tea, okay? I've got some chrysanthemum tea.

Ying Ying: What's this writing?

Lena: Mom! It's nothing. You know. It's just the things we share.

Lena murmurs: At least that's what Harold calls it. Sharing. Everything 50-50. So our love is always equal. The irony is, I was the one who started it that way.

Lena: Let's see –

Harold: Forty-one dollars.

Lena: Oh, total?

Harold: Each. What? You don't have enough?

Lena: No, it's, uh... it's just, uh, I was never very good at math.

Lena murmurs: So what if I had a salad and he had three courses? We were equals. Except that I work in his firm and he pays himself... seven times more than he pays me. Seven and a half. And then last year, when we finally decided to get married... we agreed: love, yes; false dependencies, no. With most everything, we keep track of what we spend... then split it 50-50. Of course we agreed early on not to include personal stuff... like my tampons and feminine hygiene spray... and his shaving lotion and foot powder.

Harold: Honey, isn't there a generic brand of cat food? I mean, do they know the difference? For crying out loud, $34.76.

Lena murmurs: But we still have these philosophical arguments...about the grey areas. Like magazines I subscribe to, which he reads... but only because they're there. And the cat. Even the god dam cat's fleas.

Lena: You gave her to me as a birthday gift. And now you want me to pay to get rid of her fleas?

Ying Ying: Ice cream you don't share. You don't eat ice cream. Ever since that time you got sick on strawberry and chocolate flavor together, I remember. Now you must pay for half of his ice cream? Why do you do this?

Harold: Lena?

Lena: Hmm.

Harold: Lena, when you buy charcoal, you have to buy lighter fluid. Don't you know that yet? Do I have to remind you every time?

Ying Ying: Lena cannot eat ice cream.

Harold: What? What are we talking about?

Lena: It's true. I've hated ice cream all my life. I don't touch the stuff.

Harold: Well, I assumed you were always trying to diet or something.

Ying Ying: Oh, yes, she's lost so much weight. You can't see her any more.

Harold: Hmm.

Ying Ying: One million dollars, and the walls are still crooked. It's bad luck.

Lena: Harold wanted to keep it that way for the effect.

Ying Ying: For effect? A person has to lie here thinking she's in a coffin?

(Ying Ying turns around and nearly knocks over the table.)

Ying Ying: Oh!

Lena: Careful. It's not too sturdy. Harold made it back in college.

Ying Ying: Why do you keep it? You put one more thing on top and everything falls down.

Lena: Do you need anything else?

Ying Ying: No.

Lena: Okay.

Ying Ying: No. Nothing.

TV broadcaster: ...competition. What is a drag race?

Harold: What an idiot! Regatta, not drag race! I don't believe this guy!

Lena: It's cold.

Harold: Excuse me?

Lena: I said, would you close the window, please? It's cold.

TV broadcaster: That's right for 1,000. Takes you to an even 6,000. Oh, there's the bell for "Final Jeopardy." You have 30 seconds to come up with the right question.

Harold: Honey, move. What's goin' on?

Lena: I don't think you should get credit for your ice cream any more.

Harold: Fine. You got it. End of discussion.

Lena: Why do you have to be so god dam fair?

TV broadcaster: Now at 10,400, but you're still not in the lead. Nancy –

Harold: Just what is this about exactly?

Lena: I don't know. Maybe everything. The way we account for everything. What we share, what we don't share. I'm sick of it, adding things up, subtracting, making it come out even when it's not. I'm sick of it.

Harold: You're the one who wanted the cat!

Lena: What are you talking about?

Harold: All right. If you think I'm being unfair, we'll both pay for the fleas.

Lena: This is not about fleas. That is not the point.

Harold: Then, please, tell me. What is the point?

Lena: I… I just think that we need to change things. We need to think about what this marriage is based on...not this balance sheet.

Harold: Well, I know what our marriage is based upon. And if you don't, then you better think about it...before you start to change things.

Unit 6 – Clip 1 (Outsourced)

Scene 1

Todd: When is this glass coming?

Puro: It is coming presently, sir.

Todd: Is the volume always this low?

Puro: This is low?

Todd: Well yes, you're obviously not riding on all the callers yet. Why is the MPI so bad? At 12 minutes per incidents, we're losing money on every call.

Puro: Bad?... When I started it was 15, I brought it down to 12.

Todd: This place is a disaster, if we don't get it down to 6, I'll be stuck in India for the rest of my life.

Puro: We'll get the MPI down, no problem.

Todd: Don't say no problem, when it is a problem. If we don't get it down to 6, you'll never get a promotion and you'll never get to marry what her face.

147

Puro: Who's face, sir?

Todd: Your girlfriend, Bagy Swami, whatever her name is.

Puro: Everyone, please work harder, faster. OK?

Scene 2

Todd: Before everyone takes off, I just...I like to call a little meeting. I wanna apology to all of you, especially Asha. She was right. I'd need to learn about India.

Puro: Sir, there's no need to...

Todd: No, wait. Let me finish please. Our first mistake, is trying to run this, like an American office. So I wanna ask you...How can we do things differently? What would make your work day a more positive experience, Yes, Sanjay?

Sanjay: Sir... may I bring in my family pictures, for my desk?

Todd: Yes, bring pictures of them all. I wanna see the whole family. What else? Krishna?

Krishna: Sir, may I bring murti's for my desk?

Todd: Murti's? Absolutely, whatever those are. I want...anyone can bring whatever they want to make this space their own, as long as it does not get in the way of work. Maduri?

Maduri: Sir... Puro said that, we must wear only western clothes to do western business.

Todd: Wear whatever you want. What is your good name?

Rani: I'm Rani, sir. Sir, would it be possible, to get a discount on Western Novelty products?

Todd: Is there something unparticular you were interested in?

Rani: Sir, number D100... astrology placemats.

Todd: You want those cheesy things? I'm sure... I could get you a set for free. Ah... yes?

Female worker: What about the ceramic basket?

Todd: You guys want this stuff? You like the Western you're selling?

All the staff: Yea... yea.

Todd: Alright... alright, here is what we'll do. I'll call the Company, and I'll ask them to ship us a collection of the most popular items in the catalogue. Whoever improves their MPI the most, on a given day, can get their pick in merchandise. Alright, great job everyone. Thank you.

Todd: What is that?

Puro: Massala, rock salt, cumin, chili pepper, make it better. Nice?

Todd: Oh wow! OK.

Puro: You know when I was young, Holy was the favorite day of the year. I used to await it eagerly.

Todd: For me, it was Halloween. You know Halloween? The costumes? My mom used to make these great homemade costumes... It's funny, I should think about my parents.

Puro: You miss them? Of course.

Todd: When I'm home, I don't miss them at all.

Puro: Do you see them?

Todd: Not much, hardly ever.

Puro: You don't live with your parents?

Todd: No...No, they live in Yakima... Which is about 2 hours away.

Puro: But you see them every week?

Todd: No, a few times a year.

Puro: But why? They're so close.

Todd: I don't know.

Puro: Some things I don't understand about American life. You don't live with your parents... Strange. Another thing... you hate your boss, and you don't like this country, hmm? Why not choose something else... hmm?

Todd: I don't know how to explain it. In my world, it just make sense to work your ass off... and go into credit card debt, so you can have that 50 inch plasma...

Puro: You like the HDSI or the Digiblack? Which one?

Todd: They're both good.

Sanjay: Todd sir, that's my family.

Todd: That's impressive. Asha... could you come here please? Ok, here's the deal... you're the best we have, and I've seen you giving advice to the others. After I leave, Puro's going to need an assistant-manager. Now we have to get the MPI to 6,0. Can you help us?

Asha: Of course.

Puro: You think... she can do it?

Todd: I think Asha can do anything. Congratulation on your promotion. You only have to step in on calls, when someone is really in trouble.Puro, you wanna, get her started?

Puro: You know about this?

Asha: Yes, sir.

Todd: Western Novelty, Gharapuri.

Dave: What the hell is wrong with you, Todd? You trying to bankrupt us?

Todd: What are you talking about? You've seen the MPI?

Dave: I'm talking about this request to ship hundred of our products to India. The agents can see the products online. They don't need to fondle them.

Todd: Actually they do, it's an incentive. They need to understand what they're selling.

Dave: So promise them this time. Alright. The freight got held up by a shipping delay at customs. You've got to think bottom line.

Todd: I am... That's why I wanna introduce our products to a potentially new market of over a billion people. Are you there?

Dave: I'll overnight it to you.

Todd: It's working.

Puro: Your intended program is a very good idea, sir. I'm learning so much from you.

Todd: I can't believe you're so excited about these tacky stuff.

Puro: Tacky? What is tacky?

Unit 6 – Clip 2 (Pushing Hands)

Robert: Martha, it's Robert Just to let you know to keep an eye peeled for the first reviews of your breathlessly awaited first novel. Word is, the Times is going to rave, rave, rave. Talk to you soon.

Martha: Thanks.

Linda: You look like shit. Where's Grandpa? He's so cute with the headphones on. Hi Grandpa!

Martha: No, Linda.

Linda: Hi! Do you think he remembers me? Come on, it's a steal. You've got to see it. You'll have your own room to write in. Grandpa can be out in the back chopping bricks or whatever he does out there. You'd never even know he existed.

Martha: I wish he didn't.

Linda: God, he's really getting you down.

Martha: From the way Alex has acted for the last seven years you'd have thought he didn't have a father. And then boom, a month ago this shows up on the doorstep I haven't written a word since.

Linda: Well, Alex has got to get him out of here.

Martha: It's not that simple with Alex and frankly we can't afford to get him his own place, let alone buy a mansion.

Linda: Of course you can, especially if your mother's offer is still good.

Martha: Alex will never accept money from her, you know that.

Linda: Work on him! For God sakes, Martha, you have a lot to learn about men.

Martha: And you have a lot to learn about husbands. Sorry.

Linda: It's okay. I'm getting a dog.

Unit 7 – Clip 1 (My Fair Lady)

Scene 1

Eliza: And you wouldn't go off without paying, either. Two bunches of violets trod in the mud.

Gentleman: Good heavens.

Old lady: Sir, is there any sign of it stopping?

Gentleman: I'm afraid not. It's worse than before.

Old lady: Oh, dear.

Eliza: If it's worse, it's a sign it's nearly over. Cheer up, captain. Buy a flower off a poor girl.

Gentleman: I'm sorry, I haven't any change.

Eliza: Oh, I can change half a crown. Here, take this for tuppence.

Gentleman: I told you, I'm awfully sorry, I haven't – Oh, wait a minute. Oh, yes. Here's three hapence, if that's any use to you.

Eliza: Thank you, sir.

Man: Here, you be careful. Better give him a flower for it. There is a bloke here behind that pillar taking down every blessed word you're saying.

Eliza: I ain't done nothing wrong by speaking to the gentleman. I've a right to sell flowers if I keep off the curb. I'm a respectable girl, so help me. I never spoke to him except to ask him to buy a flower off me.

Man One: Don't start. What's all the noise?

Man Two: There's a tec taking her down.

Eliza: I'm making an honest living.

Man Two: Who's doing all that shouting? Where is it coming from?

Eliza: Well...Oh, sir, don't let him charge me. They don't know what it means to me. They'll take away me character and drive me on the streets for speaking to gentlemen.

Higgins: There, there, there. Who's hurting you, you silly girl? What you take me for?

Eliza: On my Bible oath, I never spoke a word.

Higgins: Shut up. Do I look like a policeman?

Eliza: Then what did you take down my words for? How do I know you took me down right? You just show me what you wrote about me. Oh. What's that? That ain't proper writing. I can't read it.

Higgins: I can. "I say, captain, now buy a flower off a poor girl."

Eliza: Oh, it's because I called him "captain." Oh, I meant no harm. Sir, don't let him lay a charge against me for a word like that.

Man One: I'll make no charge. Really, sir, if you are a detective, you needn't begin protecting me against molestation from young women until I ask you. Anyone could tell the girl meant no harm.

Man Two: He ain't a tec. He's a gentleman. Look at his boots.

Higgins: How are all your people down at Selsey?

Man Two: Who told you my people come from Selsey?

Higgins: Never mind. They do. How do you come to be up so far east? You were born in Lisson Grove.

Eliza: Oh, what harm is there my leaving Lisson Grove? It weren't fit for a pig to live in and I had to pay 4 and 6 a week.

Higgins: Live where you like, but stop that noise.

Man One: Come, come, he can't touch you. You've a right to live where you please.

Eliza: I'm a good girl, I am. -Yes, yes, yes.

Man Three: Where do I come from?

Higgins: Hoxton.

Man Three: Well, who said I didn't? Blimey, you know everything, you do.

Old lady: You, sir, do you think you could find me a taxi?

Higgins: I don't know whether you've noticed, but it's stopped raining. You can get a motor bus to Hampton Court. Well, that's where you live, isn't it?

Old lady: What impertinence.

Man Two: Hey, tell him where he comes from, you wanna go fortune-telling.

Higgins: Cheltenham, Harrow, Cambridge and, uh, India?

Man One: Quite right.

Man Two: Blimey, he ain't a tec, he's a blooming busybody.

Man One: If I may ask, sir, do you do this sort of thing for a living at a music hall?

Higgins: Well, I have thought of it. Perhaps I will one day.

Eliza: He's no gentleman. He ain't, to interfere with a poor girl.

Man One: How do you do it, may I ask?

Higgins: Simple phonetics. The science of speech. That's my profession, also my hobby. Anyone can spot an Irishman or a Yorkshireman by his brogue, but I can place a man within six miles. I can place him within two miles in London. Sometimes within two streets.

Eliza: Ought to be ashamed of himself, unmanly coward.

Man One: Is there a living in that?

Higgins: Oh, yes, quite a fat one.

Eliza: Let him mind his own business and leave a poor girl.

Higgins: Woman! Cease this detestable boohooing instantly or else seek the shelter of some other place of worship.

Eliza: I have a right to be here if I like, same as you.

Higgins: Woman who utters such disgusting and depressing noises has no right to be anywhere. no right to live. Remember that you're a human being with a soul and the divine gift of articulate speech, that your native language is the language of Shakespeare and Milton and the Bible. Don't sit there crooning like a bilious pigeon.

Eliza: Ow!

Higgins: Look at her. A prisoner of the gutters. Condemned by every syllable She utters. By right She should be taken out and hung. For the cold-blooded murder Of the English tongue.

Eliza: Ow!

Higgins: Heavens! What a sound!

Scene 2

Higgins: All right, Eliza, say it again.

Eliza: [in cockney accent] "The rain in Spain stays mainly in the plain."

Higgins: The rain in Spain stays mainly in the plain.

Eliza: Didn't I say that?

Higgins: No, Eliza, you didn't "say" that. You didn't even say that. Every night before you get into bed, where you used to say your prayers, I want you to say, "The rain in Spain stays mainly in the plain," 50 times. You'll get much further with the Lord if you learn not to offend his ears. Now for your H's. Pickering, this is going to be ghastly.

Pickering: Control yourself, Higgins. Give the girl a chance.

Higgins: Oh, well, I suppose you can't expect her to get it right the first time. Come here, Eliza, and watch closely. Now. You see that flame? Every time you pronounce the letter H correctly, the flame will waver. And every time you drop your H, the flame will remain stationary. That's how you'll know if you've done it correctly. In time, your ear will hear the difference. See it better in the mirror. Now, listen carefully. In Hartford, Hereford and Hampshire, hurricanes hardly ever happen. Now, repeat that after me. In Hartford, Hereford and Hampshire hurricanes hardly ever happen.

Eliza: [in cockney accent] "In Hartford, Hereford and Hampshire, hurricanes hardly ever happen."

Higgins: Oh, no, no, no. Have you no ear at all?

Eliza: Should I do it over?

Higgins: No, please. Start from the very beginning. Just do this. Go: Ha, ha, ha.

Eliza: Ha, ha, ha.

Higgins: Go on, go on, go on.

Eliza: Ha, ha, ha.

Higgins: Does the same thing hold true in India, Pickering? Is it truly a habit to them, their dropping a letter like the letter H, using it where it doesn't belong, like "hever" instead of "ever"? Why is it that slavs, when they learn English, have a tendency to do it with G's? They say "linger" instead of "linger".

Eliza: Ha, ha, ha.

Higgins: And then they turn right around and say "singer" instead of "singer". I've noticed the slavs using it where it isn't needed, they learn English, they have to do it with their G's.

Pickering: The girl, Higgins.

Higgins: Go on, go on, go on. Go on.

Eliza: Ha, ha, ha.

Servants [sing]**:** Poor Professor Higgins. Poor Professor Higgins. Night and day he slaves away. Oh, poor Professor Higgins. All day long on his feet, up and down until he's numb. Doesn't rest. Doesn't eat. Doesn't touch a crumb.

Higgins: Again, Eliza. How kind of you to let me come.

Eliza: [in cockney accent] How kind of you to let me come.

Higgins: No, kind of you. Kind of you. Kind. How kind of you to let me come.

Eliza: How kind of you to let me come.

Higgins: No, no. Kind of you. Kind of you. It's like "cup of tea", kind of you. Cup of tea. Say "cup of tea".

Eliza: Cup of tea.

Higgins: No, no. A cup of tea. It's awfully good cake. This. I wonder where Mrs. Pearce gets it.

Pickering: Mm. First rate. And those strawberry tarts are delicious. Did you try the plain cake?

Higgins: Try it again. Did you try the – ? Pickering! Again, Eliza.

Eliza: [in cockney accent] Cup of tea.

Higgins: Oh, no. Can't you hear the difference? Look, put your tongue forward until it squeezes on the top of your lower teeth. And then say "cup".

Eliza: Cup.

Higgins: Then say "of".

Eliza: Of.

Higgins: Then say, "cup, cup, cup, of, of, of".

Eliza: Cup, cup, cup, of, of, of.

Higgins & Eliza: Cup, cup, cup, of, of, of. Cup, cup –

Eliza: Of, of –

Pickering: By Jove, Higgins, that was a glorious tea. Why don't you finish that last strawberry tart? I couldn't eat another thing.

Higgins: Oh, I couldn't touch it.

Pickering: Shame to waste it.

Higgins: Oh, it won't be wasted. I know somebody who's immensely fond of strawberry tarts.

Eliza: Ow!

Servants [sing]: Poor Professor Higgins. Poor Professor Higgins. On he plods against all odds. Oh, poor Professor Higgins. nine p.m., ten p.m., on through midnight every night. One a.m. Two a.m.

Higgins: Three, four, five, six marbles. Now, I want you to read this and I want you to enunciate every word just as if the marbles were not in your mouth. With blackest moss the flower-pots were thickly crusted, one and all. Each word clear as a bell.

Eliza: [mumbling] With blackest moss the flower-pots... I can't. I can't.

Pickering: I say, Higgins, are those pebbles really necessary?

Higgins: If they were necessary for Demosthenes, they are necessary for Eliza Doolittle. Go on, Eliza.

Eliza: [mumbling] With blackest moss the flower-pots...

Scene 3

Higgins: Mother, the most confounded thing. Do you...? You?

Eliza: Good afternoon, Professor Higgins. Are you quite well?

Higgins: Am I – ?

Eliza: Of course you are. You are never ill. Would you care for some tea?

Higgins: Don't you dare try that game on me. I taught it to you. Now, get up and come home and stop being a fool. You've caused me enough trouble.

Mrs. Higgins: Very nicely put indeed, Henry. No woman could resist such an invitation.

Higgins: How did this baggage get here in the first place?

Mrs. Higgins: Eliza came to see me this morning and I was delighted to have her. And if you don't promise to behave, I must ask you to leave.

Higgins: You mean to say I'm to put on my Sunday manners for this thing that I created out of the squashed cabbage leaves of Covent Garden?

Mrs. Higgins: That's precisely what I mean.

Higgins: Well, I'll see her damned first.

Mrs. Higgins: However, did you learn good manners with my son around?

Eliza: It was very difficult. I should never have known how ladies and gentlemen behave if it hadn't been for Colonel Pickering. He always showed me that he felt and thought about me as if I were something better than a common flower girl. You see, Mrs. Higgins, apart from the things one can pick up, the difference between a lady and a flower girl is not how she behaves, but how she is treated. I shall always be a flower girl to Professor Higgins because he always treats me as a flower girl and always will. But I know I shall always be a lady to Colonel Pickering because he always treats me as a lady and always will.

Mrs. Higgins: Henry, don't grind your teeth.

Servant: The bishop is here, madam. Shall I show him into the garden?

Mrs. Higgins: The bishop and the professor? Good heavens, no. I should be excommunicated. I'll see him in the library. Eliza, if my son starts breaking up things, I give you full permission to have him evicted. Henry, dear, I suggest you stick to two subjects: the weather and your health.

Higgins: Well, you've had a bit of your own back, as you call it. Have you had enough and are you going to be reasonable or do you want any more?

Eliza: You want me back only to pick up your slippers and put up with your tempers and fetch and carry for you.

Higgins: I didn't say I wanted you back at all.

Eliza: Oh, indeed? Then what are we talking about?

Higgins: Well, about you, not about me. If you come back, you'll be treated as you've always been treated. I can't change my nature. I don't intend to change my manners. My manners are exactly the same as Colonel Pickering's.

Eliza: That's not true. He treats a flower girl as if she were a duchess.

Higgins: Well, I treat a duchess as if she was a flower girl.

Eliza: Oh, I see. The same to everybody.

Higgins: Just so. You see, the great secret, Eliza, is not a question of good manners or bad manners or any particular sort of manners, but having the same manner for all human souls. The question is not whether I treat you rudely, whether you've ever heard me treat anyone else better.

Eliza: I don't care how you treat me. I don't mind your swearing at me. I shouldn't mind a black eye. I've had one before this. But I won't be passed over.

Higgins: Well, then get out of my way, for I won't stop for you. You talk about me as though I was a motor bus.

Eliza: So you are a motor bus. All bounce and go and no consideration for anybody. But I can get along without you. Don't you think I can't.

Higgins: I know you can. I told you you could. You've never wondered, I suppose whether I could get along without you.

Eliza: Don't you try to get around me. You'll have to.

Higgins: So I can, without you or any soul on earth. I shall miss you, Eliza. I've learned something from your idiotic notions. I confess that, humbly and gratefully.

Unit 7 – Clip 2 (Lie to Me)

Dr. Gillian Foster: Tell us why you think you're here, James.

James: I was out for a run, and the police thought I was running from them. So they arrested me.

Lightman: I heard you made your school's track team.

James: I didn't make it. They don't have tryouts.

Lightman: What was your best race this year?

James: I don't know. Um, probably against Jefferson last week. Why?

Lightman: I ran hurdles myself, 110 meters. How'd your quads feel during the race?

James: Good, I guess.

Lightman: And what about on your run the night you were arrested?

James: I felt fine.

Dr. Gillian Foster: Your teacher Ms. McCartney was found dead in her home. Have you ever been to her house before?

James: No, I've never been to her house before.

Dr. Gillian Foster: Ms. McCartney thought that you should be held back a year because she felt you were having some problems with your classmates.

James: What? I didn't want to get held back.

Lightman: How'd you feel when you found out she was dead?

James : I prayed for her soul. I can't know God's plan, but I didn't kill her.

Dr. Gillian Foster: Hurdles?

Lightman: Could have run hurdles?

Dr. Gillian Foster: Please.

Policeman: So you got a sense of his intent?

Lightman: When I asked James about his best race, he broke eye contact in order to remember and answer truthfully. And when I asked him about his run the night of the murder, he never broke eye contact. He wasn't recalling a memory. He was lying.

Policeman: But I thought most people avoid eye contact when they're lying.

Lightman: No, it's a myth. And quite often, they make more eye contact. They need to watch, see if you believe their lies.

Dr. Gillian Foster: The content analysis would suggest that James has been to Ms. McCartney's house before. Question: "Have you ever been to her house?" Answer: "No, I have never been to her house." Rigid repetition like that is typical of a lie.

Policeman: Okay, so you'll tell the mayor's office the murder was premeditated?

Lightman: Looks that way. But when I asked him about his teacher's death, what we saw was this: oblique eyebrows.

Dr. Gillian Foster: Sadness. Why would he be hiding sadness for her?

Policeman: Looks like guilt to me.

Lightman: It's possible he didn't mean to kill his teacher.

Policeman: Excuse me?

Lightman: Could have been an accident.

Policeman: Okay. Okay, I indulged the mayor's office in letting you talk to the kid, but now you're just making wild guesses that have no basis in hard evidence. This was no accident. And personally, I think what you do is a joke. It's a friggin' carnival act.

Lightman: Oh, yeah, yeah, I get that a lot. You know, a moment ago, I saw you smile at your colleague, flash her a glance, then shift your gaze. She responded by raising her chin boss, revealing deep embarrassment.

Dr. Gillian Foster: Cal...?

Lightman: I'll take another wild guess: you two had a fling. She doesn't want a repeat performance because, you know, what with your wife and all. But you won't move on. Oh, no, no. Keep your fingers off your nose. Men have erectile tissue there. Itches when they're hiding something.

Unit 7 – Exercise (Rush Hour 3)

Carter: All right, listen up! I need everyone's attention. I'm Detective Carter, this is Inspector Lee. We need to see Soo Yung's locker right now.

Kungfu Trainer: No one's allowed in the back without the Master Yu's permission.

Carter: Maybe you didn't hear me. We need to see that locker.

Kungfu Trainer: I'm sorry.

Lee: Wait, Carter.

Carter: Lee, I got this. Hey! Heh heh, kids, Listen. Violence will solve nothin'. Now, as the Chinese say, all great battles are won without fightin'.

Lee: Sorry.

Carter: OK?

Lee: I don't know him.

Carter: Now, let's just calm down and put this...

Martial Arts trainers(children): Haa!

Carter: Ow! God da... OK... I tried talkin'. Hoo! Now I'm about to beat the puberty out of

Intercultural Communication in Movies

y'all. You ain't gonna see it comin'. You ain't gonna see it comin', come on! Waaa! Whoo! Runnin' for your lives. About time y'all showed some respect around here. Huh?

Lee: Carter, wait for the Master Yu.

Carter: Whoa! Damn! Heh, I'm sorry, man. I thought this was the bathroom. Sorry.

Kungfu Trainer: Lee, I got a big problem, man. This boy's on steroids. He got a head like Barry Bonds.

Lee: Oh, no.

Kungfu Trainer: Come on, man.

Carter: Aaaah! Aaaaah! Ah!

Lee: Carter, are you OK?

Carter: Lee, Lee, get him, Lee!

Kungfu Trainer: Ooh!

Carter: Ahhh! Ah! Ah!

Lee: Urgh!

Carter: Lee, let's get the hell outta... Aah! My bunions! Yah! Hyah! Mm! Ungh! Grr! Rargh! Ha ha ha. Urgh! Whoo! Oh! Aaaah! Come on, man, let me go. I love Chinese people!

Kungfu Trainer: Aaaah!

Lee: Wait. I don't...

Kungfu Trainer: Ah!

Lee: Urgh!

Carter: How do you say "surrender" in Chinese?

Kungfu Trainer: Aaaah!

Carter: OK. I'm about to slice you up like a giant California roll! Like a giant California roll! Raaah! Ooh! Ooh! Ooh!

Kungfu Trainer: Ha ha ha. Funny black man.

Carter: Ooh... Oh! Shit! I'm not playin, no more.

Martial Arts trainers (children): Ahh!

Kungfu Trainer: Aaah!

Carter: Lee, let go!

Lee: Carter!

Martial Arts trainers (children): Grrrrr!

Lee: Down! Put us down!

Carter: Let me down! I'm sorry!

Kungfu Trainer: Aaaaah!

Carter: I'm sorry, man! How the hell did we get in this mess? Ugh!

Lee: Agh!

Master Yu: May I help you?

Carter: We'll be asking the questions, old man. Who are you?

Master Yu: Yu.

Carter: No, not me. You.

Master Yu: Yes, I am Yu.

Carter: Just answer the damn questions. Who are you?

Master Yu: I have told you.

Carter: Are you deaf?

Master Yu: No, Yu is blind.

Carter: I'm not blind, you blind.

Master Yu: That is what I just said.

Carter: You just said what?

Master Yu: I did not say what, I said Yu.

Carter: That's what I'm asking you.

Master Yu: And Yu is answering.

Carter: Shut up! You!

Master Yu: Yes?

Carter: Not you, him! What's your name?

Trainer Mi: Mi.

Carter: Yes, you!

Trainer Mi: I am Mi.

Master Yu: He is Mi, and I am Yu.

Carter: And I'm about to whup your old ass, man, 'cause I'm sick of playin' games! You, me, everybody's ass around here! Him!

Lee: Carter, Carter.

Carter: I'm-a kick his ass. I'm sick of this.

Lee: Carter, let me handle this.

Carter: Lee. No, Lee. No!

Lee: Carter!

Unit 8 – Clip 1 (Gung Ho)

Japanese woman: You could not tell?

Stevenson: Well, you know, I'm thinking to myself. This tastes a little bit like meatloaf, but it's too delicious to be meatloaf. In fact, Audrey leaned over and said to me, "Honey, can I have some of yours?" What, am I gonna say no? I love her, I'm gonna give it to her. There you are. Whoops!

Audrey: Thanks.

Stevenson: Sure.

Japanese woman: Are we ready for dessert?

Stevenson: Oh, boy, I know I am.

Kazihiro: In a few minutes. Right now, we have some business to discuss.

(All the Japanese wives leave.)

Stevenson: Hey, Audrey.

Audrey: What?

Stevenson: Why don't you... you know... leave?

Audrey: Actually, I'm interested in what's going on at the plant. Nobody minds if I stay, right?

See.

Kazihiro: Mr. Stevenson... How do you think things are going at the factory?

Stevenson: Honestly, Katz?

Kazihiro: Yes, please.

Stevenson: Not too well. See, you're stateside now. But you still act like Yokohama mamas. No offence.

Kazihiro: None taken.

Stevenson: Can I be frank for a second? I've heard a lot of talk about how good the Japanese businessmen are. Frankly... I'm sorry, I don't get it. I don't see it, I'm not impressed. Not one iota.

Kazihiro: You're fired.

Stevenson: What? You can't fire me!

Kazihiro: You'll go back on the line with the others.

Stevenson: Wait a minute. Explain this to me. Why?

Kazihiro: I do not understand American workers. They come 5 minutes later, leave 2 minutes earlier, stay home when they are sick. They put themselves above company. You seem to feel the same way as they do.

Stevenson: Ok, but explain something to me. When this was an American factory, production was 10% higher than now.

Kazihiro: Ten per cent? In Japan, production in same size factory is 40% higher.

Sakamoto: With superior quality.

Stevenson: Impossible. How can you work so fast?

Kazihiro: Japanese worker is very loyal. He's very proud when company does well. He's ashamed when it does poorly.

Sakamoto: Like now.

Kazihiro: In Japan, when production lags, worker stays longer in factory.

Stevenson: OK, overtime. Time-and-a-half is standard.

Kazihiro: They do not do it for pay. They do it for company.

Stevenson: Yeah, but that's there, this is here.

Audrey: Gentlemen, this is an American factory. They won't go for that.

Kazihiro: Is that how you feel, that they'll never go for it?

Stevenson: There's one guy who can get 'em to go for it, and you're looking at him.

Kazihiro: You can change their attitude?

Stevenson: If I can't, nobody can.

Audrey: Nobody can.

Stevenson: Hey, would you shut up? Goddamn. OK. You guys have a problem, right? I'm the answer man. I can work this out and make everybody happy, I always have. Come on, you gotta give me a shot.

Kazihiro: All right. We make no more changes for now.

Stevenson: There you go. Yeah. Hey, hon...

(Stevenson and Audrey are in the car.)

Stevenson: Hey, hon... wanna stop off and get some ice cream? Haagen-Dazs.

Audrey: Eat shit and die.

Stevenson: You having your period?

Audrey: Stop the car. How could you do that to me? Telling me to shut up in front of all those people!

Stevenson: I'm dealing with a delicate situation.

Audrey: So, what are you trying to do?

Stevenson: I'm trying to save jobs.

Audrey: The only job I heard being threatened was yours.

Stevenson: They picked me for this job. I didn't ask for it. They need me.

Audrey: They need to know where things stand. They don't need a guy who's trying to do it all by himself.

Stevenson: It'd be pretty nice to have a girlfriend who's a little bit supportive of me.

Audrey: Supportive? You mean some chick who'll go along with everything you say. A parrot with tits.

Stevenson: How can you bring Heather into this?

Audrey: I wasn't thinking of Heather. But apparently you were.

Stevenson: Oh, Audrey, come on. Come on, Audrey!

Unit 8 – Clip 2 (English Vinglish)

Man: This lady is so rude... must be having a bad day.

Customer One: Can I get a regular coffee... and a blueberry muffin.

Clerk: Here's your receipt... please pick up your food over there...

Customer: Okay... have a nice day.

Clerk: Next! How you were doing today?

Shashi: I want...

Clerk: I asked how you were doing today.

Shashi: Doing... I'm doing... I'm doing...

Clerk: You can't take all that time I got a long line here.

Shashi: Sorry... what to eat?

Clerk: Are you kidding me right now...please hurry up, lady.

Shashi: Vegetarian...

Clerk: Vegetarian is fine... what do you want to eat?

Shashi: Only vegetarian...

Clerk: A bagel... a wrap... a sandwich?

Shashi: Sandwich.

Clerk: And what kind of filling do you want inside? Do you want cheese... tomatoes... lettuce? Lady... you're holding up my line... this is not rocket science Cheese?

Shashi: Yes... cheese...

Clerk: Yes to cheese! Anything to drink?

Shashi: Water...

Clerk: Still or sparkling?

Shashi: Only water.

Clerk: Still or sparkling?

Shashi: Coffee...?

Clerk: Americana'? Cappuccino? Latte?

Customer Two: Lady... I ain't got all day...

Clerk: Americana'? Cappuccino? Latte?

Shashi: Nescoffee.

Clerk: What?

Shashi: Nescoffee.

Clerk: Yes, we have nice coffee... we have the best coffee in Manhattan. I'll just give you an Americana. Small or medium?

Shashi: Small.

Clerk: Small. Is that it? $10.20.

Shashi: 10 dollars...

Clerk: Hello... the least you could do is say thank you...!

Shashi: Sorry... thank you...

Customer Two: Stupid idiot!

Shashi: Sorry...

Clerk: I am not cleaning that up!

Customer Three: Don't bother... What a stupid woman!

Scene 2

Laurent: I learn English...

David: Good good! Thank you, Laurent... And now the lady in the gorgeous sari... Sit...

Shashi: Sit and talk? I Shashi... from the India.

David: From India...

Shashi: Yes sir... from the India...

David: No Shashi... not from "the" India... from India! And what do you do, Shashi?

Shashi: I also cooking... cooking... selling...

David: Are you in the catering business?

Shashi: Small business... in house only... making snacks... ladoo!

David: Ladoo...?

Shashi: Ladoo... round round...

Lama: It's a sweet...

David: We have an entrepreneur in the class! Entrepreneur... is a person who runs his or her own business. Shashi... you are an entrepreneur!

Classmates: Is that a word or a poem? What kind of a language is this! Entre... pre... near. Entrepreneur!

Scene 3

Meera: Shashi Aunty... your turn.

Guests: Yes... come on, Aunty.

Shashi's husband: Sorry... my wife's English is... not very good, so...

Shashi: May I? Meera... Kevin... this marriage is a... Oops, sorry... I started in Hindi. This marriage is a beautiful thing. It is the most special friendship... friendship of two people who are equal. Life is a long journey. Meera, sometimes you will feel you are less. Kevin, sometimes you will also feel you are less than Meera. Try to help each other to feel equal. It will be nice. Sometimes... married couple don't even know how the other is feeling. So... how they will help the other? It means marriage is finished? No. That is the time you have to help yourself. Nobody can help you better than you. If you do that... you will return back feeling equal, your friendship will return back... your life will be beautiful. Meera... Kevin... maybe you'll very busy... but have family... son... daughter... in this big world... your small little world. It will make you feel so good. Family... family can never be... never be judgemental! Family will never... put you down... will never make you feel small. Family is the only one who will never laugh at your weaknesses. Family is the only place where you will always get love and respect. That's all Meera and Kevin... I wish you all the best. Thank you.

Appendix IV   Keys to Exercises

Unit 1

Cultural Comprehension

Decide whether the following statements are true or false according to what you read.

1. F   2. F   3. F   4. T   5. T

Task 1: Fill in the blanks to the following lines spoken in the movie clips you just watched.

1. procedure   2. suspended   3. sealed   4. detain   5. represents   6. resisted

Task 2: Watch the movie clip for a second time and decide whether the following statements are true or false.

1. F   2. F   3. F   4. T   5. F   6. F

Case 1

Reflection

1. Why do you think Matthew is upset?

Answer: Matthew does not like tea, and he tried to communicate that to Mrs. Wang. However, Mrs. Wang continues to insist that he drinks tea. Matthew feels obligated to drink the tea because he does not want to make Mrs. Wang feel bad for preparing it. He thinks if he doesn't drink the tea, he is wasting both the tea and Mrs. Wang's time and energy. He drinks the tea, though it is very difficult. Just when he is about to finish the tea, though, Mrs. Wang pours him some more. Again, Matthew tries to refuse, but Mrs. Wang again disregards him. Matthew smiles, trying to be polite, but he is even more upset because he now has to drink even more. After this repeats itself a third time, Matthew feels like Mrs. Wang is being very rude for continuing to force him to drink the tea that he clearly said he doesn't want to drink.

2. What is Matthew trying to communicate with his words and body language? How does Mrs. Wang interpret his words and body language?

Answer: When Matthew says, "No, thank you," he literally means that he doesn't want to drink any tea. Again, when he says, "I have enough," he literally means that he has enough tea and doesn't want any more. Mrs. Wang, however, interprets his refusal for tea as mere politeness. She thinks "No" means "Yes." Matthew drinks the tea, not because he enjoys it but because he thinks Mrs. Wang will feel offended if he does not drink it. By drinking it, he wants to communicate his gratitude for the time and energy she spent to prepare it. He smiles at her in order to show politeness. When she sees him continuing to smile and drink the tea, however, she thinks he enjoys it. Here we see conflict that arises from two people trying to communicate from two very different cultural perspectives.

3. What is Mrs. Wang communicating with her words and body language? How does Matthew

interpret her words and body language?

Answer: Mrs. Wang originally asks Matthew if he would like tea, not because she is genuinely interested if he wants to drink tea or not but because she wants to be polite. To her, "Would you like some tea?" means "I am going to pour you some tea." Matthew, however, thinks she is genuinely asking him whether or not he wants to drink tea. Mrs. Wang insists on pouring Matthew more tea, even when he says he does not want any, because she wants to communicate to him that she is hospitable and cares about him. Matthew, however, interprets her insistence as her *not* caring about him because she disregarded his refusal for more tea.

Case 2

Reflection

1. What intercultural communication conflict has occurred in the example above?

Answer: The conflict involves differing cultural methods of communicating time, giving notice, and apologizing.

2. What cultural expectations does John have of Dai Tong when they decide to meet at 12:00? What kind of communication does he expect when Dai Tong does not show up by 12:00?

Answer: John, coming from an American culture that emphasizes punctuality, expects Dai Tong to arrive before 12:00. In America, arriving later than 12:00 would communicate that one is not considerate of the other person and does not consider the friendship very important. If Dai Tong knows he will arrive after 12:00, John expects him to call or send a text message to notify him. Additionally, he expects Dai Tong to apologize for being late. Failure to do so only further communicates to John that Dai Tong does not consider him a close or important friend.

3. What should John and Dai Tong do next time to avoid this communication conflict?

Answer: If they decide to meet at 12:00, John can specifically tell Dai Tong that he plans to arrive a few minutes early. This will ensure that Dai Tong knows that John expects him to arrive on time. Additionally, John can tell Dai Tong that he will send him a text message if he will be late. He can also ask Dai Tong to do the same. Again, this will ensure that Dai Tong understands that John expects to meet by 12:00. Other methods may be used, but what is important is that the expectations of both John and Dai Tong are clearly expressed and understood by both of them.

Case 3

In this clip, we see the effects of cultural superiority. At the banquet, the British businessman provoked the King and Anna, who expressed their disagreement and disdain. The British businessman thinks his own culture is more civilized, but he has forgotten that their own power to some extent is built on violence and the use of force. Rather than view one culture as more superior than another, we should view all cultures as having their own advantages and disadvantages.

III. Task-based Activities

Exercises:

1. b   2. a   3. b   4. a   5. b

Intercultural Communication in Movies
影视作品中的跨文化交际

Unit 2

Cultural Comprehension

Decide whether the following statements are true or false according to what you read.

1. T   2. F   3. T   4. T   5. F

Task 1: Fill in the blanks to the following lines spoken in the movie clips you just watched.

1. spoonful   2. bragged   3. criticized   4. insults   5. frequent   6. weeping

Task 2: Watch the movie clip for a second time and decide whether the following statements are true or false.

1. F   2. T   3. F   4. T   5. F   6. F

Case 1

Reflection

1. Why did the woman yell at Wang Li? What were the cars doing?

The cars were a funeral procession. In the U.S., after a person dies, a funeral is held at a church. After the funeral, everyone drives to the cemetery together, escorted by the police. The man and the woman that Wang Li met were the close relatives of the deceased person.

2. In what way was Wang Li assuming her culture was the same as American culture?

In China, a line of cars driving down the street together means it is a wedding procession. The bride and groom, along with the wedding guests, will drive to the restaurant together. Wang Li assumed that American culture was the same, and that the people in the first car were the bride and groom.

3. If you were in America and saw a long row of black cars, would you assume the same thing Wang Li assumed? What could you do to ensure you are interpreting this cultural practice correctly?

Before talking to the people that got out of the car, she should have asked someone else nearby to make sure she knew what the people were doing. In a new culture, if you are not absolutely sure what a specific cultural practice means, you should verify with others what it means before engaging with it.

Case 2

Reflection

1. In what way did Lisa assume Chen Na and Xiao Yu's culture was the same as her own? What problem did this lead to?

Lisa assumed that it was appropriate and necessary in Chinese culture for her to verbally thank her friends for their gift. She assumed that the more she thanked them, the more it expressed her gratitude for their kindness and friendship. Unfortunately, in Chinese culture, it is not appropriate for close friends to thank each other for small gifts. Verbally thanking someone means that you don't have a close relationship with them. In Chinese culture, you don't usually thank close friends. You only thank people you are not very familiar with. This led Chen Na and Xiao Yu to believe that Lisa did not consider them her close friends.

2. In what way did Chen Na and Xiao Yu assume that Lisa's culture was the same as their own?

What problem did this lead to?

Chen Na and Xiao Yu assumed that Americans pay for their own meals, as well as their guests' meals, at their own birthday parties, as is the custom in China. Unfortunately, in America, the guests should pay for the meal of the person celebrating the birthday. Since Chen Na and Xiao Yu did not offer to pay, Lisa had to pay, causing her to think that Chen Na and Xiao Yu were just using her to get a free meal and were not really her friends.

3. How could these girls avoid a similar conflict in the future?

The girls should have thoroughly researched and asked about each others' cultural customs beforehand. If the girls had all clearly understood each others' cultural expectations, they could have avoided miscommunication.

Case3

Reflection

This clip reflects the different culture value orientation on family. Firstly, western and eastern people have different family concepts, in the West, people usually have the nuclear family, which includes parents and children; while in the East, people prefer living with their extended family, which includes parents, children and grandparents. This can explain why Emma is so surprised about the big Chinese family. Secondly, it is very common in eastern countries for grandparents to babysit their grandchildren without being paid, while if eastern grandparents do that, they will be paid by their children as a reward for their work.

III. Task-based Activities

Exercises:

1. b   2. a   3. a   4. b   5. b

Assignment

Presentation 1

Please use the "The Lewis Model" to determine which country and what kind of characteristics belong to the certain type by using "√" and filling in the blanks.

Nation	Linear-active	Multi-active	Reactive
USA	√		
UK	√		
Canada	√	√	
Australia	√	√	
China			√
Republic of Korea			√
Italy		√	
Focus	**Results**	**Relationship**	**Degree of response**
Politeness	Mostly	Sometimes	Always
Challenge	Logical	Emotional	Indirect
Emotion	Ignored	Expressed	Suppressed
Communication	Written	Verbal	Face-to-face
Body language	Restrained	Open	Subtle

Intercultural Communication in Movies
影视作品中的跨文化交际

Linear-actives seem to inhabit cooler countries, while multi-actives inhabit hotter climates, as reflected in their greater emotional attentiveness. The USA and UK are mostly linear-active. Canada lies between linear-active and reactive. Australia lies between linear-active and multi-active. European countries mostly range between linear-active and multi-active, with Northern Europeans tending to be mostly linear-active, but with reactive leanings.

Presentation 2

Just like an iceberg, some cultural aspects are visible, while many are invisible. Think of cultures you've visited or learned about. Fill in the following blanks with at least five words and present them to the class, explaining each word.

Visible cultural characteristics	*Invisible cultural characteristics*
artifacts	ethical codes
architecture	

Visible cultural characteristics include behaviors and practices: clothing, dance, language, physical features, food, music, architecture, gestures, greetings, devotional practices and more. Invisible cultural factors include perceptions, attitudes, values and beliefs: spiritual beliefs, worldviews, rules of relationships, approach to the family, motivations, tolerance for change, attitudes to rules, communication styles, modes of thinking, comfort with risk, separation between public and private, gender differences and more. The visible elements of a culture are driven and shaped by the invisible elements of the culture.

Unit 3

Cultural Comprehension

Decide whether the following statements are true or false according to what you read.

1. T   2. T   3. T   4. T   5. F

Task 1: Fill in the blanks to the following lines spoken in the movie clips you just watched.

1. not even   2. protect   3. authorized   4. you're supposed to   5. laugh at   6. poured

Task 2: Watch the movie clip for a second time and decide whether the following statements are true or false.

1. F   2. F   3. T   4. T   5. F   6. F

Case 1

1. How did James expect his students to act in class? How does this reflect the Western value orientations of human activity, social relations, and the relationship of man and nature?

James expected his students to ask questions if they didn't understand something. He also expected his students to talk to him when he asked them questions. These expectations are reflected by the Western value orientation of human activity because Americans typically emphasize "doing". Americans believe one must "do" in order to get success. In class, this means that students must often ask questions and respond to the teacher's questions if they are to be successful. The Western value orientation of man conquering nature also means that James expects students to be active, not passive, in class. They cannot expect "nature" to magically put English knowledge into their brains. They must "conquer" English by participating in class and asking questions in order to learn it. Moreover, the Western view of social relations means that James views the students as each person participating in the class as an individual. Each student has the individual responsibility to participate. When the students do not do this, James thinks either the students are failing or he is failing as a teacher.

2. Was James right about why the students acted the way they did? Why did they act like they did? How do their actions reflect the Eastern value orientations of human activity, social relations, and the relationship of man and nature?

No, James was not right about why the students acted like they did. The students were simply reflecting the Eastern value orientations. In social relations, Chinese people tend to emphasize hierarchy or lineality. They have a high view of leaders, which means they view James very highly (even though James thinks they don't respect him). As a result, they do not see themselves as active participants in English class, but rather see James as the only active participant. While Westerners see students as "actors" and teachers as "directors", Chinese see students as the "audience" and the teacher as the "actor". James' students think it's his job to teach and their job to listen. So, when James expects them to participate, they do not feel comfortable. Moreover, Chinese do not emphasize "doing" as Americans, but rather "being". For most of the students, it is enough that they are simply "being" English students. They do not see a need for "doing" too much. Similarly, Chinese do not have the Western view of man conquering nature. They see man's duty as living in harmony with nature. As a result, they tend to be more passive in class. If they simply come to class and listen, they think they will be able to absorb English knowledge without having to actively ask or answer questions in class.

3. What can James do to become a more effective English teacher in China? What can the students do to help him?

James can clearly communicate his expectations to the class so that the students know how they should act. The students can help him by adopting a more Western approach to teaching and learning by being more active in class. James can also become familiar with the Chinese value orientations so that he doesn't become too upset when students aren't actively participating.

Case 2

1. How did Kelly's actions on the date reflect the value orientations of Americans toward human nature, human activity, and social relations? Why didn't she think Jay liked her?

Americans think humans are inherently evil. As a result, they are suspicious of everyone and do not naturally trust them. This is why Kelly was not comfortable with Jay's suggestion to go to a fancy restaurant for their first date. Americans value authenticity, so they tend to choose to go on dates to places where people can "be themselves". At a fancy restaurant, everyone dresses up and does not act natural. But at the park, she can see what Jay is normally like. Jay will be less likely to act unnatural (and possibly deceive Kelly) at the park than at a fancy restaurant. Kelly was also uncomfortable when Jay gave her a gift because she suspected that he had some bad motives. Perhaps he wanted to manipulate her by giving her a gift. Americans typically do not give gifts on the first date because they do not know each other well enough yet. Such "friendly" behavior on the first date, therefore, is seen as suspicious. In social relations, Americans emphasize individuality. And in human activity, they emphasize "doing". This is why Kelly did not want Jay to carry her purse. Jay's offering to carry Kelly's purse suggested to her that she was too weak to carry it herself. In America, it is important to respect a woman's independence. Trying to help her too much is not good. Finally, Kelly thought Jay didn't like her because he never told her he liked her. Americans value "doing", which means they are typically straightforward in expressing their feelings. An American man will often tell an American girl, "I like you" on the first date to express his feelings. Since Jay didn't do that, Kelly assumed he didn't like her.

2. How did Jay's actions on the date reflect the value orientations of Chinese toward human nature, human activity, and social relations? Why didn't he think Kelly liked him?

Chinese people think people are inherently good. So, Jay assumed the best of Kelly. He was not suspicious of her, but rather wanted to express his respect for her by treating her to a nice dinner, bringing her a small gift, and carrying her purse. Since Chinese do not emphasize individualism, Jay did not know why Kelly refused to let him carry her purse. Chinese also emphasize "being" much more than "doing", which is one reason why Jay did not directly tell Kelly that he liked her. To him, the fact that he was on a date with Kelly (as well as his giving her a gift and offering to carry her purse) meant that he liked her. But since he never verbally communicated it, Kelly assumed he didn't like her.

3. If your Chinese friend was going to date an American, what advice would you give him/her?

Do not wait for fate to connect you with them. Be pro-active in pursuing them. Respect the other person's independence. Be direct in expressing your thoughts to the person, but do not be too aggressive in the beginning. Remember that the other person is naturally suspicious of you. Be as genuine as possible. Act as you would act around anyone else. Do a common activity together for the first few dates (homework, exercising, drinking coffee, etc.).

Case 3

Chinese parents attach great importance to the success of their children, and they like to compete with each other through the achievements of their children. If a child gets a prize, his or her parent will take great pride in it and even brag about it. On the one hand, Chinese parents make many decisions for their children that can help them to grow; but on the other hand, it deprives children of the right to make their own decisions, which can be harmful for their future independence. On the contrary, Western parents prefer encouraging their children to make their own decisions.

III. Task-based Activities

Exercises:

1. a   2. b   3. b   4. a   5. b

Assignment

Presentation 1

Orientation	Chinese values	Western values (Americans)
1) Human Nature	Basically good	Mixture of Good and Evil
2) Relationship of Man to Nature	Harmony with nature	Humans control Nature
3) Sense of Time	Past orientation	Future orientation
4) Human Activity	Being (who you are)	Doing (what you are doing)
5) Social Relationship	Hierarchy	Individual

Presentation 2

Dating

1. Human Nature

Americans are naturally suspicious of other people.

Americans value transparency and authenticity.

2. Human Relationship with Nature

Americans generally don't believe in fate; therefore, they will often be very pro-active in pursuing a partner.

It is the individual's responsibility to find a partner.

3. Individuality and Independence

Women do not like it if men try to help them too much because it makes them feel week. Therefore, it is important for the man to respect her independence.

4. Straightforwardness

Americans generally value being very straightforward; therefore, affection is often showed on the first date.

"I really like you."

Hug and/or kiss

Unit 4

Cultural Comprehension

Decide whether the following statements are true or false according to what you read.

1. T   2. T   3. F   4. F   5. T

Task 1: Fill in the blanks to the following lines spoken in the movie clips you just watched.

1. blow up   2. packed   3. get around   4. stride   5. conformity   6. unique

Task 2: Watch the movie clip for a second time and decide whether the following statements are true or false.

1. F   2. T   3. F   4. F   5. T   6. F

Case 1
Reflection

1. How does the above scenario reflect the differences in power distance in American and Chinese cultures?

The waitresses' actions reflect the low power distance inherent in American culture. Since Americans view all people equally, the waitress treated Mr. Wang the same as she treated the other students. From an American perspective, treating Mr. Wang with more honor since he is a CEO would be disrespecting the students. Mr. Wang, however, comes from a high power distance society, which considers people of greater achievement worthy of more respect. In China, Mr. Wang would have sat at the head of the table, and his needs would have been considered first because he is an accomplished CEO while the students are just students.

2. Was the waitress really being disrespectful? What might the waitress say if she was accused of disrespecting her customers?

One cannot conclusively say whether the waitress was being disrespectful without considering which cultural lens one views her actions through. "Respect" is relative to every culture. In China, she would be acting disrespectfully. However, if someone confronted her in America, she would say that she was actually respecting the customers because she treated all the customers the same. From an American perspective, if she had showed favoritism toward Mr. Wang, she would have actually been treating the customers disrespectfully since she would have been neglecting the inherent worth and value of the students.

Case 2
Reflection

1. What would Tom expect from his Chinese colleagues at the meeting?

Tom expects his Chinese colleagues to freely express their independent ideas about the new plan. Because American people highly value individualism , they prefer to express their personal ideas and feelings in public, and different ideas are always welcome in the discussion.

2. Could you analyze the response of Chinese colleagues to Tom's proposal?

Because in China, people highly value collectivism , they like to keep face for others, so they don't like to express their personal ideas and feelings in public, and different ideas are considered improper in the discussion.

3. If you are on the Chinese staff, what you will do? Or suppose you know both of their cultures quite well, could you please give them some advice in order to help them understand each other well?

I think they should have a better understanding of each other's cultures , which would be beneficial for both parties.

Case 3
Reflection

This clip reflects the different power distances between eastern countries and western countries. In the clip, Siam is an ancient Asian country where there is high power distance. The emperor has the supreme power and all the subjects in the kingdom must obey his orders. Anna, on the other hand, comes from Britain, a democratic western country where there is low power distance. In the beginning of the movie, the emperor promises Anna to provide a house outside the palace; however, he later does not fulfill his promise. Anna urges him to keep his promise, but since Siam has a high power distance, Anna's demand irritates the emperor. In Siam, the emperor is not normally challenged by other people.

III. Task-based Activities

Exercises:

1. b   2. a   3. b   4. a   5. b

Group Work

Discussion 2

1. Low power distance   2. Low uncertainty avoidance   3. High long term orientation
4. High MAS   5. Collective

Assignment

Presentation 1

Geert Hofstede identified five dimensions that he claimed summarized the differences between different cultures. According to Hofstede, the power distance dimension focused on how a society deals with the fact that people are unequal in physical and intellectual capabilities. The second dimension identified by Hofstede, individualism vs. collectivism, focused on the relationship between the individual and his or her fellows. Hofstede's third dimension, uncertainty avoidance, measured the extent to which different cultures socialize their members into accepting ambiguous situations and tolerating uncertainty. Fourthly, Hofstede's fourth dimension, masculinity vs. femininity, examined the relationship between gender and work roles. Finally, Long-term/short-term orientation refers to whether the focus of cultural values is on the future, the past, or the present.

And if you never plan or schedule for upcoming work or activities, you belong to high uncertainty avoidance.

Presentation 2

A.

Characteristics of Individualism and Collectivism

Individualism	Collectivism
"I" identity	"We" identity
independence	interdependence
competition	group harmony
self-realization	fitting into the in-group
direct communication	indirect communication

Intercultural Communication in Movies
影视作品中的跨文化交际

Unit 5

Cultural Comprehension

Decide whether the following statements are true or false according to what you read.

1. T   2. T   3. T   4. F   5. F

Task 1: Fill in the blanks to the following lines spoken in the movie clips you just watched.

1. basically   2. traveler   3. broke up   4. sharing   5. split   6. get rid of

Task 2: Watch the movie clips for a second time and decide whether the following statements are true or false.

1. F   2. T   3. F   4. T   5. F   6. T

Case 1

Reflection

1. Do John and Wang Peng come from high or low context cultures?

John comes from a low context culture. Wang Peng comes from a high context culture.

2. How do John's actions and reactions reflect his high or low context culture? Why did he want Wang Peng to ask for directions? Why did he feel disrespected by Wang Peng and feel like he lost his trust?

John's actions reflect a low context culture because he wants to solve the problem very directly. If they are lost, he thinks it is most reasonable to ask for directions. He felt disrespected by Wang Peng because he interpreted Wang Peng's refusal to ask for directions as wasting his time and making him needlessly walk around town. He felt like he lost Wang Peng's trust because Wang Peng deceived him. Wang Peng knew they were lost, but he refused to admit that to John. In the future, John will suspect that Wang Peng is now deceiving him.

3. How do Wang Peng's actions and reactions reflect his high or low context culture? Why did he refuse to ask for directions? How was he trying to show respect toward John?

Wang Peng's actions reflect a high context culture because he did not communicate in a direct way. He refused to ask for directions because it would make John upset, especially since this place was in Wang Peng's hometown. Wang Peng was afraid that it might reflect badly on his relationship with John, since it would show that Wang Peng did not adequately prepare to host John. Wang Peng, therefore, is attempting to show respect toward John by trying to make him not get upset. He hopes that by hiding the fact that he is lost he can keep peace and harmony in their relationship and avoid conflict.

Case 2

Reflection

1. How does Xiao Li reflect a high context culture in how she handles the situation with James?

Xiao Li wants to communicate very indirectly. She is afraid that communicating too directly will create unneeded conflict. First she attempts to communicate her refusal to date James by remaining silent and not responding to his email. Later, though, she attempts to communicate to him through a "middleman", namely April.

2. How do James and April reflect a low context culture in how they handle the situation?

James reflects a low context culture because he very directly asked Xiao Li to date him. April reflects a low context culture because she does not think it is respectful to James for Xiao Li to communicate to him through a "middleman". Instead, she thinks it is Xiao Li's duty to respond directly to James.

3. Give an example of something Xiao Li could say to James that would clearly communicate to him that she does not want to date him but that would not make him feel disrespected.

Xiao Li should communicate directly, but she should be careful not to communicate too directly. She should still be polite in her communication. Saying "I don't want to date you" sounds too direct to an American – even rude. Instead, she should say something like, "I think you are a nice guy, but I am not currently interested in dating you. Thank you for asking me, though."

Case 3

Reflection

This case is about high context culture in Chinese society, where people prefer to state their views indirectly rather than directly. In the clip, Lester is the director manager and is going to retire from the company. But before he goes, he is responsible for the design and furnishing of the company's offices. At the meeting, he asks several staff members if they would like to do the job. Although they do not refuse him directly, each of them has his/her own excuse. Even before the meeting, Rose refuses the task by saying that she has to have an operation, but in actuality there is no operation. Since Chinese people live in a high context culture, they like to save others' face by refusing indirectly and in a way where meanings are not expressed explicitly.

III. Task-based Activities

Exercises:

1. a 2. b 3. b 4. a 5. b

Discussion 2

The difference between the two cases is that the speakers in the second case try to always express their preference in order not to impose anything on each other. It would be impolite to refuse a clear proposal. There is a strong sense of compromise as it is more important to find a solution that is good for all than to satisfy the individual needs. In the first case, it is seen as perfectly acceptable to clearly say what one prefers and to find a solution that fits both as much as possible, even if it means separating for some time. This solution is not seen as a failure but as the optimal way to find maximum satisfaction for both and thus a good solution.

A: two people from a low context country

B: two people from a high context country

Intercultural Communication in Movies
影视作品中的跨文化交际

Unit 6

Cultural Comprehension
Decide whether the following statements are true or false according to what you read.

1. T   2. F   3. T   4. F   5. T

Task 1: Fill in the blanks to the following lines spoken in the movie clips you just watched.

1. stuck in   2. positive   3. incentive   4. cute   5. chopping   6. would have thought

Task 2: Watch the movie clip for a second time and decide whether the following statements are true or false.

1. F   2. T   3. T   4. T   5. T   6. F

Reflection

1. Why does Susie get so upset at the people staring, the man taking the photo, and the woman touching her son?

Susie is upset because each of these people is invading the privacy and personal space of her son.

2. How does this reflect American proxemics?

Americans generally prefer a large distance between them and strangers. This is especially so when one's own child is involved. Eastern countries tend to require a much smaller personal space and are accustomed to staring at children of other people, commenting on them, and touching them. In America, though, this is seen as disrespectful at best or child endangerment at worst. Parents may even call the police if they think someone appears to be taking too much of an interest in their child.

3. How should the Chinese people have acted when they saw her boy playing?

The Chinese people in the park can look at and admire the child, but they should not stare. They should not take any photos without the mother's permission. And they should never touch another person's child unless they are family members or very close friends.

Case 2

Reflection

1. Why do you think Michael is upset and feels disrespected?

Michael expects Zhang Peng to plan well in advance for his visit; however, Zhang Peng has barely planned any activities. He feels disrespected because to him, Zhang Peng's lack of planning means he did not consider Michael a very important friend. If Michael was important in Zhang Peng's eyes, Zhang Peng would have planned better. Also, Michael feels like Zhang Peng deceived him. He promised to have plans, but he never fulfilled that promise. Michael feels like Zhang Peng lied to him just to get him to visit his family.

2. How do Michael and Zhang Peng's actions reflect the Western and Eastern orientations toward monochronic and polychronic time?

Michael comes from a very monochronic culture, which emphasizes planning ahead for activities. As a result, he wants Zhang Peng to plan each day of his visit before he arrives. He wants to know exactly how he will be spending his time. Uncertainty about the future makes Michael hesitant to go. Zhang Peng, however, comes from a very polychronic time that tends to value relationships more than time. As a result, he does not consider it important to plan all of the events of Michael's visit. To him, the important thing is just that Michael is there with him.

3. What do you think Zhang Peng should have done?

Zhang Peng should have planned as many events ahead of time as possible and told Michael so that Michael could make a well-informed decision about whether or not to go. If he cannot think of many activities or things to do, he should not ask Michael to stay for two whole weeks since Michael would likely get bored. Two or three days would be better.

Case 3

Reflection

In the clip, the policeman talks about four different distance zones in American culture. Firstly, the public distance is far more than 360 cm; secondly, the social distance is between 120 cm and 360 cm; thirdly, the personal distance is between 45 and 120 cm; finally, the intimate distance is from 0 to 45 cm.

According to the distance Lin Weisheng keeps between himself and the woman, the policeman concludes that they have an intimate relationship. What's more, the fact that the woman crosses her feet and leans near Lin Weisheng reveals that she loves him. From this clip, we can see how people's gestures and facial expressions can convey information to others. Policemen can recognize criminals by reading their body language.

III. Task-based Activities

Exercises:

1. a   2. b   3. a   4. a   5. b

Unit 7

Cultural Comprehension

Decide whether the following statements are true or false according to what you read.

1. T   2. F   3. T   4. F   5. T

Task 1: Fill in the blanks to the following lines spoken in the movie clips you just watched.

1. policeman   2. articulate   3. pronounce   4. held back   5. eye contact   6. mean to

Task 2: Watch the movie clip for a second time and decide whether the following statements are true or false.

1. F   2. T   3. T   4. T   5. F   6. T

Case 1

Reflection

1. How did misunderstandings about eye contact lead to cultural conflict between the

lieutenant and Wang Gang? What was Wang Gang trying to communicate? How did Lieutenant Mark interpret it?

Wang Gang and his family were not making eye contact because in Chinese culture this represents respect to someone whom one considers in a high or prominent position. They were trying to show honor to the lieutenant. But the lieutenant is American and therefore thinks that they are not making eye contact because they are disinterested in what he is saying. He thinks they are showing disrespect.

2. How did misunderstandings about gestures lead to cultural conflict between the lieutenant and Wang Gang? What was Wang Gang trying to communicate by his gestures? How did Lieutenant Mark interpret it?

Wang Gang and his son were making the "V" sign with both hands as they were taking a picture, which is a common gesture in Chinese culture. In China, "V" typically is understood to mean "victory" or is simply just a fun hand gesture. But in America, the "V" sign means peace. So, when Lieutenant Mark saw them making the peace sign next to an army tank, he thought they were mocking the army. Americans are sensitive to people from other countries criticizing the American military for fighting too much, so the lieutenant thought Wang Gang was making fun of that "fighting culture" by making the peace sign beside the tank.

3. How did misunderstandings about object language lead to cultural conflict between Wang Gang, his wife and John? What was John trying to communicate? How did Wang Gang and his wife interpret it?

John bought a green hat so that Wang Gang would have a piece of military clothing to add to his military collection. He just wanted to make his friend feel better after getting kicked out of the military base. But in China, if someone gives a married man a green hat, it means that his wife is in a secret relationship with another man. This is why Wang Gang and his wife were embarrassed and upset by John's gift. But John had no idea that this "object language" carried this meaning.

Case 2
Reflection

1. What kind of misunderstandings occurred between William and Zhang Tao in their verbal communication? What meanings are given to the phrases "Thank you!" and "Waiter!" in their respective cultures?

In American culture, "Thank you" is simply a polite phrase to express gratitude to anyone. This phrase is used often, no matter who one is expressing gratitude towards. Failure to say "thank you" is actually disrespectful. But in China, a friend will not say "thank you" to another friend for most things – especially small things like opening the door. When Zhang Tao hears William say "Thank you!" he thinks that means William is treating him like a stranger and not a friend because in China people are only that polite to strangers or those with whom one does not have a deep relationship.

Likewise, in China, it is common to yell "Waiter!" to get the waiter's attention. But in

America, this verbal phrase is very rude. In America, one should simply raise one's hand or walk over to the waiter or waitress and politely ask them for help. Thus, William expresses disapproval at Zhang Tao's language.

2. How do Eastern and Western understandings of proxemics (space) account for William's being irritated by Zhang Tao when he places food on his plate and removes the chopsticks from his rice?

In China it is common for friends to put food on each other's plates because the proxemics of Asian culture is much closer than that of Western culture. In Chinese culture, people can interact much closer with others – even touching them – without the other person feeling uncomfortable. But in American culture, people have a large area of "personal space" that one should not invade. Thus, when Zhang Tao puts food on William's plate, William feels like Zhang Tao invaded his privacy and possibly "contaminated" his plate with his food. Additionally, when Zhang Tao reaches over and removes William's chopsticks from his bowl, William feels like Zhang Tao invaded his privacy. William thinks Zhang Tao is not allowed to touch his personal property – in this case, his chopsticks.

3. How does object language account for Zhang Tao's removing William's chopsticks from his rice? What was William communicating to others in the Chinese restaurant by placing his chopsticks in his rice?

William placed his chopsticks in the rice simply for convenience. But in China, chopsticks sticking out of rice looks very similar to incense that is stuck in the ground and burned for dead relatives. Thus, Zhang Tao is afraid people in the restaurant will be offended if they see William's chopsticks sticking up out of his bowl.

Case 3
Reflection

This clip is about the role of verbal language in communication. Non-native speakers often have difficulty pronouncing foreign names and words. In this clip, the master's surname is Yu (余), but Carter is a native English speaker and can't pronounce it correctly; thus, he pronounces the master's name as "You". The man in the black clothes is Mi (米), but Carter thinks the man is saying "me". From this, we can see that verbal language, though it may sound similar in different cultures, may vary drastically in meaning between cultures. We also see the importance of understanding culture. If Carter had known that "Yu" and "Mi" were surnames in China, he likely would have been able to understand what the two men were saying. But since he was not culturally aware, he misunderstood what they were saying.

III. Task-based Activities

Exercises:

1. b   2. a   3. a   4. b   5. c

Intercultural Communication in Movies
影视作品中的跨文化交际

Unit 8

Cultural Comprehension
Decide whether the following statements are true or false according to what you read.
1. T   2. F   3. T   4. T   5. T

Task 1: Fill in the blanks to the following lines spoken in the movie clips you just watched.
1. interested in   2. acting like   3. dealing with   4. holding up   5. own business
6. help yourself

Task 2: Watch the movie clip for a second time and decide whether the following statements are true or false.
1. F   2. T   3. T   4. T   5. F   6. F

Case 1
Reflection

1. Is Xiao Min right in assuming that Claire is upset because she did or said something wrong to her? Why has Claire changed so much?

No, Xiao Min is not right. Claire has changed so much because she is experiencing culture shock.

2. Using the U-curve, analyze what stages of culture shock Claire has experienced.

According to the U-curve, Claire was excited about China in the beginning because she was in the honeymoon phase. But later, she entered the crisis phase, which explains why her views have changed and why she is much more easily angered and annoyed. During this phase, it is natural for people to want to isolate themselves, which explains why she wants to be alone.

3. What are some specific things Xiao Min can do to help Claire?

First, Xiao Min can explain to Claire that what she is experiencing is normal. She can share her insights about culture shock and the U-curve. Xiao Min can try to show extra patience toward Claire, knowing that Claire might say or do some things that offend her. She can try to bring Claire some things that will remind her of home, such as Western food, Western music, or Western movies. Finally, Xiao Min can help Claire try to adapt to Chinese culture by explaining the underlying beliefs and values that lead to many of the customs that Claire does not like. Through mutual understanding, Claire and Xiao Min can develop their intercultural competence.

Case 2
Reflection

1. Do you think life back in China will be as wonderful as Song Hao and his mom believe it will be? Why or why not?

While Song Hao may experience the "honeymoon stage" after the first few days back home, he will quickly enter a new "crisis stage", which will make life back home quite difficult and stressful.

2. How might the W-curve give Song Hao and his mother a more realistic picture of what life

for Song Hao will be like when he returns to China? What should they expect?

The W-curve shows that Song Hao will likely experience a "honeymoon stage" for the first few days back home, but very soon he will enter a "crisis stage" that will make him very stressed. He likely will not want to be around people and may become critical of his own culture as he compares it to American culture. Over the long run, though, he will readjust and adapt to Chinese culture.

3. Using the W-curve and your knowledge of culture shock, give Song Hao's mother some suggestions about how best to help Song Hao transition back into life in China. How should she change her plans?

Song Hao's mother should express joy in her son's returning home, but she should be careful not to assume he can instantly transition back to Chinese life. She should not plan so many activities with friends and family because Song Hao will quickly feel very stressed and will want to be alone. While it would be good to cook him Chinese food and give him other experiences of Chinese culture, she should not overload his life with these things. She may want to consider taking him to a Western restaurant every once in a while or watch an American movie, since he will be more accustomed to Western culture than Chinese culture for the first few weeks. By doing this, she can help him slowly adjust to Chinese culture again.

Case 3

Reflection

From this clip we can see two kinds of culture shock. The first kind relates to the prohibition of alcohol for teenagers. In China there are no strict regulations on it, although parents know it is harmful for young people to drink. But in the U.S.A., it is illegal. The second kind of culture shock relates to spanking. There is an old Chinese saying: "棍棒底下出孝子", which means spare the rod, spoil the child. In Chinese education, therefore, spanking is common. But in America, it is often looked down on – even illegal in some parts of the country.

III. Task-based Activities

Exercises:

1. b   2. b   3. b   4. a   5. a

Bibliography

[1] ADLER P S. The transitional experience: An alternative view of culture shock [J]. Journal of Humanistic Psychology, 1975, 15(4): 13-23.

[2] ARON WOLFE SIEGMAN. Nonverbal Behavior and Communication [M]. Mawah, NJ: Lawrence Erlbaum Associates, Incorporated, 1987: 637.

[3] BICCHIERI C. The Grammar of Society: the Nature and Dynamics of Social Norms [M]. New York: Cambridge University Press, 2006.

[4] BRENT D RUBEN, DANIEL J KEALEY. Behavioral assessment of communication competency and the prediction of cross-cultural adaptation [J]. International Journal of Intercultural Relations, 1979, 3(1): 15-47.

[5] CYNTHIA JOYCE. The Impact of Direct and Indirect Communication [N]. The University of Iowa Edition of the Independent Voice, the newsletter of the International Ombudsman Association, 2012.

[6] DAVID PINTO. Intercultural Communication – A Three-step Method for Dealing with Differences [M]. Antwerpen-Apeldoorn: Garant Uitgevers, NV, 2000.

[7] LINELL DAVIS. 中西文化之鉴[M]. 北京：外语教学与研究出版社，2010.

[8] DUNN L J. Non-verbal communication: information conveyed through the use of body language [D]. St. Joseph, Missouri: Missouri Western State University, 1999.

[9] EDWARD T HALL. Beyond Culture [M]. Garden City, NY: Anchor Press, 1976.

[10] EKMAN P, FRIESEN W V. The Repertoire of Nonverbal Behavior: Categories, Origins, Usage, and Coding [J]. Semiotica, 1969(1): 49-98.

[11] FRED EDMUND JANDT. An Introduction to Intercultural Communication: Identities in a Global Community [M]. 6th ed. New York: Sage Publications, Inc, 2009.

[12] GUDYKUNST W B, TING-TOOMEY S, NISHIDA T. Communication in Personal Relationships across Cultures [M]. New York: Sage Publications, Inc, 1996.

[13] GUDYKUNST W B, TING-TOOMEY S. Culture and Interpersonal Communication [M]. New York: Sage Publications, Inc, 1988.

[14] GULLAHORN J T, GULLAHORN J E. An Extension of the U-curve Hypothesis [J]. Journal of Social Issues, 1963(19): 33-47.

[15] HALL E T. The Silent Language [M]. New York: Doubleday, 1959.

[16] HALL E T. The Hidden Dimension [M]. New York: Doubleday, 1966.

[17] HALL E. Beyond Culture [M]. New York: Doubleday, 1976.

[18] HALL E, HALL M. Understanding Cultural Differences: Germans, French and Americans [M]. Yarmouth: Intercultural Press, 1990.

Bibliography

[19] HILLS M D. Kluckhohn and Strodtbeck's Values Orientation Theory [EB/OL]. http://dx.doi.org/10.9707/2307-0919.1040, 2002.

[20] HOFSTEDE G. Culture's Consequences: International Differences in Work Related Values [M]. Beverly Hills, CA: Sage, 1984.

[21] HOFSTEDE GEERT. Cultural Dimensions in Management and Planning [J]. Asia Pacific Journal of Management, 1984(1): 81-99.

[22] HOFSTEDE G. National Cultures and Corporate Cultures [C]// SAMOVAR L A, PORTER R E. Communication between Cultures. Belmont, CA: Wadsworth Publishing, 1984.

[23] HOFSTEDE GEERT, BOND MICHAEL HARRIS. The Confucius connection: from cultural roots to economic growth [J]. Organizational Dynamics, 1988, 16(4): 4-21.

[24] HOFSTEDE G, BOND M H. The Confucius connection: from cultural roots to economic growth [J]. Organizational Dynamics, 1998 (Spring): 5-21.

[25] HOFSTEDE G. Culture's Consequences [M]. 2nd ed. New York: Sage Publications, Inc, 2001.

[26] JURGEN RUESCH, WELDON KEES, SHIRLEY WEITZ, WELDON KEES. Nonverbal Communication: Readings with Commentary [M]. Berkeley, CA: University of California Press, 1969.

[27] KLUCKHOHN FLORENCE R, FRED L STRODTBECK. Variations in Value Orientations [M]. Evanston, IL: Row, Peterson, 1961.

[28] KROEBER A L, KLUCKHOHN C. Culture: A critical review of concepts and definitions [D]. Cambridge: Harvard University Peabody Museum, 1952.

[29] LANDIS DAN, BENNETT JANET, BENNETT MILTON J. Handbook of Intercultural Training [M]. New York: Sage Publications, Inc, 2004.

[30] LEDERACH J P. Preparing for Peace: Conflict Transformation across Cultures [M]. Syracuse, NY: Syracuse University Press, 1995.

[31] LEWIS R D. When Cultures Collide: Leading across Cultures [M]. 3rd ed. London: Nicholas Brealey Publishing, 2007.

[32] LYSGAARD S. Adjustment in a foreign society: Norwegian Fulbright grantees visiting the United States [J]. International Social Science Bulletin, 1955(7): 45-51.

[33] MARK KNAPP, JUDITH HALL. Nonverbal Communication in Human Interaction [M]. 2nd ed. Belmont, CA: Wadsworth Publishing, 1978.

[34] OBERG KALERVO. Culture Shock [EB/OL]. Presentation to the Women's Club of Rio De Janeiro, Brazil. [1954-8-3]. http://www.smcm.edu/Academics/internationaled/Pdf/cultureshockarticle.pdf.

[35] OBERG KALERVO. Culture Shock: Adjustment to New Cultural Environments [J]. Practical Anthropology, 1960(7): 185.

[36] RICH ANDREA L. Interracial Communication [M]. New York: Harper & Row, 1974.

[37] RON SCOLLON, SUZANNE B K SCOLLON. Narrative, Literacy, and Face in Interethnic Communication [M]. Norwood, NJ: Ablex, 1981.

[38] SAGARIKA GOSWAMI. Eastern culture vs. westerern culture [J]. The Journal of

Department of Applied Sciences & Humanities, 2011 (11): 33-36.

[39] SAMOVAR LARRY A, PORTER RICHARD. Communication between Cultures [M]. 4th ed. New York: Thomas Learning Publications, 2001.

[40] SAPIR E. The Status of Linguistics as a Science [C]// MANDELBAUM D G. Culture, Language and Personality. Berkeley, CA: University of California Press, 1958.

[41] SMITH A L. Transracial Communication [M]. Englewood Cliffs, NJ: Prentice-Hall, 1973.

[42] STELLA TING-TOOMEY. Communicating across Cultures [M]. New York, London: The Guilford Press, 1999.

[43] STELLA TING-TOOMEY. Communicating across Cultures [M]. New York: Guilford Press, 1999.

[44] TANNEN DEBORAH. Talking from 9 to 5 [M]. New York: William Morrow and Company, Inc., 1994.

[45] TING-TOOMEY STELLA. Communicating across Cultures [M]. 上海：上海外语教育出版社，2007.

[46] WARD C. The A, B, Cs of acculturation [C]// MATSUMOTO D. The Handbook of Culture & Psychology. New York: Oxford University Press, 2001.

[47] WHORF B L. Science and Linguistics [J]. Technology Review, 1940, 42(6).

[48] 毕继万. 跨文化非言语交际[M]. 北京：外语教学与研究出版社，1999.

[49] 胡文仲. 跨文化交际学概论[M]. 北京：外语教学与研究出版社，1999.